Examining Philosophy and Ethics

Answers for A level

Patrick J Clarke

Text © Patrick J. Clarke 2002
Original illustrations © Nelson Thornes Ltd 2002

The right of Patrick J. Clarke to be identified as author of this work has been asserted by him in accordance with the Copyright, Designs and Patents Act 1988.

All rights reserved. No part of this publication may be reproduced or transmitted in any form or by any means, electronic or mechanical, including photocopy, recording or any information storage and retrieval system, without permission in writing from the publisher or under licence from the Copyright Licensing Agency Limited, of 90 Tottenham Court Road, London W1T 4LP.

Any person who commits any unauthorised act in relation to this publication may be liable to criminal prosecution and civil claims for damages.

Published in 2002 by:
Nelson Thornes Ltd
Delta Place
27 Bath Road
CHELTENHAM
GL53 7TH
United Kingdom

05 06 / 10 9 8 7 6 5 4 3

A catalogue record for this book is available from the British Library

ISBN 0 7487 6009 1

Page make-up by Northern Phototypesetting

Printed and bound in Spain by GraphyCems

Acknowledgements

With thanks to the following for permission to reproduce photographs and other copyright material in this book:

Corbis – pp 26, 38, 58, 86, 125. All other photographs – Nelson Thornes archive.

Every effort has been made to contact copyright holders. The publishers apologise to anyone whose rights have been inadvertently overlooked, and will be happy to rectify any errors or omissions.

Contents

Contents

About this Book

This book is designed to help students of philosophy of religion and ethics. The essays are not meant to be model answers, or a definitive guide to how examination questions should be answered. Examiners happily acknowledge that there is no definitive, or single, way to form an answer, and are open to 'any reasonable interpretation' of a question. At the same time, examiners *expect* to see certain topics and issues dealt with, and they look out for the way in which these are presented, together with an awareness of how far certain views can be supported or challenged. I hope you will find the essays in this book as much a stimulus to *thought* as a helpful source of knowledge and understanding. But I hope they contribute in the end to the three vital skills of **knowledge**, **understanding** and **evaluation**.

Factual **knowledge** of course is of crucial importance, since a basic familiarity with the facts, concepts and ideas of the subject under question is a fundamental requirement. But you must avoid being carried away with giving factual knowledge. Knowledge must not be used it for its own sake, but as a means to showing the vital skill of **understanding**. This is the ability to see the logical *implications* of whatever facts, theories and beliefs you are dealing with. A useful guide is to remember that understanding is shown in the *linking* of facts, not the *listing* of facts.

Closely related to understanding is the skill of **evaluation**, an important component in all examination questions at A/AS level. All three skills are in fact *interlinked*. Understanding shows knowledge, and evaluation shows understanding. In its totality, your essay should show a knowledge of the question, of the strengths and weaknesses of the arguments, and 'how far', or 'to what extent', the view in question can or cannot be upheld. It is also important to remember that any *personal view* is not to be an expression of what 'I think', but must be integrated within a knowledgeable understanding of the overall question. Remember too that the best conclusions are never absolute, but provisional and hypothetical. Words and phrases such as 'if', 'provided that', 'depending whether' and 'in so far as' are ways in which to show the provisional nature of your conclusion.

The essays in this book are written primarily to meet the AS and A2 philosophy of religion and religious ethics options of Religious Studies specifications for the OCR, AQA and Edexcel examination boards. These are based on philosophical and ethical issues arising from the main religious influence in the West, the Judeo-Christian tradition. The essays are broadly divided into five main topics: (1) the existence and nature of God; (2) religion and science; (3) religion and language; (4) religion and ethics; and (5) medical ethics.

A final reason why the essays are not to be taken as model answers (although your own essays may be modelled on them!) is their *length*. Most of the essays are much longer than you would be able to write in the standard time of 45 minutes, the time allowed in the examination for each question. As a handy guide, a good essay written within this time should reach somewhere around 1000 words. Many of the essays here are much *longer* in order to provide you with a greater *selection* of material. I hope you will find them a useful resource for philosophy of religion and ethical studies.

About this Book

Outline of Topics

The Existence and Nature of God

This is the subject of the first group of essays. The employment of different kinds of reasoning to argue for God's existence, the strengths and weaknesses of the arguments, the influence of **David Hume** and **Immanuel Kant**, and the importance of **empirical** evidence to the modern mind all form important themes in this area. How the attributes of God emerge as logically necessary for God to be God is the basis of so-called classical theism. The empirical problems raised by some of God's attributes, especially the problem of evil, are an important factor in the modern denial of God's existence. One key question is how successful is the case for God's 'defence', known as theodicy. This topic appears again later in the book.

Issues of Faith and Philosophy

This group of essays deals with how, and to what extent, faith is related to **reason**. Is faith something independent in itself, or must it be dependent on reason, or on some evidence from experience? There are important views on both sides. The proposal known as Pascal's Wager poses an interesting question: Does it represent an astute *use* of reason to acquire faith, or does it signal the *limits* of reason to acquire it?

Religion and Experience

The perceived failure of **rational** attempts to prove God's existence led to a turning inward, to a more experiential or emotional approach. This is called **religious experience**. Whether, how and to what extent the divine impinges on human experience is the main focus of this group of essays. The religious experience recorded in the Bible, which provides the basis for the divine communication known as **revelation**, is an important theological issue with important philosophical implications.

Claims for religious experience have been a particular focus of attention since the rise of the human sciences. The problem for the believer is to show that these claims are any more than *human* phenomena. This is the challenge of those who claim that religion is the result of human conditioning, an illusion or a form of wishful thinking. Thus the **sociological** challenge posed by the theories of Marx, Durkheim and Weber, and the **psychological** theories of Freud and Jung, need to be seriously assessed.

Religion and Science

This group of essays examines the relationship between religion and science in the light of discoveries that appear to undermine some traditional religious assumptions about the origins of the universe and life itself. Part of the focus of these essays is whether **Darwinism** or the findings of modern **cosmology** create difficulties that threaten to undermine religion. How successfully modern theologians have responded to these difficulties, by appealing to the function of religion to *interpret* rather than explain life, is a major question.

vi

Religion and Language

Attempts to limit language to 'facts about the world' have had important implications for the language of faith. With the modern preference for **empirical**, or provable, truth in the wake of the popularity of science, many have found that the language of religion, in attempting to express the invisible world of faith, has serious deficiencies. Defenders of religious language claim that the use of everyday terms to speak of God has a long history and is a valid use of language.

Analogy, and other forms of **symbolic** language are claimed to bridge the gap between the material world and the spiritual, and express religious truths about God. But the challenge represented by **logical positivism** is that the only **meaningful** use of language is to express what is empirically verifiable. This is known as the **verification principle**. How far this challenge ignores more profound aspects of human nature is an important theological and philosophical question.

Ethics/Moral Philosophy

This takes us to the second major part of the book. The first group of essays, covering what is called **metaethics**, will examine the ideas and concepts used in ethical debate. This means examining the extent to which ethics can be called a rational, intuitive, emotive or indeed religious enterprise. Also to be examined is the extent to which the moral life is one of freedom, or whether it is instead determined by factors that limit moral freedom; whether ethical principles are absolute or relative, and how far the moral life is decided by conscience, rather than by some external authority such as God.

We will then assess the different **ethical theories** that compete in claiming to represent the best way to live the moral life. The relationship between ethics and religion is a key question that will form the background to many of these issues, but will be examined on its own in two specific essays. How ethical theories relate to each other in terms of similarities and contrasts will also be examined. In the final chapter, a major area in ethical decision-making will be considered; namely, medical ethics.

Medical Ethics

In the end, ethics is about *action* rather than *thought*. One of the most crucial areas where ethical decisions have to be made is the field of medical ethics. In this area, a host of issues have become commonplace in recent years. Scientific procedures such as embryo creation, embryonic stem-cell harvesting and various forms of fertility treatment have given rise to serious ethical questions arising from fears about the power of science. What is becoming scientifically possible is being increasingly distinguished from what is morally correct. Equally, certain surgical procedures such as **abortion**, and questions about the individual's right to **euthanasia**, put the focus on principles such as **personal autonomy** and the **sanctity of life**.

Philosophy of Religion

All areas of human study and exploration make claims to knowledge. It is the task of philosophy to examine those claims and to assess their validity, their scope and their limits. Thus the philosophy of science examines the ways in which scientific knowledge is obtained, and what sort of knowledge this is. The philosophy of history looks at the nature of historical knowledge, and the influences that shape its meaning or its character. The philosophy of language looks at the way in which language is used, and examines the different truth-claims that lie behind our use of words.

The philosophy of religion examines the meaning of religious faith, and how far some of the key ideas of religious belief stand up to rational analysis and the test of experience. In this book we shall be looking at some of the standard areas examined in philosophy of religion:

- the existence and nature of God
- the nature of faith, and the extent to which it is related, or not related, to human reason
- how religion impinges, or does not impinge, on human experience
- the extent to which religious beliefs can or cannot be expressed in language
- how religious belief is affected by the discoveries of science
- the extent to which religion is related to, or separate from, ethics.

The conclusions that emerge from philosophy of religion are quite diverse. For some, the conclusion is that religion is false; while for others the conclusion is that religion stands up well to the test of reason and experience. For some, religion is upheld or discredited on the strengths or weaknesses of the traditional arguments for theism. For others, religion is better approached as a matter of experience. But this is an area fraught with difficulties, especially since the rise of the social sciences. Both psychology and sociology claim to be able to explain religion as a human phenomenon, something that can be explained in terms of human forces and unconscious dynamics, which make it possible for what is false and illusory to be mistaken for real. For others, it is the physical sciences, such as biology or astronomy, which create the greatest challenge to the credibility of religion. Ironically, some new insights resulting from science have offered the possibility of solving some of religion's own problems – such as how to interpret and understand the Bible.

The philosophy of religion is an area of study that continues to exercise a remarkable, but not surprising, fascination. Perhaps no other area of study has attracted the attention of so many of the greatest minds in the history of Western thought. These have included both atheists and believers, theologians, philosophers and scientists, and the participants have ranged across the spectrum of religions, to include influential contributions from Jewish, Muslim and Christian philosophers.

Why this has been so can partly be explained by the human relevance of the subject. It is not just for *academic* interest that people would like to know the reasons why

God is said to exist, or not exist, why faith is held to be true, or not true, and whether life after death is credible or impossible. Faith gives one answer to all these questions, but the task of the philosophy of religion is to examine the credibility of its claims against the test of reason and experience.

1   *The Existence and Nature of God*

Questions about the existence and nature of God have engaged philosophers and theologians since the earliest times. **Plato** and **Aristotle** had already laid down the ideas that were built on by later thinkers. **St Augustine** and **St Anselm** were influenced by Plato's dualistic theory of **ideal forms**, in which the realm of true reality was located beyond the shadowy world of the senses, while **St Thomas Aquinas** was influenced by Aristotle's concern with the **empirical** world as the here and now, and therefore the most practical reality. But here Anselm argues that *thought*, not experience, leads to what is most real, God.

The Ontological Argument

The ontological argument is unique in the way in which it approaches the idea of God from an *a priori* position. This means that it takes something like a mathematical approach. In mathematics we deal with ideal things – straight lines, angles, shapes and so on. We do not deal with the real world of experience, although we apply its measurements to the real world. In a similar way Anselm, and later **René Descartes**, go from the ideal world of *thought* to the real world of *existence*. God is the ideal being who exists so perfectly that His non-existence is inconceivable.

Assess the value of the ontological argument as a proof of the existence of God.

The roots of the ontological argument appear in the thought of **St Augustine**, who spoke of God as that being to which none was superior. **St Anselm** made this the basis of the argument that is famously attributed to him. The argument is about the *being* of God – hence the name **ontological**, from the Greek word for 'being'.

Anselm's argument is puzzling inasmuch as it is begins as *a priori* (analytical, prior to experience), but ends up as **existential** (*a posteriori*, synthetic, about the real world). In its *a priori* beginning, it speculates on what God's nature must be like if He is to exist. For God to be God, He must be 'that than which nothing greater can be conceived', and to qualify as such He must be able to exist of Himself (*a se*). This is to say that he must *necessarily* exist, or have necessary existence. Otherwise, something greater could be conceived.

In his first formulation of the argument (*Proslogion*, Chapter 2), Anselm claims that everyone has an idea of God in their minds – even the fool in the psalm, who says in his heart 'there is no God'. The idea of God is of a being greater than which cannot be thought. However, the greatest conceivable being must not just exist in the mind, but also in reality. Any lesser being couldn't be God. It is clear from this that Anselm sees God as uniquely having the perfection of being able to exist in reality.

This becomes further clarified in his second formulation of the argument (*Proslogion*, Chapter 3), Anselm addresses God as existing, and declares that he could never conceive of His non-existence. It might appear at first sight that Anselm is simply rephrasing his first formulation: the impossibility of God not existing amounts to saying that He necessarily exists. But, looked at again, Anselm's language has become more *existential* than logical. An existential claim asserts that something exists in fact, as opposed to a logical *a priori* claim that if God is God, He must necessarily exist. This is why Anselm's reasoning seems to have a baffling fluidity, and appears to drift from *a priori* to a statement of fact. In the first form of the argument, Anselm speaks about what God must be like; while in the second, he speaks about what God is like. The latter is called *a posteriori* reasoning, based on some existing evidence, such as the evidence of the Bible.

This might explain the continuing controversy over whether Anselm was offering a proof of God's existence to the non-believer, or whether his argument is simply a meditation on the greatness of God as revealed to faith. If it is the latter, there can be no doubt about the argument's illuminative value. It puts into philosophical language what the believer already accepts. At the very least, Anselm's argument effectively establishes God's necessary existence, given the meaning of God.

One of the problems of the argument, but probably its strength, is undoubtedly the unique nature of its subject. A failure to appreciate this led Anselm's contemporary, the monk **Gaunilo**, to challenge Anselm's reasoning by bringing up the idea of 'the most perfect island'. The move didn't work, because an island is a contingent object that belongs to the empirical world, and anything contingent can never be 'perfect' in any absolute sense. At best, an island could only be the most perfect of its kind. By contrast, God is a spiritual reality, and is unique in being absolutely perfect above and beyond all kinds of beings in the world. This is entailed from the fact that God is in no way part of the contingent world – and therefore cannot be compared to an island, or to anything else in the world.

Descartes later produced his own version of the ontological argument, but the nature of his reasoning also raises some questions. On the one hand, he appears to be using *a priori* reasoning when he compares the necessity of God's existence to the mathematical necessity of a triangle having three angles that equal 180 degrees. On the other hand, he argues that the idea of God is an innate idea (already in the mind) and, in his view, innate ideas only come from the 'substance' of the things that they represent. This means that the idea of God comes from the actual existence of God. This seems like existential reasoning. But in either case God is perceived as a being whose perfection requires the quality of necessity, or **aseity**; that is, the ability to be the source of His own existence.

Aquinas understood Anselm's argument to be *a priori*, an exercise in metaphysical logic that he took as sound but unconvincing since, in fact, people question God's existence. As an empiricist, Aquinas believed that God's existence needed to be proved by reference to experience (*a posteriori* reasoning) before His nature could be discussed at all. It appears that Aquinas thought that Anselm had got things the wrong way around, but we must remember that Aquinas, under the influence of Aristotle, was more concerned with showing how theism arises from facts about the world. He believed it was necessary to begin from outside of God – not from inside, as Anselm had done.

In the first three of the **Five Ways**, Aquinas himself argues to God's nature as a necessary being from the contingent nature of all earthly things. As experience shows, every event gives rise to a causal chain that runs backwards. For Aquinas, since an infinite regress (never-ending movement backwards) is impossible – and certainly impossible to imagine – it follows that, ultimately, all events in the world require a crucial first cause for the chain of events to start at all. The fact that the world has evolved from a point of space–time singularity, popularly called the 'Big Bang', to a state of profound complexity appears to lend some scientific support to Aquinas' rejection of an infinite regress.

Immanuel Kant was a noted critic of the argument, on the basis that Anselm's key idea – existence – was not a predicate; that is, a quality or perfection that can be added to the idea of something. For example, you cannot say that a unicorn is an animal with one horn *and also* that it exists. The concept of a unicorn is valid, says Kant, whether or not a unicorn exists. To add existence is to make an additional claim; namely, that the concept is *instantiated*, which means that there *is* an instance of a unicorn existing, say, in Ireland. It is quite different to say that if a unicorn existed it would have one horn. But saying this adds nothing to the concept, and says nothing about whether or not something exists. Thus to say that the greatest possible being also exists is a misuse of the word 'exist' by treating it as a predicate.

This objection seems to have been anticipated by **René Descartes**, who agreed that in the case of empirical things one can say that if they existed, certain things would follow. For instance, if a mountain existed it would be bounded by a valley. But in speaking about God things are different. In the case of God, there can be no hypothetical 'if', since God is not a contingent thing – because He *necessarily* exists. Therefore Kant's objection misses the point by not allowing for the unique nature of God, whose essence, or nature, is actually to self-exist. Ironically, this was the conclusion reached by Aquinas, but only after he established God's real existence!

More recently, **Norman Malcolm**, in his treatment of the argument, has focused on Anselm's second formulation, in which God is impossible to be thought of as not existing. This has meant a shift from the idea of *logical* necessity to the idea of *existential* necessity. He argues that God necessarily exists existentially; that is, as a matter of fact, not as a matter of logic. His argument runs along the lines that God's existence is either necessary or impossible. If God's existence were to depend on something else, it would be contingent. But the idea of a contingent God is an absurdity, and thus impossible. But we know that a world exists that is contingent, and anything contingent cannot be the cause of itself (in medieval language, an *ens se*). Therefore the necessary existence of God is presupposed by the existence of a contingent world. It is not difficult to see from this what Kant meant when he said that the cosmological argument depends on the ontological argument.

Malcolm, however, does not believe that the ontological argument is persuasive in itself. He believes that some other insights are required from within human experience, such as a sense of the passing nature of all contingent things, before a person can understand the insights of religious faith. This brings him into line with other thinkers, who hold that the necessary insight into God's existence comes not from logical speculation but from within human experience. By looking at certain characteristics of our nature, such as our moral awareness (**Kant**), our sense of absolute dependence (**Friedrich Schleiermacher**), our sense of the absurdity of life (**Søren Kierkegaard**), our fallenness, but our potential for moral improvement (**Rudolf Bultmann**), our restless searching and capacity for **transcendence** (**Karl Rahner**) and our sense that there must be a Ground to the being of everything (**Paul Tillich**) – from all these we get a glimmer of the reality of God's existence.

In a different vein, **D. Z. Phillips** supports the ontological argument for its logical clarification of the concept of God. He accepts that Anselm was attempting to express what he already believed, but his argument is no less enlightening for all that. God is unlike all contingent things, and is not part of any class or kind. The key to the ontological argument, says Phillips, is in the way Anselm expresses the unique *sense* of the word 'God'. The word has a unique 'grammar', and it is therefore a mistake even to say 'God exists' in any ordinary sense. God does not 'exist' alongside other existing things – hence Phillips' preference for so-called *non-realism*. God, as believers claim, 'is up there listening', but not in the crude realist sense of an 'old man in the sky'. In what *sense* God is there is something that, Phillips believes, calls for a profound level of understanding that only faith can provide.

Other modern thinkers such as Paul Tillich and **John Macquarrie** have tried to convey the same idea by using the concept of **Being Itself**, to distinguish the unique being of God from the 'beings' that make up the contingent world. The **apophatic** way (the way of silence) favoured by the mystics was a similar attempt to overcome the tendency to speak of God as if He were just another worldly phenomenon who 'might' or 'might not' exist. In **Meister Eckhart's** puzzling words, 'God is the not-person, not-thing ... the nameless nothingness, the superessential darkness'.

In conclusion, we can say that the ontological argument has the merit of clarifying the nature of God for believers. God is a necessary being who possesses **aseity**, or necessary existence. For Malcolm, the truth of the argument is seen as too remote for many, and does not guarantee a religious response. For Phillips, the argument highlights the unique nature of God, and provides a warning about speaking about God as another being in the world. For **Karl Barth**, the argument was primarily a meditation by a believer for believers. He held that the argument's value lay in its capacity to highlight the unique mystery of God's nature, and why He is worthy of worship, aspects that can only be appreciated by faith. In this sense, its value may be illustrated by the stained glass windows of a church, which cannot be viewed from the outside. Only being visible from the inside is a parable of faith.

Related questions:

1 Assess the strengths and weakness of the ontological argument.

2 How justified is the claim that the ontological argument is merely an exercise in *a priori* reasoning?

3 Evaluate the view that the ontological argument clarifies the nature of God as a necessary being.

The Cosmological Argument

The cosmological argument goes back to **Plato** and **Aristotle**. It was later developed by Arab philosophers such as **Avicenna** and **Averroes**, before its classic formulation in the first three of the Five Ways of **Aquinas**. It is based on the notion that an infinite regress (going backwards forever) is impossible, and that the existence of everything must be traced back logically to a first cause, God. In contrast to the ontological argument, which is mostly *a priori*, the cosmological argument is based on the cosmos – the world – and so is *a posteriori*. The argument comes in three forms; namely, motion or change, causality and contingency.

How persuasive is the cosmological argument for God's existence?

The cosmological argument is so-called because it is based on the evidence of the cosmos, or world. From an examination of the world, it is claimed, we can prove the existence of a being who must have created it. This is called *a posteriori* reasoning; that is, reasoning that follows experience, or reasoning based on experiential data.

However, it has been objected that the argument also relies on *a priori* reasoning; that is, reasoning that precedes experience. For instance, the claim that every event *must* have a cause is not the same as saying that every event in our experience *has* a cause (the former is *a priori* and the latter *a posteriori*). As **David Hume** said, perhaps the world has no cause, since we have no experience of universes being caused. This was considered a rather weak point even in Hume's day. The belief that every event must have a cause cannot either be proved from experience or proved as logically necessary. It is simply a basic assumption, or axiom, without which no reasoning could take place at all. Besides, it is a matter of empirical observation that every event does have a cause, a fact that seems to more than justify the inductive belief that every event must have a cause.

Although the cosmological argument goes back to the Greeks (**Plato** and **Aristotle** had reflected on the impossibility of the world explaining itself), its best known formulation is set out in the Five Ways of **St Thomas Aquinas**.

The *first way* argues from motion or change in the world, and leads back to the notion of an unmoved mover, which is called God. The argument survives the claim that movement and change are natural features of matter (**Isaac Newton**). This is because motion and change occur in causal, as opposed to random, sequences. This legitimises the idea of a logically first, or 'prime', mover. Even the apparently random causality observed in quantum physics needs a framework within which to operate, and outside that framework it has no application. The notion of a possible first mover being explained by a prior mover, which itself needs to be explained, is rejected as an absurdity by the argument, which is why an infinite regress is also rejected.

The *second* form of the cosmological argument is from causality, and proceeds to the conclusion that there must have been a first cause of everything, which is called God. The argument has attracted a number of criticisms. **Bertrand Russell's** ridicule that 'because every human being has a mother, the human race must have a mother' shows that he misunderstood Aquinas. Aquinas was not saying that the whole series of cause and effect had to have a cause, but merely that its beginning had to have a cause that itself is uncaused. Such a first cause was logically, or ontologically, necessary to explain how the causal chain ever got started.

Another criticism is the idea that an infinite regress is possible, a notion central to the 'Steady State' theory of **Fred Hoyle**. This makes little sense when analysed, because it fails to deal with how a contingent (chance) series of contingent causes could ever have started. To presuppose that it never needed to start is simply an assertion, and raises the question of how a contingent series could appear from nowhere – or why it should have come into existence only 15 billion years ago, the time when the universe began. Whether the fact that many people can live with the idea of an infinite regress is more a fatal flaw in peoples' thinking than a flaw of the argument is something that could be hotly debated.

The question of origins is touched on again in Aquinas' tantalising *third way*. Here Aquinas argues from the fact that everything in the world might not have existed and, indeed, at one time did not exist. If this is the case, it follows that at some time nothing existed. Since nothing can come from nothing (*ex nihilo nihil fit*), there must have been a being that always and necessarily existed, which is called God. As **John Hick** has pointed out, Aquinas is not talking about *logical* necessity, as **Anselm** was, but *factual* necessity. Without the fact of God's existence, nothing could ever have come into existence. However, this distinction seems unnecessary if we bear in mind that the argument moves towards a logical conclusion. It seems that the existence of God is just as logically necessary as it is factually necessary.

Another objection is contained in the question 'Could not the universe be eternal?' This question is really a variation of the notion of an infinite regress. In a famous radio debate with **Frederick Copleston** in the 1940s, Bertrand Russell defended this possibility by saying that the universe was just there, and that's all there is to it. Copleston saw this as an evasion. He agreed that the universe could be eternal, but only as long as it was granted that God was ontologically the originator of it, meaning that the universe owed its existence ultimately to God. This would allow for the possibility of a universe that was eternally existent with God, but still dependent on Him for its existence. Science, however, does not support an eternal universe.

The so-called *kalam* argument, set out by Muslim philosophers, highlights this point. The sequence of causes that resulted in our world cannot be infinite, since infinity, in fact, cannot be known or conceived. Experience also shows – and science has proved – that the universe had a finite beginning. The resulting conclusion is that the universe is ultimately dependent on the agency of a **personal will**, which is called God.

Gottfried Leibniz produced a variation of the cosmological argument with the idea that everything in the world must have a sufficient reason for its existence. Since nothing in the world is the sufficient reason for its own existence, because everything requires a material cause, it is necessary to go outside the world, to a being who is the sufficient reason of its own existence, called God. We can see that Leibniz is treading much the same ground as Aquinas, but using different terminology. Both are clearly driven by an awareness that the world cannot explain itself.

The Enlightenment critiques of **David Hume** and **Immanuel Kant** dealt a serious blow to the cosmological argument. They rejected all metaphysical speculation on the grounds that we could never know what lies outside the range of human experience. Kant called causality a necessary (*a priori*) perception, without which experience could not be possible at all. This restricted the notion of causality to the world of space and time. There could be no such thing as a cause that operated outside experience.

However, the idea that the intellect should be satisfied to stay within the limits of experience was to prove highly presumptuous, as **Descartes** had already shown. Besides, the contemporary philosopher **William Lane Craig** has questioned Kant's logic in limiting causality to experience, and ruling out its application beyond the horizon of experience. By doing this, Kant has actually gone outside experience to rule out causality. The most he can say is that we cannot confirm it by experience. But, as we saw, Aquinas showed that causality is presupposed in understanding how things ever began at all.

Another blow to the argument came with rise of science, with its emphasis on causal empirical explanations. The notion of **ultimate** causality was overtaken with more down-to-earth scientific concerns about how the world is, and how it works – not where it came from (as Russell showed). Defenders of the argument might reply that its aim is not to challenge science, but to point out the inadequacies of human, natural or mechanical reasons as ultimate explanations of how the world is. This is why modern scholars still hark back to the cosmological argument in seeking to highlight such things as our inability to explain ourselves, or to account for our **spiritual** complexity, our contingent nature, our ceaseless moral striving, our sense of the artistic and the aesthetic or, indeed, our insatiable thirst for more and more knowledge.

The cosmological argument may be properly situated as part of the search for the truth behind the world; and its conclusions, being both logically coherent and consistent with experience, will continue to command respect. The fact that the God it reaches is a 'philosophical God' is a religious criticism of the limited knowledge that it provides of the God that the argument establishes. But this is not a rational shortcoming, since the God of faith presupposes the God of philosophy. Yet it must be admitted that no philosophical conclusions can necessarily compel religious faith, a fact indeed readily acknowledged by all its defenders.

For this reason the argument has many weaknesses, beginning with its reliance on cold reason, and in its inability to settle decisively the metaphysical question that it takes on. By itself, the argument may be considered an academic exercise, with little practical impact even on the religious faith of the ordinary believer. But it still raises awkward questions that remain provocative: in some form or other, it continues to be a stubborn last line of defence in the philosophical justification of theism.

Related questions: _____

1 Discuss the view that the cosmological argument shows that faith and reason are in agreement about God's existence.

2 Is the theory of an 'infinite regress' fatal to the validity of the cosmological argument?

3 To what extent does science offer a convincing alternative to the cosmological argument?

The Teleological Argument

The **teleological** argument is based on the appearance of order, beauty and purpose in the universe. Some like to make the distinction between **order** and **regularity**, but one implies the other. The regularity of the seasons, coming from the order in the regularity of the heavenly bodies such as the sun and the moon, has traditionally been the main reference point of the argument. Other aspects of nature, such as the wonder of reproduction, the workings of human faculties such as the eye or the marvel of animal instinct, have provided the material for the teleological argument in its later forms.

The argument came to suffer a serious decline after the criticisms of **David Hume** and, later, after the discoveries of **Charles Darwin** which were followed by a growing confidence in the ability of science to explain everything. This led to the conviction that scientific explanations would eventually replace all religious ones. Therefore, a major weakness of the argument is its reliance on a certain degree of wonder about the workings of nature, a wonder that science has helped to dispel. But the argument has not gone away.

Modern forms of the argument centre on the two main questions. First, how did the universe create the unlikely conditions that resulted in human life, the very **precondition** for understanding the universe at all? This is the **anthropic principle**, which to science is a brute fact of no great significance. To some philosophers and theologians, however, the universe was so unlikely to produce life – let alone **conscious** life – that the fact that it did so is nothing short of a mystery. The other question centres on the meaning, aim or *'telos'* of our existence. How is it that our capacity for knowledge, understanding and achievement can never be fully satisfied? And how is it that we are driven to seek the **good**, the true and the beautiful? Such questions cannot be answered by science, which is limited to the empirical world of cause and effect.

Assess the main strengths and weaknesses of teleological arguments for the existence of God.

The roots of the teleological argument are to be found in the thought of **Aristotle**, who argued that **soul** or **mind** was the origin of everything, 'the cause of good and evil, the base and honourable, just and unjust, and of all other opposites ...'. The 'World Soul' was what lay behind the universe, and was a 'principle of wisdom'. This argument forms the *fifth* of the Five Ways of **St Thomas Aquinas**. He argued that everything in the world, animate and inanimate, was directed to a purpose or end (*'telos'*). The evidence of order and purpose in the world pointed to the hidden presence of a guiding Intelligence: 'This all men speak of as God'.

William Paley famously used the analogy of a watch to argue that just as something so complex, ingenious and purposeful as a watch points to a watchmaker, so does the world point to an intelligent designer. Paley's intention was to highlight the unlikelihood that the universe, let alone wonders such as the human eye, could be chance occurrences. His analogy was not intended to suggest that the world was like a mechanical object, but merely that such a complex but organised totality suggested an intelligent creator. However, he could not have foreseen that many of the wonders that he spoke about would later be explained in terms of the laws of nature – thus not needing, as **Pierre Laplace** said, any *religious* hypothesis.

This is what happened with the arrival of Charles Darwin's theory of evolution, a theory whose credibility was strengthened by geological and archaeological studies that revealed the earth to be millions of years old. This has encouraged some modern scientists to suppose that, given enough time, it will be possible to explain everything by science. The findings of Darwin, and the rise of naturalistic explanations for what had previously been thought to be 'miracles of nature' – such as planetary regularity, animal instinct or the workings of the human eye – greatly weakened the force of the teleological argument. So-called 'design' came to be seen as the natural outcome of gravitational forces, or the interaction of living things with their environment over long periods of time.

Earlier, **David Hume** had already argued for the possibility of various natural explanations for the phenomena of apparent order and purpose in the universe. Even granted that it was the work of a designer (which could never be proved anyway), the universe gave no reason to suppose that the designer was an infinite or perfect God. This could be seen from those aspects of the world that showed poor design, especially those that gave rise to evil and suffering. If he existed, said Hume, a good deity could at least have arranged to mitigate the suffering caused either by human wickedness or natural disasters.

John Stuart Mill, following in the critical tradition of Hume, thought that animal suffering, particularly that which arose within the animal kingdom itself, could be given no rational justification, and counted heavily against 'a Being of infinite power'. But while the argument in its classical form has suffered some decline, the questions that it has tried to address have returned in new guises.

Hume is almost certainly playing devil's advocate with the argument, showing correctly that its conclusions are not convincing because empirical facts cannot support religious conclusions. But in some places he appears to miss the point. Even if the world was created by angels or other beings (which is not completely ruled out by the Bible), it would merely push the question of its origin further back. Part of the argument is surely to make the link between the nature of the world and the conclusions of the ontological and cosmological arguments. By focusing his concern on showing that other explanations of the world's existence, design and teleology are just as feasible as the traditional religious one, Hume avoids the bedrock ontological issue of how the world came about in the first place. This probably goes to show that for the teleological argument to be fully understood it cannot be isolated from the other arguments for God's existence.

Despite Hume's challenge, the argument has continued to attract attention. Its supporters refuse to accept that a world resulting from chance is a credible concept, because such an explanation would do little justice to the mystery of human existence. So **F. R. Tennant** highlights the aesthetic dimension of the world, which only humans can appreciate. Beauty is something we recognise, he says, but it is an aspect of the world that need not be there. Its presence in art, music, architecture or nature evokes, for him, a kind of awe and wonder that most appropriately leads to a religious response.

Austin Farrer argues along similar lines that wonders such as the beauty of nature or the phenomenon of reproduction are 'more consistent with a theistic view than with any other'. **John Polkinghorne** has used the **anthropic principle** to argue that chance is an unlikely theory to explain how, or why, the exact conditions occurred that were required for the universe to produce conscious life. Even the atheist **Thomas Nagel** has questioned the adequacy of evolution to explain the complexity of human consciousness and rational thought. He finds it puzzling that the universe should be credited with producing the rationality required for us to understand it! Nagel does not draw any religious conclusion from this, but his question clearly provides the basis for some modern formulations of the argument.

In the end, teleological arguments will always suffer from the weaknesses exposed by Hume: empirical explanations can always be offered as a provisional explanation for the way things are – and without the problem of evil or suffering arising for them. In the age of evolutionary **naturalism** begun by Darwin, and continued by contemporary writers such as **Richard Dawkins**, scientific explanations will always have more immediate attraction than ultimate, religious explanations.

Yet the sheer fact of a world open to scientific investigation – a world of art, beauty and moral vision – is not something that everyone is prepared to take for granted, because such aspects need not be there. For believers in particular, the teleological argument helps to confirm faith in a God that they already know through faith, whose existence they naturally see reflected in the teleology that the world exhibits. This exposes the overriding philosophical *weakness* of the argument: it only makes sense to the already converted, and has little power to move the unbeliever. But this can also be seen as its *strength*. As **Thomas McPherson** put it, the value of the teleological argument 'lies in its power to confirm faith, not create it, and in its power to set up a habit of mind, suitable for religious believers, in which there is a disposition to see design in the things about them'.

A final criticism of the argument is the fact that it fails to point to a God that is recognisably the God of religious faith. But perhaps this is to overlook the fact that the argument makes no claim to do so. The so-called **God of metaphysics** – or what **Blaise Pascal** disparagingly called the **God of the philosophers** – is indeed only a pale shadow of the God of either Christianity, Judaism or Islam. Aquinas explicitly acknowledged that only by **revelation** could the trinitarian God of Christian faith be fully known. However, since the God of religious faith logically implies the God of metaphysics, it is not difficult to see how the argument *a posteriori* can evoke, for the believer, a recognition that this is the same God as the God of faith.

Related questions:

1 What are the strengths and weaknesses of the teleological argument?

2 To what extent has modern science undermined the validity of the teleological argument?

3 How valid is the criticism that the teleological argument can only make sense to believers?

The Moral Argument

The **moral argument** for God's existence switches from a consideration of the outside world that surrounds our existence and turns within, to a consideration of existence itself. Central to the argument is the claim that certain features of our inner experience call for an explanation. One such feature is our capacity for moral awareness. Where does this awareness come from, and can it be explained merely by reference to human factors, such as our personal needs or wishes, or our social needs in the world? For **Immanuel Kant**, the most famous proponent of the argument, we are mysteriously lords of our environment – not merely products of it as the evolutionary naturalism of **Charles Darwin** appeared to suggest. As moral beings, we transcend our surroundings and want to put the world right. It is these facts that lead Kant to draw conclusions that transcend our existence in the world, conclusions that are indeed religious.

 Assess the strengths and weaknesses of Kant's moral argument for God's existence.

Kant produced what is called the **moral argument** for God's existence after he had joined with **David Hume** in exposing the futility of the traditional **rational** approaches exemplified by the cosmological and teleological arguments. For Kant, it was a question of turning away from the first thing that ever filled him with wonder, 'the starry heavens above', to the second, 'the moral law within' (the words engraved on Kant's tombstone).

St Paul had hinted at the possibilities of a moral argument when he spoke of the Gentiles having 'the divine law written on their hearts'. But Kant drew no direct inference for the existence of God from moral obligation alone, and studiously avoided seeing the moral law as anything but a human rational phenomenon. For Kant, the **moral law** was a universal experience that touched every human being, regardless of religious belief or disbelief. Ironically, it was the fact of human moral experience that led Kant, on later reflection, indirectly to introduce the idea of God.

Kant explicitly stated that his moral argument was not a 'proof' of God's existence in the ordinary rational sense. Kant distinguished between the theoretical and the practical reason. The theoretical reason that was used in the traditional arguments was shown to be unable to provide such proof. But he believed it was possible to turn to the practical reason, and here to find a basis for understanding why God must exist. For Kant, reason had two aspects: it was a light telling us what we could know (knowledge) and what we should do (will). The latter was the role of the practical reason, which makes us aware of questions raised by our inner moral life, what we usually call our **conscience**.

Central to Kant's argument was the **categorical imperative**, or the absolute sense of **duty** that we all experience in certain situations. This 'compulsion to do the morally right thing' was for Kant something of a mystery. Where does this sense of duty come from, and where does it lead? Either the natural world is at the mercy of blind forces or it is not. If, as **Jean-Paul Sartre** claimed, God does not exist, then the moral life is absurd, since in such a world 'everything would be permitted'. If it is not, then the moral life is worthwhile. But it requires faith to believe this, because experience shows that happiness does not necessarily come from following the moral law.

Kant knew that the contradictions of the moral life, with its absolute demands on the one hand, and its frustrations and apparent unfairness on the other, raised questions that were difficult to answer by the light of reason alone. Somehow, we cannot avoid the conviction that happiness should only belong to those who deserve it; that is, those who have followed the dictates of their conscience. This conviction is rooted in our awareness of the *summum bonum* (the highest good). This is our inner compass needle, our sense of **justice** that **virtue** should be rewarded with happiness. If the *summum bonum* exists – that is, if justice is ever to be done in the moral life – it must be in another realm beyond the present world, because it doesn't happen in this world.

Put another way, the *summum bonum* is the reward of a good will used in the pursuit of the moral law. But for the *summum bonum* to be realised it has to be supposed that God exists to guarantee it. Kant's argument is therefore based on faith and trust, not on reason or logic. It does not have the strict character of a rational proof, but it highlights the stark choice between seeing the moral life as having a just fulfilment, or seeing it as an instance of the absurdity of human life. Kant believed that it provided a basis for trusting that life was not absurd. And here lies the weakness of the argument.

Critics of Kant say that he presupposes too much, and that his faith in the *summum bonum* being realised in the future is greatly misplaced. From an **atheistic** standpoint, this life is all there is, and any belief to the contrary can easily be explained as a projection of our human powers on to an imaginary God, as **Ludwig Feuerbach** held. Religion might be a kind of opium to dull mankind into thinking that this life doesn't need to be changed, because everything will come right in some future life, as **Karl Marx** believed. Or religion might be an **illusion**, or wishful thinking, that creates the imaginary comfort of a heavenly father who can forgive our wrongdoing, as **Sigmund Freud** held. Perhaps life is unjust and carries no ultimate rewards, and that is the brute fact of the matter (**Bertrand Russell**).

Critics of Kant also argue that his idea of an objective moral law is without foundation. Morality, it is argued, is man-made, and arises from our human needs as individuals and as members of society. It can really be explained in terms of our need for survival as individuals and as a group. This accounts for the way in which moral rules shift and vary between times and cultures. If this is true, and morality is a human survival tool, then there is no such thing as a 'moral law' independent of our needs as human beings.

Experience, however, shows that we do have an inner sense of **obligation** to do certain things or behave in certain ways, a sense not easily explained in purely rational terms. The validity of this sense does not necessarily depend on Kant's particular understanding of the moral law. In other words, the categorical imperative is a fact of life regardless of how we understand its content. Two people facing the same situation may see their duty in different ways. For one person, family commitments may come first; for another, the demands of job or country. But for Kant it is the sense of duty that is significant, not its material content. Therefore the idea of a fixed 'moral law' is not crucial to Kant's argument. We still have a basic **moral sense** that requires a metaphysical explanation.

Kant held that the moral life without God simply leaves too many questions unanswered. Our human spiritual ability to receive moral insights, and pursue them by our free will and sense of duty, raised for Kant the whole question of whether our destiny could be reduced to a matter of blind chance. This admittedly called for faith, but a faith in which God would be seen as the vital key to making sense of some important facts about ourselves.

Predictably, support for Kant's argument has come from believers. The argument is remarkably in accord with Christian beliefs about divine law, and the rewards of the moral life in the hereafter, as stated in The Bible. **J. H. Newman** saw **conscience** as the basis of a similar argument for God's existence. Our moral conscience is a source of obligation that has the character of making us feel subject to a personal law-giver, which we call God. Both **Huw Parri Owen** and **Maurice Wiles** have suggested that the demands of the moral law have the character of *personal* demands. These demands, whatever the difficulties in getting them 'right', are perceived not as impersonal forces or as merely human conventions, but as coming from a personal law-giver that we call God.

Other theologians have, in different ways, taken up the Kantian approach of making a link between morality and faith. **Rudolf Bultmann** has argued that the moral life is a central issue for everyone's existence, and sees its resolution in the inspiration provided by the example and destiny of Jesus Christ.

Paul Tillich was concerned to answer **Friedrich Nietzsche's** criticism that religion weakened and constricted the human will, and halted moral progress. Religion, with its belief in the after-life, he suggested, helped to make more sense of moral demands, and provided a more effective dynamic for changing the world for the better through brotherly love and self-sacrifice. In conclusion, Kant's moral argument may provide a less than watertight case for God's existence, as many thinkers have shown. But its challenge to draw some transcendent or spiritual conclusion from the compelling experience of the moral life cannot easily be dismissed.

Related questions: _____

1 Evaluate the criticism that Kant's moral argument is a form of wishful thinking.

2 How valid is the claim that Kant's argument depends on the existence of an objective moral law?

3 How significant is the connection between Kant's argument and the claims of religious faith?

4 Explain how Kant's argument could form part of a cumulative case for God's existence.

The Attributes of God in Philosophy

The classic profile of God that is called classical theism is based on the *a priori* (logically required, or prior) qualities that God must possess in order to be worthy of

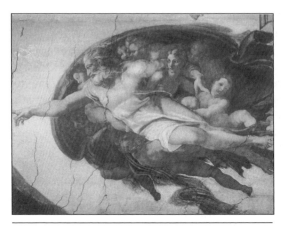

God, from the Sistine Chapel, by Michelangelo

the worship due to a deity. If God was to lack any of the attributes set out in classical theism, He could not be God. Thus God needs to possess attributes that include omnipotence, omniscience, absolute **goodness** and necessary existence. First, how are these attributes to be understood? Then, how far they can be challenged in the light of certain aspects of human experience? This takes us to the major question of evil and suffering, which will be dealt with again later.

Q Explain the main attributes of God in Western philosophy.

This is a philosophical question, which refers to those attributes that God must possess in order to be God, using only the tools of reason, not of faith. **St Thomas Aquinas**, although a theologian, took on the role of philosopher using reason alone when he set out to demonstrate the existence of God in his famous Five Ways.

Although the Five Ways are meant to establish the existence of God, a logical profile of the God that they establish can be built up using the tools of reason. The end result is known as the God of classical theism. The attributes that God must possess include: having necessary existence, being all-good, all-powerful, all-knowing and all-perfect, and being a living spirit. In this essay we shall consider three aspects of God that have been central to classical theism.

Necessity   We begin with **necessity**. Necessary existence means that God must of necessity exist. In **Anselm's** ontological argument, God is 'that than which nothing greater can be thought'. Anselm argues that the notion of God implies His necessary existence, since the greatest possible being must not just exist as a notion in the mind, but also exist in reality. Therefore a being that didn't exist of himself (*a se*) couldn't be the greatest possible being. In this line of reasoning, Anselm brings together the ideas of logical necessity and existential necessity (existence as a matter of fact).

Aquinas arrives at God's necessity by a different route, in the cosmological argument. Experience shows that everything requires a prior cause. Indeed, the search for prior causes is the mission of science. But a chain of contingent things, causally related in an infinite regress, is an intellectual absurdity, say

Plato, **Aristotle** and Aquinas. Therefore, a necessary being that does not need any prior cause of its existence is required to account for how the causal sequence got started at all.

The notion of God implies a being that cannot come into existence, since this would presuppose that something had been there prior to God to account for His existence. Equally, God cannot cease to exist, since this would presuppose a superior power that could bring His existence to an end. This was what **Norman Malcolm** meant when he said that either God's existence is necessary or it is impossible.

As Anselm argued, existence belongs to the very definition of God. After demonstrating God's existence by *a posteriori* reasoning, Aquinas restated the ontological argument by saying that God's essence is necessarily to exist. **René Descartes** admitted that he could no more conceive of God not existing than he could think of a triangle without its three angles adding up to 180 degrees. To believers, God's necessary existence has implications for human life. They see this an essential perfection that makes God both infinite and eternal, and uniquely the object of human worship. In this sense, the God of the philosophers contributes to the understanding of religious faith.

Yet the notion of necessity remains puzzling. Linguistic philosophers insist that only propositions can be called necessary – that is, those that are *a priori* – are logically true. Atheists dismiss the idea of a factually necessary being as incoherent, since all facts are contingent. This is not so simple, however, when we consider that all established facts (such as the existence of the sun) are also necessarily true. Atheists prefer to accept the possibility of an infinite regress in, say, explaining how the world originated. However, the idea of an infinite causal chain that goes backwards and forwards to eternity is ironically close to the religious notion of infinity that only God can possess! This remains an important sticking point in the conflict between theism and atheism.

In conclusion, those who defend the notion of God's necessary existence can do so either from the perspective of the ontological argument on the one hand, or from that of the cosmological argument on the other. If the former, God is seen as having *logical* necessity, since his existence is viewed from an *a priori* position; that is, not dependent on experience. If the latter, his existence is viewed from an *a posteriori* or existential position, and his existence is seen as having *existential* necessity. The problem remains, however, that those who might accept the notion of God's logical necessity do not necessarily feel compelled to accept the notion of God's existential necessity. It is the latter claim that distinguishes the believer from the non-believer.

Omnipotence   Amongst His attributes, God is held to be all-powerful. To suggest otherwise is to say that God has some limitations, which is self-contradictory. The difficulty with omnipotence arises from the experiential fact that God appears to be 'powerless' in controlling certain events in the world, such as disproportionate suffering, and the apparent free rein of evil. The traditional theistic answer, that God's power is constrained and limited by mankind's free will, begs the original question 'Why?' If it appears obvious from experience that God does not interfere with human free will – as when Hitler and Stalin were allowed to commit some of the worst crimes in history – the conclusion for many is that this simply shows that no God exists.

Yet, philosophically, there is no contradiction in God allowing evil while remaining omnipotent. An omnipotent and good God might be able to see human evil and suffering in a different perspective to human beings, and ensure that justice is always done in the end. Reasons produced by theologians from **Irenaeus** and **St Augustine** to **Richard Swinburne** and **John Hick** centre on the notion that free will was a gift given by God to allow humans to live freely and virtuously (good), regardless of the risk of evil that might result from its misuse. This so-called 'free will defence' makes human freedom a necessary condition of our acting virtuously before God, and so makes it worthwhile.

But the cost of putting a practical limit on God's omnipotence is to reduce, for many, the credibility of His existence as a likely fact. Linking omnipotence with God's nature results in the unbeliever finding empirical evidence, if not proof, that no omnipotent power such as God exists at all.

For this reason, some theologians have suggested that the notion of God's omnipotence is somewhat too philosophical, and therefore too misleading. The biblical notion that God is **almighty** is seen as much more meaningful. In this view, although God allows humans free will to do good or evil, He is firmly on the side of good and, crucially, is still in charge of the ultimate outcome of all things. In this view, God is not to be judged on the empirical evidence of the here and now, because His power extends beyond the present world. As **Immanuel Kant** held, in a world that appears chaotic, with no balance between good and evil, only an almighty God can ensure the final triumph of justice and right. This is a compelling argument, but it is open to the criticism that **faith** is required to accept it. For the **unbeliever**, this begs too many questions.

Logically implied as part of the attribute of omnipotence is the attribute of **omniscience**. If God is all-powerful, He must be all-knowing. But if God is all-knowing, why did He decide to create a world that would contain evil and suffering? There are three possible approaches to this question. (1) Aquinas held that God could know the future, but that such knowledge need not necessarily interfere with human free will. In other words, humans cannot complain just because God may know how they used their freedom. (2) **Keith Ward** thinks that, in any case, God cannot know that part of the future that depends on the free decisions of human beings. In this view, the future is beyond the horizon of God's knowledge, so that not knowing the future is not necessarily a limitation on the part of God. (3) **Richard Swinburne** puts forward a similar idea, but with a slight variation. He argues that God could freely choose to limit His knowledge to avoid any interference with human free will. In this view, God blots out the future, to leave human beings psychologically free. Although all three theories attempt to grapple with the problems raised by God's omniscience, in the end they fail to explain to the sceptic why an all-knowing God could not have ensured the existence of a world that more clearly reflected His goodness.

A living spirit   From a philosophical point of view, the notion that God is a living spirit is implied by the other attributes. The idea of a lifeless God would be self-contradictory, since a God who lacked life would lack the essential perfections implied in being His own cause, being of good will (benevolent) and being omnipotent. A being so lacking couldn't be God. Hence, from the earliest times, the notion of God implied a living God, a divine characteristic central to the Bible. Plato sensed the need for a living origin of all things when he attributed the creation of the world to a self-moving principle that he called the **World Soul**.

Plato's term **soul** calls attention to God's essential attribute, spirit. Philosophically, God's essence cannot include a material body, since a body is composed of parts that are contingent and perishable. In medieval philosophy, God is not a 'this' or a 'that', and is not subject to analysis. As Aquinas showed, God's nature is spirit, because only a spirit is simple (*simplicitur*) and not composed of parts (*compositum*). Plato also argued that soul is the most powerful thing, able to create good and evil, truth and lies, and beauty and justice, as well as their opposites. Therefore the origin of everything is appropriately soul, or life.

The alternative to a living origin of the world is, of course, a theory of eternal matter, which in turn entails the explanation of reality and its development in terms of pure chance. Such a theory raises a host of philosophical problems (which appear under the arguments for God's existence, above). At the very least, it leaves the world at the mercy of blind lifeless forces. For Kant, this would rule out the notion of any ultimate significance to personal human morality. For some, such as **Karl Rahner** or **Wolfhart Pannenberg**, it would fail to account for certain dynamic and intellectual aspects of human consciousness (**transcendence**).

For others, the concept of God as a living spirit with a personal will is crucial to the notion that the world had an ultimate **beginning**. The alternative is that the world is the cause of itself, or never had a beginning. As **William Lane Craig** has argued, the former was disproved by Aquinas, while the latter has been disproved by science. This means that God can only be described as personal, an idea that is confirmed in the Bible.

The Jewish philosopher **Martin Buber** has sought to underline this by showing that an 'I–Thou' relationship with God (that is, a personal relationship) is the key to understanding God. He compares this to the rather detached 'I–It' relationship (that is, a relationship to an object) which we form with things and possessions. However, Buber was aware that the application of the word 'person' to God creates problems.

When God is described as a 'person', the word is used analogically (by way of comparison) in an attempt to apply to God the highest form of reality known to our experience; that is, ourselves as living persons, characterised by freedom and intelligence. However, a human person possesses a body, is materially visible and is located in a particular space at a particular time. God is often thought of, or imagined, in this way – as when people say that He is 'up there in the heavens'. To take this literally is to forget that language is used symbolically here, for the purpose of showing a respectful attitude to God as the highest being.

In more recent times, attempts have been made by theologians such as **Rudolf Bultmann**, **Paul Tillich** and **John Macquarrie** to shift the idea of God back into a more spiritual framework. This was to avoid the problems of 'objectifying' God, and to restore the essential mystery of a divine spirit whose inner being cannot be fully described in human language. Yet it has to be said that many people continue to reject the idea that reality needs an ultimate explanation such as God. Thus the divine attributes, while philosophically coherent, continue to be rejected as metaphysical speculation by those who deny God's existence.

Related questions:

1 Explain and assess the meaning of God's necessary existence as understood by Anselm, Aquinas, Descartes and Malcolm.

2 What problems are attached to the claim that God is omnipotent and omniscient?

3 How far does human experience encourage belief, or disbelief, in the idea of a personal God?

Problems with Classical Theism

What problems have been raised about certain attributes of God in Western philosophy?

Among the attributes of God which have caused problems in Western philosophy are God's **benevolence**, **omnipotence** and **omniscience**. These attributes have been criticised as being inconsistent with the evidence of human experience. Although all three attributes are interrelated, we begin with the interrelation between benevolence and omnipotence. According to classical theism, God is of necessity benevolent; that is, He possesses an absolutely good will, and is absolutely good and loving. Since evil is a lack of perfection, an evil or malevolent 'god', as Aquinas said, would be self-contradictory, and such a being could not be God.

The claim that God is benevolent is challenged on empirical grounds by the existence in the world of evil and suffering. If God were benevolent, it is argued, He would not have created a world in which people suffer unfairly, because he would want to show his infinite love and goodness. If God were omnipotent, it is argued, He would have the power to end evil and suffering. Thus the existence of evil and suffering shows that God is either not willing or not able to do anything about it. Thus, the conclusion follows, no God exists.

The Christian response is to offer an answer within the terms of religious faith, and to see evil and suffering as something that can be reconciled with God's justice. This is called **theodicy**, which means *justifying* God. God allows evil and suffering to happen as part of a world in which human beings are given freedom. Much evil is caused by the misuse of freedom, starting with Adam and continuing ever since. But free will can also be used correctly to bring about good, and the possibility of the good use of freedom, and the moral benefits it brings, outweighs its misuse. This is known as the **free will defence**.

In this view, the apparent unfairness of suffering is a mystery, but trust in God entails the acceptance of unavoidable evil as part of God's plan for the world. Theologians such as **Jurgen Moltmann** insist that evil and suffering should be fought against, and that God's guiding influence and inspiration is a key factor in this fight. First, the universal recognition of what evil is is rooted in a moral awareness that is encouraged and supported by religious faith. Secondly, religious (Christian) faith is geared specifically to the love of neighbour, and will always be a driving force in the fight against evil and injustice.

The demands of faith, however, are sometimes too much even for believers. Some are so outraged by evil that they refuse to believe any longer, as exemplified by the character of Ivan in **Fyodor Dostoyevsky's** *The Brothers Karamazov*. Ivan Karamazov refuses to believe in a God that allows innocent children to suffer. The Holocaust has become the classic modern example of this problem, raising for many the poignant question 'Where was God in Auschwitz?' More recently, the existentialist writers **Jean-Paul Sartre** and **Albert Camus** have declared their unbelief on the evidence of evil and suffering.

A different approach has been proposed by so-called **process theology**, which sees God as part of the world, involved in its affairs and sharing in its suffering. Through His presence in the world (typified by the life of Jesus), God is constantly working against evil and suffering, and persuading the world to overcome evil by the power of His law and grace. In this view, God is immanent

Where was God in Auschwitz? Atheists say that there is no such reality, but believers see this as a poignant and tantalising question

in the world, working and suffering with human beings. This is also called **process theology**.

The cost of this comforting view of God is the risk of eliminating His omnnipotence, and making Him appear more human than divine . For this reason, process theology has lost ground as a convincing theory, since it downplays God's **transcendence** to an unacceptable degree. If God is not transcendently God in the traditional sense, He is not all-powerful, and so cannot be challenged as the all-powerful God who allows evil and suffering to happen. Thus the problem of classical theism is solved by surrendering some of its key claims.

The problems raised by the third attribute, **omniscience**, relate to why God did not use his foreknowledge to ward off the undesirable aspects of His creation. The criticism is that if God were all-knowing He would have foreseen the evil and suffering that afflict the world, and so should have done something to prevent it. For example, if God knew that Adam was going to fall from grace, why did He put him to the test in the first place? From this if follows that if God could have foreseen the evil and suffering of His creation, he cannot be absolved from responsibility for its happening.

The believer's answer is that God's omniscience may be puzzling, but it is not inconsistent with God's love. With regard to natural evil – such as floods, disease and road accidents – a world of fixed laws will inevitably give rise to suffering when things go wrong. But these are natural risks in an uncertain world, and as **John Hick** and **Richard Swinburne** have argued, without such risks we could never be truly human, or grow into mature and responsible adults. Other risks follow from the misuse of free will, which causes moral evil, such as murder and violence.

John Hick has added the notion that believers are at an **epistemic** distance from God. This means that God may seem absent or non-existent, resulting in a clouded vision that makes evil and suffering appear to lack any obvious purpose. This view is rejected for moral reasons by those who deny that suffering necessarily leads to moral growth, or 'soul-making'. This is confirmed they say, by the example of Jesus, who saw suffering as a misfortune and tried to alleviate it. It is also rejected for another moral reason by those who point to the injustice of its disproportionate, erratic, random and apparently senseless distribution. To reply that this is the 'mystery' of evil is simply to beg the question why it is indeed such a mystery.

The classical theodicies of **St Augustine** and **Irenaeus** both implicitly accept that God could have foreseen the arrival of evil in the world. However, this foresight would also have included foresight of good. Although Swinburne argues that God could have deliberately shut Himself off from any knowledge of how mankind was going to act, it may be that God saw the risk of the good outweighing the evil sufficiently to make creation worthwhile. Additionally, if God is omnipotent, then He is able to compensate in the after-life those who suffer unfairly or unavoidably in the here and now. Since God is believed to be infinitely just, this offsets the possibility of any ultimate 'unfairness' in suffering, as Ivan Karamazov alleged. But again the sceptic will ask on what evidence can this be accepted? The trusting convictions of faith will hardly suffice.

In conclusion, we have seen that the divine attributes of benevolence, omnipotence and omniscience have been challenged by the existence of evil and suffering. The believer is able to counter this challenge by giving theodicic reasons why God – who is infinitely good – allows the world to be as it is. However, the challenge to the attributes of God will remain as long as the unbeliever continues to see these aspects of life as sufficient evidence that a loving and good God does not exist.

Related questions:

1 Evaluate the view that 'this is the best of all possible worlds' for the realisation of God's purposes.

2 How valid is the claim that evil and suffering prove the non-existence of God?

3 How far are evil and suffering consistent with belief in God's attributes?

Faith and Reason

Søren Kierkegaard said that faith was like being suspended over 60 000 fathoms, but was he a fideist?

One of the more persistent questions in philosophy of religion is the relationship between faith and reason. Non-believers predictably see faith as unsupported by reason. This leads to the conclusion that faith is a fabrication, an invention, an illusion, something that is not true. However, believers do not uniformly see faith as something based on reason. For religious reasons, some distance themselves from any use of reason to support faith. According to this view faith, if it is to be a saving faith, or a faith that brings merit, must not be tied up with any strings of rational security. To do so would be to undermine the trust in God that they see as the essence of faith. Other believers are happy to use reason to assure themselves, or show others, that faith is a responsible and therefore rational choice in the face of questions raised by the nature of the world, and in particular of human life. **Blaise Pascal's** proposal that, for those who cannot penetrate the mysteries of faith by means of reason, a sensible option is to make a wager – in other words, to bet on faith – raises an interesting question. Does it amount to using reason by the back door?

(a) To what extent does faith have, or need, the support of reason?

(b) How far can faith be philosophically justified?

(a) For some believers, faith should not have any support from reason. To rely on reason is to contaminate the purity of faith by making it dependent on a human power that is in any case corrupt. Famous supporters of this view, which is known as **fideism**, include **St Augustine**, **Blaise Pascal**, **Martin Luther** and **Søren Kierkegaard**. The Catholic tradition, which looks to **St Thomas Aquinas**, permits the use of reason to show that faith is not irrational. However, there is considerable overlap and agreement between both sides about the religious nature of faith. Whether or not it is seen as supported by reason, faith is still a religious act that has its own inner spiritual dynamic which, in the end, makes it more than a human act of the will.

In the strict sense, fideism is the view the view that faith is a free personal choice to believe in God and His revelation, independent of rational evidence. At its most extreme, this approach means that faith contains its own justification, and does not rely on reason to provide any basis for it. In this view, faith is considered to be an act that is unsupported by rational evidence. It is not surprising, therefore, that fideism is often identified with irrationality and fanaticism. Considering that the most famous exponents of fideism mentioned above, including more recently **Karl Barth**, were all persons of acute intellect and unquestionable integrity, one has to suspect that fideism might not be so irrational as is often supposed. When looked at more carefully, fideism turns out to be a far more complex position than it might at first appear.

St Paul had already sown the seeds of fideism when he described faith as 'folly to the wise'. **St Augustine**, following Paul, held the view that faith was superior to reason, and provided a more lofty vision of what he called 'the truth that matters'. This explains his famous expression, 'I believe in order to understand' (*credo ut intelligam*). In this view, faith is beyond, an addition to, or above reason – not against it.

Martin Luther had a low estimate of reason as a human faculty, because he considered it to be corrupted by **egoism** and sin. Like St Augustine, he held that faith, being above reason, was a more reliable path to truth. But, if it was to be a saving faith, it required taking the risk of trust (*fiducia*). Søren Kierkegaard, following Luther, famously saw faith as a decisive, and somewhat reckless, leap of the will, a leap unsupported by the security of any rational evidence, like the feeling of being 'suspended over 60 000 fathoms'.

Yet, for Kierkegaard, the leap of faith was far from being absurd or 'foolish'. Given the existential cul de sac in which we find ourselves, the decision to make the leap of faith is a responsible and morally intelligent decision, which enables us to find religious enlightenment in a world of frustration and mystery. In this sense, faith is not at all irrational, but a sensible, wise and rewarding decision. Yet because the object of faith is a **paradox** – the paradox of God's love shown in a human being, Christ – it calls for a suspension of our normal tendency to seek reasons for reassurance. For Kierkegaard there can be no reassurance, because what is believed is 'the strangest thing in the world', as he called it. In this sense, faith goes partially against reason.

Others have argued that fideism should not be called irrational because, in some form or other, it is part of reason. **John Calvin** spoke of how reason itself is imbued with 'a sense of the divine' that can lead, say, to seeing God's handiwork in creation. This would suggest that reason (no doubt aided by grace), can enable mankind to 'see' with the eyes of faith, thus blurring the distinction between faith and reason. The need for divine grace is acknowledged by all fideists, and was curiously touched on by **Ludwig Wittgenstein** when he once remarked that it takes 'love' to believe in the Resurrection.

Pascal accepted that reason could never prove faith, but the decision to choose faith was responsible and worthwhile. Faith was a wise bet or gamble, given the shortness of life, the length of eternity and the importance of the stakes.

William James, who at first criticised Pascal, went on to defend fideism as something demanded by our 'passional nature'. We live in a time frame that is limited, where urgent decisions have to be made and risks taken. We cannot always wait for rational justification of everything, and if we did our ordinary human relations with others would be severely impaired (such as questioning a friend's honesty). Faith and trust without immediate supporting evidence (that is, some form of fideism) are therefore necessary, not only in religion but in everyday affairs.

Alvin Plantinga attempts to give fideism some rational basis by calling belief in God a **basic belief**. He is not speaking so much about belief in God's *existence* as belief in God's love, goodness, forgiveness, mercy and so on. A basic belief is one that makes fundamental sense to the holder, and need not be justified by any other beliefs. Fideists would agree that God cannot be objectified, or held up for inspection, and therefore cannot be the object of reason in the ordinary sense. As Kierkegaard said, the issue in a court case is not the existence of the prisoner, but whether or not he is a criminal. Besides, God can only be apprehended in the mode of address, in the same way as another person is known only through a relationship with them. This is the meaning of **Martin Buber's** point that God's reality can be grasped only in an 'I–Thou', and never in an 'I–It', relationship. In a real sense, then, all these forms of fideism can be called *responsible* fideism, because some justification accompanies the decision to believe.

There is also a form of fideism that is more directly related to reason as traditionally understood, which may be called *rationally justified* fideism. In this form of fideism faith is an option, but reason can be used, not as a justifying precondition, but merely to show that the option of faith is not irrational. In contrast to more strict fideism, reason is seen as a God-given faculty that mankind is meant to use in the search for truth. The tradition of rational fideism certainly includes **St Thomas Aquinas**, who saw reason as capable of providing the intellectual foundation of faith, not *a priori* but *a posteriori*, much as philosophy provides an intellectual foundation to theology. His Five Ways were an attempt to demonstrate that belief in the existence of God has a solid foundation in reasoned thought.

But both sides would agree that even if faith can be supported by reason, it doesn't need to call on reason. Aquinas was a believing Christian who saw faith within the context of a relationship with God. For him, faith was an act that was based on accepting 'the authority of God who reveals', a view that reserves a place for trust or *fiducia*, something central to the more strict fideism of **Luther** and **Kierkegaard**. As a philosopher, Aquinas was merely trying to demonstrate that faith had rational foundations that were transparent from the outside and visible to all.

Finally, there is what is called **Wittgenstein's** fideism. This is the view that faith is immune to criticism from those who do not understand the 'language game' of faith. In this view, faith can neither be supported nor undermined by reason, largely because the object of faith (God) is unlike any object in the contingent world. Reason can only be used to understand faith, not to criticise it. It must be remembered, however, that Wittgenstein was merely giving an account of how faith is perceived, practiced and expressed; he was not saying whether or not faith was rationally justified.

(b) The question whether faith can be philosophically justified has been central to the tradition of natural theology. Following the Enlightenment criticisms of **Hume** and **Kant**, rational-style natural theology, in the tradition of Aquinas, fell into disfavour. This was replaced by a new approach based on experience, suggested originally by Kant in his moral argument, but really pioneered by **Friedrich Schleiermacher**. Turning from reason to the senses, he argued that our deeply felt sense of 'absolute dependence' within a contingent universe made the idea of God possible to grasp. He believed that God could be perceived in the experience of contingency, and that this provided a more accessible basis for faith than rational thought.

Kierkegaard later argued that faith arises in the experience of the bleakness of existence that each person faces as an individual in the world. Either one turns to faith or one faces life as a complex and baffling series of frustrations and contradictions. Faith is therefore a risk that one takes, but the risk is worth taking in order to make sense of our existence. Other thinkers, influenced by Kierkegaard, and alarmed by the limiting effects of scientific atheism, have proposed that faith is a more than reasonable option in the light of the apparent absurdities and *Angst* of life. They would grant that atheism might be a valid, but negative, option; while science has little to offer as a solution to what Wittgenstein called 'the problems of life'.

Rudolf Bultmann believed that the inspiration of faith was necessary to make an authentic moral life possible. **Paul Tillich** argued that a life focused on a personal God, as the 'Ground' of our being, can inspire humans to have the 'courage to be', and help to counter the debilitating pull of the material world. Both of these approaches attempted to face head-on the criticisms of **Friedrich Nietzsche** in particular, who argued that faith in a God who was 'dead' was an obstacle to living a morally courageous life, and was ultimately an impediment to the full flourishing of the human spirit.

Those who deny that faith can be philosophically justified fall into two main categories: agnostics and atheists. Agnostics are products of the **Enlightenment**, and hold that knowledge of what lies beyond the empirical world is unattainable. The word comes from the Greek, meaning 'not to know'. In practice, they differ little from atheists, since they normally see religious faith as something for which there is insufficient evidence.

Atheism is a term that bears more directly on the question of God's existence, since the word means 'against God' (a-theism). Atheists believe that the physical or material world is all that there is, and that the empirical methods of science are the only basis for true knowledge about reality.

The modern atheistic tradition is usually traced to **Ludwig Feuerbach**, whose ideas about religion being a human projection of the mind had a great influence on later thinkers. The positivist tradition begun by **August Comte** gave a further boost to anti-religious ideas. The use of discoveries in sociology, led by **Emile Durkheim**, the influence of economics on peoples' beliefs as shown by **Karl Marx**, and the role of the unconscious in accounting for human drives and wishful thinking as shown by **Sigmund Freud**, gave a great impetus to the rejection of faith, and a preference for scientific, as opposed to supernatural, explanations of events in the world. As a result of these movements, all forms of fideism came to be rejected as irrational.

In conclusion, the question of whether faith can be philosophically justified is both defended and challenged. Theists and atheists remain divided on whether faith can be rationally or experientially justified. Believers argue that life without faith must remain largely unexplained. Non-believers argue that only the explanations provided by science have any credibility. Both sides claim to offer sound reasons for their world-view. In terms of the question, however, it is clear that there is a responsible tradition that holds faith to be philosophically justified, both in theory and in practice.

Related questions:

1　Explain the relationship between faith and reason.

2　Explain and evaluate the criticism that fideism is irrational.

3　'Fideism is a choice that has rational foundations, and is therefore reasonable.' Discuss.

Pascal's Wager

Evaluate the view that Pascal's Wager makes faith a matter of 'mechanical calculation'.

Blaise Pascal tried to show that life was an arena of risk, a battleground on which winning the prize of eternal salvation was at stake. Those who win the battle will win a prize of eternal value, while those who lose will risk facing a

30

future of eternal damnation. The size of the gap between winning and losing is so great that the sensible thing to do is to bet your life on winning, not on losing.

This is called **Pascal's Wager**, and it has been criticised by some as cold and calculating, bordering on the irreverent and the unworthy. **William James** said if he was in the place of the deity he would exclude from salvation anyone who tried to gain it through such 'mechanical calculation'. At the same time, James agreed with Pascal that some things are too important to await the arrival and security of confirming empirical evidence. We would lose many friends if we adopted such a suspicious and untrusting approach to life. James was therefore sympathetic to Pascal's appeal to **trust**, even if by the dubious route of taking a gamble. However, there seems more to the gamble than first meets the eye.

Pascal was a man who so valued his religious faith that he wanted to persuade others to risk everything in order to possess it. As a realist, and keenly aware of the frailties of human nature, he knew that no appeal to clever reasoning, or rational thinking, would cut any ice with his worldly contemporaries. In fact, the wager was the outcome of a period in Pascal's life when he lived in Paris, in the company of free-thinkers, gamblers and men of the world, among whom he was a worthy member.

Under the influence of **St Augustine**, he was convinced that reason was no path to religious faith. This approach, endorsed by **St Paul**, was 'folly'. Ideally, faith had to be accepted on its own terms. But there was one aspect of it that could appeal to ordinary 'men of the world': the great reward that religious faith held out for those who accepted it and lived by it, and the great loss that might await those who rejected it.

Pascal knew that the language of winning and losing was what his race-going and card-playing contemporaries would understand. Risk living a life of faith now and winning the prize of eternal life. Live a life without faith, and risk the terrible fate of facing an eternity of damnation. After all, life is short but eternity is long. The gamble required is only a temporary and limited investment, but the win or loss is for ever. 'If you win you win everything, if you lose you lose nothing', he pointed out.

But what exactly did Pascal mean? Was he calling for a life of sham and hypocrisy? Was he saying 'go through the motions of a life of faith and the prize will be yours'? To think this is to misunderstand Pascal, for whom faith was not just a matter of belief but also a matter of action. Faith was something that involved a real investment in moral and spiritual living. While Pascal recognised that the outward signs of faith – such as church-going, confession, holy water, saying prayers and so on – only made sense to believers, he believed that those who went through such practices would eventually benefit from them. Such outward practices could be a door to inner, religious faith.

It was the inner, more spiritual, or moral aspect of faith that was decisive for winning the wager. This was the struggle between good and evil, which Pascal believed was the ultimate essence of faith. It was this inner life that Pascal was more concerned about. In this arena of **moral living** there was no place for sham and hypocrisy – only honesty, discipline and dedication. Here was where the outlay of the wager took place. Live a life of decadence and egoism now, and risk an eternity of damnation; or live a life of discipline and goodness, as if you had faith at the intellectual level – and then you stand the chance of winning the lottery of life for eternity.

Viewed in this way, Pascal's Wager cannot be reduced to a matter of detached mechanical calculation, as James at first seems to have thought. Many theologians today agree with Pascal that faith is essentially about moral investment, the opposite of the 'cheap grace' criticised by **Dietrich Bonhoeffer** (referring to the way in which nominal believers often appear to rely on worship and sacraments). Other thinkers such as **Rudolf Bultmann** identified faith with the project of living an authentic, morally dedicated life. Noted for his view of faith in terms of moral living, **Karl Rahner** produced the concept of what he called 'anonymous Christianity', the theory that faith is about fidelity to conscience, the struggle to live a life of personal integrity, regardless of whatever label one wears, whether it be theist or atheist, Christian or non-Christian.

In the end, Pascal's Wager is about the implications of the possible existence of God. In effect, Pascal is saying that if God's existence is a possibility, then it is important to face up to the implications. Pascal thus anticipates **Kant**, whose moral argument also raises the question of God's existence, and for whom moral commitment comes before religious conviction. Pascal therefore called attention to the relationship between faith and life, and in doing so to the way in which faith is ultimately an act not of the intellect, but of the will.

It was 'the will to believe' that Pascal knew was the difficult part, and it was this that he tried to activate. Knowing human nature as he did, he knew that faith is less about the search for truth than about how it is perceived to impinge on personal convenience, as illustrated by the notorious Frank Mitchell. Once thinking about embracing the Jewish faith, he suddenly changed his mind. 'I like me bacon', he said. 'And Jews don't get none in Dartmoor.' For Pascal, being prepared to sacrifice temporary convenience is part of the wager.

We can conclude that those who criticise Pascal's Wager as cold and calculating fail to do justice to the subtlety of his proposal. Far from putting a premium on hypocrisy by appealing to the self-interest of his listeners, he calls for a real personal investment in terms of commitment to the moral standards of the Christian life. Looked at carefully, the wager is no soft option. Rather, it is a call for a personal act of faith in the value of upright living, one that Pascal thought might lead to a more devout kind of faith, but would in any case be enough to win the eternal prize.

Related questions:

1 What light if any does Pascal's Wager throw on the relationship between faith and reason?

2 How fair is the criticism that Pascal's Wager is an unworthy approach to the problem of faith in a rational age?

3 How far is Pascal's Wager consistent with the view that reason can be used to justify faith?

3 Religion and Experience

Revelation, Faith and the Bible

In theological language, **revelation** means a communication of God to mankind. Faith is the acceptance of this revelation. Philosophically, if God exists, it would not be unexpected if He were to manifest Himself to human beings. In fact, this is what believers claim He has done. The Bible is seen as the sacred book that records the history of God's revelation to mankind. Classic instances of revelation recorded in the Bible include the call of Abraham, Moses before the burning bush, and the religious and moral insights of the prophets.

The life and death of Jesus is generally regarded as the high point of revelation which, along with other parts of the Bible, has also been called **special revelation**. This is to distinguish it from what is called **general revelation**, the understanding of God obtained from reason or experience (obtained, say, from the arguments for God's existence, both rational and experiential).

In its earlier form, revelation was understood as the message that was extracted from the biblical writings – summed up in various truths, dogmas or propositions such as 'God made the world', 'God gave Moses the Ten Commandments' and 'Jesus was sent by God to redeem the world'. This view, which became known as the **propositional** view of revelation, reflected a concern with the religious facts about God and His relationship to mankind. It suggested a one-way communication from God to human beings. **Faith** was seen as the acceptance of these truths out of reverence for the God who revealed them.

More recently, revelation has also been viewed from a more human perspective. This has led to revelation being seen as a two-way process in which God communicates and human beings respond. This is really a recovery of the original way in which God 'spoke' in the Bible. In each case there was a human response to the address of God. In this respect, many see the life of Jesus as a model of how revelation happens. Jesus was less interested in issuing truths than in relating with His listeners in such a way that they understood what He was trying to say.

In this view, the focus of interest is on the nature of revelation as an insight into the personal nature of God, not a series of facts about God. Revelation is thus recognised as a historical rather than a miraculous happening, involving divine address and human response. One possible reason for this shift to what is called the **non-propositional** view of revelation is the modern decline in religious understanding. While formerly it was possible to assume the significance of the message of revelation, today it is acknowledged that the ground needs to be better prepared for the message to be received. As **Paul Tillich** put it, if the message is not received there is no revelation. For this reason, it may be argued that some form of general revelation is needed before the insights of special revelation can be understood.

Q (a) **Explain the relationship between revelation and the Bible.**
(b) **How far is revelation a philosophically intelligible notion?**

(a) Although **revelation** is a technical term that has always been central to Christian theology, its understanding has undergone a revision in recent years. With the formation of the Church there arose serious concern with the purity and correctness of the Christian message. Against this background, the Bible came to be seen as a sacred book whose contents needed to be secured and protected against attack from heresy and unbelief. This concern led to the formulation of 'truths', 'dogmas' and 'propositions' which would enshrine and codify the essential 'truths' of what **John Macquarrie** called God's **primordial**, or **special**, revelation. From this resulted the so-called **propositional** view of revelation.

Under the impact of this view, the original manner of revelation became obscured. Overlooked was the way in which God's presence was perceived by people over time and history, partly in forms of general revelation. This insight was one of the results of new biblical theories promoted by **D. F. Strauss** in nineteenth-century Germany. From these came the understanding that the Bible was a much more *human* book than was previously thought. Scholars discovered that the contents of the Bible were seen much more as a *story* than a series of isolated events. Besides, as a record of these events, the Bible came under the same cultural and period influences as all other ancient books. This gave rise to a different understanding of the Bible's contents.

In this view, the Bible is not a ready-made oracle of divine truths issued from above, but more a record of how God revealed Himself through the perceptions of people at the time. Such a revelation took time, and only in the course of time was it possible to see its pattern. Today, we call the pattern the **history of salvation**. The final stage of this story is seen in the coming of Jesus Christ, whose redeeming death provides the final pieces of the 'puzzle' of revelation.

But Jesus is also significant for another reason. If He was God's Son it might be expected that He would have issued definitive 'truths' or 'propositions' that encapsulated important messages from God to the human race. But He did not seem to do this. By relating with people in an ordinary human way, Jesus was more interested in creating the conditions in which a message from God might be *understood*. From this came a recovery of the original insight that revelation was about a particular understanding, or *vision* of life, gained from ordinary events.

The fundamentals of this vision are recorded in the Bible, and are accessible to the eyes of faith. Within this faith-vision, certain events were seen as bearing the imprint of God. Collectively, these events came to be called the history of salvation, stretching from Creation and the Fall, to the life and death of Jesus Christ. But as **John Hick** pointed out, it was only later that the *religious* significance of this history became apparent as the revelation of God.

In this **non-propositional** view, revelation is not something that can be isolated or frozen into propositions or dogmatic truths. Rather, it is a process of communication, first between God and human beings through ordinary events which are seen as extraordinary. As **Søren Kierkegaard** put it, the paradox of faith is that an ordinary *man* living an ordinary life became the revelation of *God*. But the communication requires human mediation – human beings influencing other human beings to share this faith perspective.

In this view, revelation in its broadest terms is a non-coercive, faith-based vision, through which life is seen under the direction of God, and in which human beings are given assurance of an ultimate satisfaction of their deepest moral and religious instincts. The beginnings of this revelation may be of a more secular or general kind. Theologians have called attention to the way in which revelation answers some fundamental human questions about life and its meaning.

For this to be made intelligible, theologians have pointed out that some fraternal or socio-religious context – such as the experience of worship, or belonging to a faith community or church – is required before revelation can be fully understood in its more special form. In this new understanding, revelation can be seen as a two-sided coin. On one side is the revealed message or facts of God's historic communication (propositional view), and on the other the awareness of God as an answer to human searching for fulfilment (non-propositional view). In this more inclusive view, the message of revelation (for example, in the Church's Creed) still plays an important part in preserving the story of God's doings, but it cannot be isolated from a sense of the need for God that can arise from life itself, and which, it may be said, Jesus tried to provide.

In conclusion, we have seen that although the Bible has always been regarded as 'the source of revelation', there has been a new understanding of what this means. From being originally seen as a source of 'truths', which in turn became codified into 'propositions', it is now seen as more of a record of how God reveals *Himself* to human beings. It is not by way of oracles and teachings, but through a faith-guided perception that He is involved in human history. In this vision the Bible record is seen as a real history, the *history of salvation*. But following the logic of the Bible, how the story is communicated today calls for the same reflective approach to life, as well as the mediation of human beings to transmit an awareness of God to others.

(b) Some modern theologians such as **Karl Rahner**, **Rudolf Bultmann** and **Paul Tillich** have argued that revelation is an answer to certain questions thrown up from within human experience – such as 'Why am I here?', 'What is my life for?' and 'What is the good life and how can I lead it?'

Earlier, **Blaise Pascal** saw the connection between the message of revelation and the meaning of life, which led to his 'wager'. Kierkegaard saw the message of revelation offering the only route out of the painful dilemmas and *Angst* of an otherwise meaningless life. **Wolfhart Pannenberg** has argued for the historical truth of the Resurrection as a key moment of revelation. He points out that when it happened it was recognised as revealing the secret of one of life's greatest mysteries, the reality of life after death.

Richard Swinburne has argued that if God exists there are clear *a priori* reasons why He would want to help mankind to achieve the goal of existence, a life lived in accordance with His will. This would involve such truths of revelation as God's atonement for human sinfulness, his eternal destiny with God in heaven (salvation), and the possibility of its alternative, damnation, for those who choose evil.

All of these thinkers have stressed how the message of revelation provides an answer to questions about the meaning of human existence. Such questions are posed by the fact of death, the futility of human endeavour and the frustrations of the moral life. As Rahner has pointed out, if revelation had no existential significance it would have no point, would never have found a human response, and would never have been 'heard'. For these reasons, revelation, when seen as something that offers insight into the meaning of human life and its final end, is an understandable notion within the realm of real possibility.

Critics of revelation question how a human being could successfully establish that God ever spoke to him or her. If God were to speak, how could the recipient know that it was God? For these reasons, atheists reject the notion of revelation as impossible to establish. To this, the believer will reply that revelation is not such a difficult notion to grasp if God exists. It is therefore not unreasonable to believe that He might have communicated with mankind to help to clarify the meaning of life. Unless revelation was a philosophically coherent notion, the biblical claims that revelation has taken place would make no sense.

Related questions:

1 Explain the relationship between faith and revelation.

2 Explain and evaluate the propositional and non-propositional views of revelation.

2 To what extent can revelation be said to be contained in propositions?

Religious Experience

Religious experience has a variety of meanings. It can mean the direct experience of God, or it can mean an ordinary experience in the world in which the presence of God or the supernatural is indirectly perceived. The main problem with claims for religious experience is the difficulty of verification. Where claims are made that a human experience touched on the objective world of the supernatural, how can this be confirmed as anything more than subjective imaginings? The difficulty of claiming that God was in some alleged experience was remarked on by **Thomas Hobbes** when he asked what the difference is between 'God spoke to me in a dream' and 'I dreamt that God spoke to me'.

In his play 'Joan', George Bernard Shaw saw the voices of the Maid as no more than evidence of a vivid imagination, but since she was not 'malicious, selfish, cowardly or stupid' her sanity was never in doubt

Modern theories that attempt to explain away religion as false naturally impact on claims of religious experience. The sociological theories of religion of **Karl Marx** lead to the conclusion that religious experience is a form of displacement, or alienation, that arises from certain needs that are felt as a result of being part of **society**. The psychoanalytical work of **Sigmund Freud** leads to the conclusion that religious experience is an **illusion** that arises from feelings of frustration and helplessness in the course of family upbringing. Yet the work of **Kant**, **Schleiermacher** and **Rudolf Otto** raises the claim that religion is a genuine form of perception that cannot be explained away by subjectivist theories. Rather, religion comes as much from outside the individual as from inside. As we saw above, this is confirmed for believers by revelation, the insight into God's reality obtained from reason and inspired personal experience, and confirmed publicly by the Bible.

(a) Explain what is meant by personal religious experience.
(b) How far can claims of such an experience be taken seriously?

The term 'religious experience' has different meanings. First, there is an experience that in many respects is an ordinary everyday experience, but for some may have a religious or 'mystical' dimension. The mountaineer Chris Bonnington has spoken of being aware of a 'mysterious presence' during his climb of Everest. Similar experiences are spoken of by poets and nature lovers, but **David Hay** has pointed out that such experiences need not be given a religious interpretation or be seen to have any religious significance.

Secondly, there is the kind highlighted by **Friedrich Schleiermacher** in his book addressed to the 'cultured despisers of religion'. He followed **Kant** in rejecting the old rational approach to religion, but disagreed with him that God was best found in **moral** experience. He turned instead to a third way, the way of inner *feeling*, which arises from what he called the 'sense of absolute dependence'. This is a kind of natural, but deep-seated, intuition by which we become aware of our finite nature and contingency within a universe that is also contingent. This intuition gives us a sense of the unity of all things, a perception of the 'All' that carries with it a feeling of dependence on a fundamental reality that we call God. In principle, we all have the capacity for such feeling, the capacity for a true 'God consciousness'.

Thirdly, there is the kind of experience highlighted by **Rudolf Otto** in his book *The Idea of the Holy*, written 100 years after Schleiermacher. Otto argues that we can experience what he calls the **numinous**, a sense of hidden mystery parallel to our sense of the beautiful. The numinous is the mysterious presence of the **holy**, which is perceived as being both attractive and repellent, both fascinating and awe-inspiring. Otto claims that all the great religious experiences recorded in the Bible – such as the vision of Moses at the burning bush, the vision of Isaiah in the Temple and the divine experience of Jesus – are instances of this experience of the numinous. However, while there may have been an element of the numinous in these experiences, it may be argued that they involved a much more direct encounter with the divine than Otto speaks about.

Another form of religious experience is identified by **Ninian Smart**, who uses the word numinous to describe the everyday devotional experiences of believers during prayer, worship or the reading of the Bible. Whether such meditative or prayerful experiences can qualify as recognised forms of religious experience is open to doubt. To judge at least by the testimony of believers, such moments are not generally claimed to be of sufficient intensity as to qualify as properly so called religious experience.

Fourthly, there are the kind of experiences that are called **mystical**, which belonged to those who are called **mystics**. Well-documented experiences of mysticism are found in the lives of the saints **Teresa of Avila** and **John of the Cross** in Spain, **Julian of Norwich** in England and **Meister Eckhart** in Germany, to name but a few. Such experiences are associated with those who have lived lives of asceticism and religious dedication. A somewhat similar experience is that of the **vision** or **apparition**, the classic example of which was the vision of **St Paul** on the road to Damascus. Other recipients of visions include **St Ignatius of Loyola**, **St Bernadette** in Lourdes, and others at Fatima in Portugal and Knock in Ireland.

Fifthly, there are the exceptional experiences of a mystical kind that have led to the founding of major religions. The experiences described in the Bible of Abraham, Moses, Isaiah and Jesus, and in the Muslim tradition the experience attributed to **Muhammad**, have been historically decisive. An important element in these experiences is some kind of communication from God called a **revelation**, the record of which forms sacred books such as the Bible or the Qur'an.

(b) Claims for religious experience of whatever kind are open to an obvious challenge. How can such experiences be verified as authentic? Is there any reason to take them to be any more than subjective experience, or even halluci-nations? **A. J. Ayer** dismissed them as merely 'expressive of someone's state of mind'. But in doing so he begged the question of whether the state of mind was merely an expression of some self-induced psychological condition. Maybe it was exactly what the mystic or visionary claimed it was, an encounter with the divine or the supernatural. In the absence of verifying proof to the contrary, empiricists such as Ayer predictably argue for the most likely **natural** explanation of such experiences.

All naturalistic explanations of this kind usually claim some interaction between the mind and some *imagined* object. The so-called **nature mystic** who senses the presence of God in lakes and forests may be simply disposed, or 'tuned in', to see things like this, while another person may not. The sense of the numinous may be available to those who are sufficiently introspective to feel so deeply, like someone who can see patterns of beauty where others cannot. The religious mystic may have reached certain heights of spiritual awareness that lead to a *sense* of oneness with the divine. In each case it is possible to locate the experience in, and limit it to, the subjective consciousness of the recipient. **Bertrand Russell** made this point when he said that 'we can make no distinction between the man who eats little and sees heaven, and the man who drinks too much and sees snakes'. In each case the experience is assumed to be imagined, and the empiricist's conclusion is that 'there is nothing there'.

Naturalistic explanations of religion received a boost from the psychoanalytical theories of **Sigmund Freud**, who dismissed mysticism as evidence of regressive infantile obsessions, resulting in desired dream-like sensations. **Carl Gustav Jung** was less dismissive when he suggested that Paul's vision may well have had neurotic origins, related to his repressed guilt for opposing the new followers of Jesus. Jung's explanation is indeed interesting and perfectly legitimate, but it does not necessarily undermine the claim that the experience was a religious one. If God exists, it would not be surprising that He should act through natural means, whether rational, psychological or emotional. On **Richard Swinburne's** principle of **credulity** and **testimony**, those who make such claims have a right to be taken seriously. If a recipient of such an experience is normally a person who is sincere and trustworthy, the likelihood is that their testimony has strong credibility.

William James supported this idea in his assessment of the **character** of many of the mystics from the 'fruits' that their lives produced. He rejected any attempt to interpret their claims as evidence of some kind of mental incapacity, and ruled out the idea that such experiences were signs of a 'degenerative brain'. He saw them as **noetic** (involving experience of something perceived as external), despite being **ineffable** (difficult to express in words). Even from a philosophical perspective, if faith is a form of insight into reality, as **Ludwig Wittgenstein** granted, it is not illogical to allow that this insight might play a role in the way a person perceives that reality. However, this view veers towards a subjectivist account of how an ordinary experience can be mistakenly taken for a supposed religious experience.

In conclusion, therefore, subjectivist interpretations of feelings, events or levels of awareness are possible, and non-believers insist that no compelling evidence exists to warrant belief in religious experience. On the other hand, believers insist that religious experience is always a real possibility, and that historical evidence supports claims for such experiences. It seems that at the very least religious faith can engender a religious colouring of some events, resulting in some form of religious perception. Whether in the end this is to say that religious experience is a merely **subjective** phenomenon is not proven.

Yet, in the absence of empirical evidence that would verify them as encounters with the supernatural, sceptics will continue to question such claims. But then the question remains: What sort of empirical evidence could ever establish the truth or otherwise of claims for religious experience?

Related questions:

1 a Describe a religious experience that you have studied.
   b How might a religious experience affect a person's religious faith and moral behaviour?

2 Evaluate the claim that religious experience is merely the product of an unbalanced mind.

3 a Explain the views of Schleiermacher, Otto and James on religious experience.
   b Evaluate the criticisms of Ayer and Freud of claims for mystical experience.

Religion and Psychology

The advent of psychological studies created new possibilities for the understanding of religion. It also created new possibilities for its *explanation*. In the hands of **Sigmund Freud**, religion becomes reduced to a psychic mechanism by which the individual falls victim to *illusory* hopes and dreams that have no foundation in reality. Religion can therefore be dismissed as an **infantile obsessional neurosis** arising from childhood experiences. These experiences centre on neurotic fears connected with the father figure, who looms large in the life of the developing child. The result is preoccupation with an idealised **cosmic** father figure, who will guarantee protection from the fears and anxieties of an otherwise meaningless life. This is the essence of religion – an understandable, but ultimately illusory, world of make-believe.

Sigmund Freud (above) and Carl Gustav Jung both studied the nature of religion, but they reached different conclusions. Is Freud guilty of committing the genetic fallacy?

Not everyone reached so negative an assessment of religion. Freud's colleague in the field of clinical psychology, **Carl Gustav Jung**, agreed with his mentor that religion was problem-solving, but disagreed that it could be dismissed as illusory. Religion was not something that could be explained exclusively in terms of fears imposed from *outside* the individual, by way of experience, as Freud had held.

Rather, religion was something for which the individual was already fitted, an **archetype** of the soul that nothing could take the place of. In this way, Jung placed religion far deeper in the human psyche than Freud allowed for. However, neither theory provides the means of either conclusively disproving or supporting the truth-claims of religion.

How far do psychological theories of religion undermine its truth-claims?

Psychological theories of religion are found especially in the writings of **Sigmund Freud** and **Carl Gustav Jung**. As one-time colleagues, both made important discoveries about the role of the unconscious in the formation and functioning of the human personality. Inevitably, both had theories about the nature of religion, and about how it functioned within the overall make-up of the human psyche.

Freud saw religion in a very negative light. Under the influence of **Ludwig Feuerbach** and, later, of the findings of **Charles Darwin**, he set out with the personal conviction that religion was a human phenomenon with human origins that could be explained **psychologically**. In his clinical experience he found that religion was often associated with mental illness and neurosis. His aim was to search for the possible roots of religion in the life of the **psyche**, and to show that it was in reality a symptom of an infantile obsessional neurosis. He believed that he found the key to human drives and wishes in the **Oedipus Complex**, an unconscious infantile trauma which, if unresolved, leads to emotional conflicts and neuroses. This, he believed, was the key to the nature of religion. The Oedipal theory is that each person grows up with a sense of foreboding towards a *father* figure who is both loved and feared. This becomes the basis of the (religious) need for a **cosmic** father figure who offers protection and salvation, but who in the meantime needs to be appeased by devotion and sacrifice. Freud saw confirmation of this in the prominence of ritual sacrifice and forgiveness of **sin** in Christianity.

Religion therefore amounts to a purely human phenomenon that can be outgrown as the individual shakes off his infantile dependency and moves towards maturity. Freud stopped short of calling religion a **delusion** (something false), but instead called it an **illusion**, something that *could* be true. This left open the possibility that religion was a real phenomenon but, as he saw it, the narcissistic (self-centred) nature of religion made it too much of a coincidence, for it not to be seen as wishful thinking. For this reason, he made no secret of his atheistic conclusion that religion was no more than a childish clinging to illusory hopes.

Because Freud's theory of religion could never be falsified, it could be argued that, in principle, it fails to be truly scientific. But from an empirical standpoint it fails to do justice to more balanced forms of religion, of which Freud seems to have little awareness. In particular, it ignores the altruistic, or other-regarding, nature of much traditional religion, where the individual is drawn away from selfish concerns, often to the extent of showing unconditional self-sacrifice. Such forms of religion are a long way from the neurotic 'comfort' religion that Freud speaks about.

Secondly, the idea of a loving father figure, so central to Freud's concept of God, is noticeably absent from many of the earliest tribal religions. Many scholars point out that the Judeo-Christian tradition represented a distinct innovation in its understanding of God as a father figure. A shift to the notion of God as a mother figure would seriously undermine Freud's Oedipal theory. Besides, since his theory centres so much on the male conflict, it hardly does justice to the understanding of the female religious impulse.

However, Freud correctly observed the way in which religion can become tainted with selfish neurotic elements that, in many cases, can be criticised as infantile and self-centred. Religion can often build on an individual's faulty psychological make-up, and have obsessional elements that indeed appear to justify Freud's analysis. But this is clearly not true of all forms of religion, and it fits in badly with **William James'** neutral observation that religion is often the inspiration of outstanding, well-balanced individuals whose lives have left a positive mark on history.

By means of a different interpretation of the Oedipus Complex, which is so central to Freud's theory, his illusory view of religion can be turned on its head. Perhaps the *real* illusion is to think that religion is *false*. This is a view put forward by **Paul Vitz**, who has argued that modern **atheism** could equally be shown to have Oedipal origins. He argues that the 'God is dead' tradition that goes back to Feuerbach can credibly be traced to the Oedipal urge to 'kill the father'. Behind this urge is the wish to remove the father and replace him with the son. By so doing, the son can enjoy greater personal liberty. This he sees as an accurate image of the modern desire to be free from the constraints of religion, which is popularly seen as psychologically repressive and morally restrictive. These are indeed unwelcome aspects of religion, but no more so, perhaps, than the restrictive aspects of natural law theory, or **Kant's** categorical imperative, or the promptings of conscience.

Jung, on the other hand, had a much more positive view of religion, even though he agreed with much of what Freud had said. His break with Freud came from his conviction that his former master was too prejudiced in favour of reductive scientific **naturalism** (reducing everything to natural explanations), a result of falling under the spell of modern evolutionary atheism. In contrast, Jung resented the claims of science to pretend to explain the human mind completely. Whereas Freud tried to explain everything scientifically in terms of drives, Jung saw the psyche as an area that was shrouded in mystery. The inner workings of the psyche couldn't be 'explained' by empirical theories or methods. Jung was openly critical of scientific attempts to reduce the mind to an object of investigation. This approach leads to ignoring what he called 'the wisdom which comes from the soul'. He was therefore much more receptive than Freud to what he learned from his patients about the nature and role of religious faith.

Jung saw religion as part of the **collective unconscious**, a predisposition towards the **sacred** that he saw as crucial in helping the individual to overcome neurotic fears and conflicts. Showing the influence of **Rudolf Otto**, Jung believed that religion was rooted in a profound sense of the **numinous**, which some seem to have to an extraordinary degree. Jung believed that it was possible to encounter this religious sense by getting in touch with the great **symbols** used within religious communities, such as the cross, light, bread and so on. Unlike Freud, who saw religion as an aberration, Jung valued it for its **psychological truth**. By this, Jung meant that religion was an operational phenomenon that was active in human experience. Regardless of its origin, it was too significant as a psychological reality to be ignored. And because of its power to bring wholeness, integrity and peace to the troubled mind, he thought it churlish to explain it away as mere myth or illusion.

Jung has been criticised for adopting a utilitarian view of religion; that is, for limiting its value to its use to the human psyche. As a clinician, he can hardly be faulted for this. He saw it as the task of others to deal with its metaphysical truth-claims – claims that, incidentally, he himself did nothing to criticise or undermine. Despite their disagreements, both Freud and Jung recognised that religious faith has an important influence on the life of the psyche. For Freud, it was something that did harm to the individual; whereas for Jung, it was a mysterious reality that fulfilled a psychological need that nothing else could satisfy.

We can conclude, therefore, that psychological theories of religion do show the way in which religion is sometimes acquired, how its form can be identified, and how it can be either a positive or negative influence depending on how it is integrated into a wider understanding of life. For Freud, the way in which religion answered our deepest wishes made the conclusion inevitable. For Jung, the question of its theological truth was secondary to the reality of its psychological power to bring about mental and emotional health. In the end, the closed mind of Freud stands in contrast to the more open mind of Jung, showing that the issue of the truth-claims of religion is beyond conclusive resolution by psychological theory.

Related questions:

1 How convincing is the view that Freud's theory of religion can equally be applied to modern atheism?

2 Compare critically the views of Freud and Jung on the nature of religious belief.

3 Discuss the view that psychological theories of religion have dealt a fatal blow to those who claim to know, from experience, that God exists.

Religion and Sociology

While psychology examines the impact of religion on the *individual* psyche, sociology looks at its impact on the human *group* that we call society. **Karl Marx** attempted to show that religion was the outcome of social conditions such as poverty and enslavement. Conditions of **material poverty** create other-worldly wishes and desires that turn people away from solving the problems of the here and now. Such wishes and desires are what religion typically encourages and offers to fulfil. Because they are illusory wishes, and they distract people from the real task of removing the conditions that create them, they need to be exposed and destroyed. Once the social conditions of poverty – and the class divisions that perpetuate it – are removed, religion will no longer be needed and will wither away.

A different understanding and explanation of religion was given by the so-called father of sociology, **Emile Durkheim**. He saw religion as the product of the need for **social unity**, which goes back to the earliest times. The outer symbols of religion, beginning with the totem pole, functioned to bring people together by providing a common focus for respect and adoration. But all this was a form of displacement. The objectified symbol was merely a substitute for something *within* the group itself. Thus religion was the result of a mistaken understanding of something purely *human*. What people attributed to God should really be attributed to their own powers as members of human society. The focus of this essay is how far these theories can stand up to the criticisms levelled against them.

Karl Marx's view of religion was highly influenced by the ideas of Ludwig Feuerbach

With reference to Marx, Durkheim and Weber how convincing are attempts to explain religion as merely a sociological phenomenon?

There is an important difference between explaining religion as a sociological phenomenon, and explaining it as merely that. The former is perfectly justified, since religion is unquestionable a social phenomenon. The investigation of the social influences that led to particular religious forms is therefore sound and legitimate. The attempt to reduce religion to a sociological process is known as **reductionism**; that is, explaining a phenomenon exclusively in terms of its psychological, natural or in this case social origins. This is also known as the **genetic fallacy**, the assumption that because the origin of something can be traced, the thing in question is only apparent and not real. Because the origin of religion can be traced to human social tendencies, **Emile Durkheim** concluded that its reality was false.

Accordingly, religion is here claimed to arise from social needs, and is merely a human invention arising either from the satisfaction or the frustration of those needs. One corollary of this is that if these needs did not exist, then neither would religion. Another corollary is that if these needs are identified and removed, religion will disappear. This was the view of **Karl Marx**.

Under the close influence of his contemporary, **Ludwig Feuerbach**, Marx was convinced that religion was a projection of mankind's powers on to an imaginary supernatural being, God. His own contribution was to carry this theory further and explain in greater detail how this projection took place. Marx set out to show that religion was a product of the socio-economic conditions under which people became enslaved, oppressed and alienated.

Instead of engaging in a positive struggle to fight against their alienation and improve their material lot, people were mistakenly led to look for comfort in a transcendent being who would reward them in the hereafter. Religion was therefore an unfortunate displacement of human hopes from this world to the next, much as Feuerbach had argued.

Seeing its offer of false comfort as an obstacle to the social liberation of the masses, Marx famously called religion 'the sigh of the oppressed creature, the heart of a heartless world, the soul of a soulless environment, the opium of the people'. When the enslaving social conditions were removed, predicted Marx, religion would no longer be needed and would wither away. This was of course a mistaken forecast, and even by itself contains the seeds of doubt about how convincing Marx's theory could claim to be.

Marx could be forgiven for some of his hostility to religion. As he saw it, religion had become too institutionalised, and the Church of his day (in Britain and Germany) appeared to do little to challenge the political causes of the social injustice that he saw around him. Later, **Vladimir Lenin** would use Marx's ideas to castigate the Church in Russia for the way in which it seemed more concerned with the 'pie in the sky' spiritual benefits of the next life, than with helping to overcome the desperate material conditions of its adherents in this life. All in all, religion was a displacement of human energy both *caused* by economic conditions and, in turn, *causing* those conditions to continue.

Religious critics of Marx, while sympathising with his social and political aims, have rejected his criticism that religious belief is a major obstacle to economic progress. While he was right to say that in conditions of material poverty people often do turn to religion as a source of comfort, he was wrong to conclude that material despair is the only root of religious faith. He was also presumptuous to see in religion a primary cause of making the poor remain satisfied with their lot. While it is true that religion tends to elevate the spiritual over the material (and for a materialist like Marx this was an absurdity), it is equally true that religion does not condemn material ambitions. It is obvious that the Good Samaritan could not have helped the roadside victim without the material resources to do so. In both the Old and New Testaments, it is selfishness and material injustice that is condemned, especially the **exploitation** and oppression of the poor by the rich, and not material prosperity as such.

Marx also ignores the capacity of religion to inspire the social ideals of equality and justice that he believed in so much, and indeed its power to challenge the status quo on behalf of the poor. This capacity has been shown not only by social reformers from **William Wilberforce** and **Mahatma Gandhi** to **Martin Luther King**, but to an heroic degree by movements such as **liberation theology**, which famously looked to the Gospels for its inspiration, and which, ironically, was criticised by many for being 'too Marxist'.

47

Marx also failed to consider that religion might have other sources besides the need for other-worldly consolation. He could have found confirmation of religion's concern with this world, through its emphasis on moral living and concern for the neighbour. Such an emphasis was evident in the lives of the saints, martyrs and above all the prophets. Besides, by concentrating on a one-sided link between poverty and religion, Marx ignored the fact that religion can also thrive in conditions of material prosperity. The fact that it can thrive in this way might suggest that the values it stands for cannot be replaced by material substitutes. In the end, Marx's attempt to explain religion in terms of material poverty fails before the facts.

In contrast to Marx, **Emile Durkheim** studied the behaviour of ancient peoples and found a quite different reason to explain religion. He did not see any connection between religion and social deprivation, as Marx did. Rather, he was struck by the way in which people characteristically formed themselves into clans, or tribal groups. They did this by means of some unifying symbol that came to be regarded as sacred. From this, Durkheim concluded that religion was a displacement of a natural sense that people are interdependent on each other. People knew that society was an essential part of the human condition, but mistakenly turned to religion as the basis of a primitive but effective way of bringing about social interdependence. This was achieved through paying allegiance to some transcendent power, or sacred being, that functioned as a centralising focus to enhance the unity of the group.

For Durkheim it is society, not God, that stands transcendent over the individual, and it is this unconscious awareness of the human need for a transcendent power that is the origin of religion. The transcendent power is society, the collective group of which the individual is only a minor part. All so-called moral and religious ideals are essentially unifying forces within the group, but they originate not from some being called God, but from human beings themselves.

To create and reinforce group solidarity, human beings use communal rituals. At the primitive stage, some object taken from the material world became totemic or sacred, and acted as a unifying focus for the group. In secular society today, where religious consciousness has largely declined, these same dynamics can be seen at work in the use of flags, anthems, national ceremonies and other ritual celebrations. Today, it is clear that human beings have a natural inborn drive to reinforce their social interdependence, whereas in the past they used religion to achieve this.

For this reason, Durkheim sees religion as a displacement of those forces that unite people into social groups, on to an imaginary focus of ideals called God. The similarity between society's need for unifying codes of law, moral values and a sense of common purpose and religion's ethical laws, regulations and code of unifying beliefs was too much for Durkheim to overlook. He concluded that one was the mirror image of the other. Religion was the earliest and most primitive way of bringing about the collective solidarity that mankind needed. Thus, he says, 'religion is superimposed on what is natural', 'the religious life is really the forces of society at work', 'the idea of society is the soul of religion' and 'religious forces are human forces'.

Not surprisingly, Durkheim's idea of religion was confirmed by what he saw as its unifying power to form religious communities. He saw religion as 'a unifying system of beliefs and practices relative to sacred things ... which unite (its adherents) into one moral community called a Church'. Religion is therefore distinctive for its functional power to bring about social solidarity. Religion is the product of the human as a social animal, and God is in reality only an imaginary focus that helps us to create the social bonds that are vital to human life in the world. The day will come when religion will disappear, as we stand on our own two feet and realise that we must maintain our social cohesion and identity through the use of our own resources.

But what of so-called religious truths, what Durkheim called the speculative function of religion? This will be the first to disappear, he thought, as science continues to make inroads into explaining everything, including (through the new 'science' of psychology) even the inner dynamics of the mind. This suggests that Durkheim was influenced by materialist theories that attempt to explain the mind as a function of brain activity. If this view is held, there is no reason to doubt that the functioning of the brain can ultimately explain even religion!

Durkheim attempted, therefore, to explain religion by way of reduction to human social needs, a move that takes him back to Feuerbach's theory of projection, but suffers the same fate. Because religion serves mankind's need for social interdependence, this can provide no basis for saying that religion is merely a human invention for the satisfaction of this need.

First, because it only accounts for one aspect of religion – its communal aspect – Durkheim's theory fails to take sufficient account of the individual and personal nature of religion. This was one of its essential and distinctive charac-teristics underlined by Kant, Schleiermacher, Kierkegaard and Otto. For **Rudolf Otto** in particular, religion is the outcome of a solitary sense of the numinous, and only later acquires a social dimension. Durkheim's observation that all private experience eventually becomes communal is little more than saying that all significant experience tends to be shared. So the experiences of Moses, Jesus or Paul were shared because they were recognised as privileged insights into reality, a reality valued in its own right.

Secondly, his theory leaves out of account mankind's capacity to see ethical demands as something more than conventional adherence to social rules. For Durkheim, ethical awareness is merely a function of social needs. Kant had seen the inner power of the categorical imperative as something that had obvious social implications, but was not fully explicable in social terms. Rather, it had a transcendent aspect that drove the individual to fulfil the demands of duty as a personal, not social, obligation. For this reason, the categorical imperative could not be reduced to keeping conventional social rules, or be confined to the service of human needs.

Thus **ethical values** are seen to transcend the individual regardless of their social value, a fact that Kant saw as having underlying religious implications. While for Durkheim religion could be explained in terms of covert social forces acting on the individual, for Kant the individual alone possessed a sovereignty that embodied moral and religious insights which owed nothing directly to his or her own needs or the needs of others.

Thirdly, there is the plain fact that religion has not been, and is not likely to, be replaced by society, as Durkheim had predicted. Both have run parallel to each other since the beginning, one based on the recognition of the need for social values and conventions, and the other based on the recognition of religious values and realities. To say therefore that religion is a displacement from what is 'really' society is contrary to the common experience of human beings throughout history.

For this reason, Durkheim's theory can be stood on its head. Perhaps the dynamics of society are derived from religion, and not the reverse. Perhaps human society is only the visible reflection of what religion aims to achieve, namely the bringing together of all those who recognise transcendent values in a Kantian kingdom, in which people treat each other with dignity and respect (as ends), known to religion as the kingdom of God. From this viewpoint, secular society is no more than the human manifestation of that yearning for social solidarity and collective security that is ultimately rooted in the perceived sense of a higher, divine reality, known to believers as God.

In contrast to Durkheim, the distinguished sociologist **Max Weber** made no speculation about the metaphysical truth value of religion. He rejected the theory of Marx that religion had a single source in the human experience of material poverty. Instead, he made interesting observations on the various social factors that influence religious movements, and that determine particular forms of religious belief and practice. Christianity, for instance, was initially a religion of the non-elite classes who were hungry for salvation from oppression and misery. Later, its appeal was extended to the more prosperous, better educated, and more critical classes, whose need for salvation was understood in more sophisticated ways. Its appeal to political leaders partly lay in its power to enhance ethical awareness among the subjects, and thereby to engender greater respect for law and authority.

But the correspondence between the appeal of religion and the spiritual and social benefits that it promised did not lead Weber to fall into the reductionist trap laid by Durkheim. For many, therefore, Weber's contribution has been more interesting, enlightening and provocative: first, by showing how religious forms take shape from the social and historical conditions that prevail at a particular time; and, secondly, by examining how religious beliefs can in their turn influence social movements.

A particular case in point is how the religious theory of **John Calvin** influenced a social movement such as the **Protestant work ethic**, which became the basis of capitalism. Calvin had held that human beings were already **predestined** by God to either salvation or damnation. But an encouraging sign of future salvation was material success or prosperity. This belief fuelled a new interest in material success. Those who worked productively in this life would be the more likely candidates for salvation in the next.

In conclusion, we can readily accept that religion is indeed a sociological phenomenon. With Durkheim, we can agree that all major religions have a strong communal emphasis, and have features that link them to the way in which societies are formed and how they operate. They have a central focus in a code of beliefs and values, as society has a code of laws and purposeful aims. However, to accept this does not entail any necessary conclusion that religion is merely a functional means for reinforcing our sense of our communal need for others. Both religion and society have recognised and distinct places in our understanding of our nature, lives and destinies, and religion cannot therefore be explained as a mistaken substitute for the power of society.

With Marx, we can agree that the sense of alienation created by unfortunate material and social conditions can sometimes make people more conscious, and perhaps more trustful, of *spiritual*, rather than material, rewards. But there is no evidence to show that religion is necessarily linked to material poverty. Neither is the conclusion justified that turning to religion as a source of spiritual uplift makes it false. With Weber, we can accept that social and political factors can influence particular *forms* of religious belief and practice, without making this a basis for pronouncing on its truth or falsity. We therefore conclude that all sociological theories of a **reductionist** kind beg too many questions to undermine the truth-claims of religion.

Related questions: _____

1 What conclusions can be drawn from sociological observations on the nature and practice of religion?

2 How valid do you find the conclusions reached by Marx and Durkheim about religion?

3 Evaluate the criticism that both Marx and Durkheim ignore the transcendent nature of religion.

God and the Problem of Evil

The empirical fact that evil and suffering exist in the world has led many to conclude that the claim of religion that a good God exists is simply false. For believers on the other hand, evil and suffering present a 'problem' inasmuch as it can be granted that they do not easily fit in with the claims of religious faith. The classic response of believers is to 'justify' God in the face of evil. This is known as **theodicy**, and consists of finding theories that might explain how a good God permits such things to happen. In one approach, God is seen as offended against by a misuse of human free will, which results in a change of the world from original perfection to a state of disintegration. Another approach sees evil and suffering as God-given opportunities for human growth in virtue and goodness. Both approaches include the so-called **free will defence**. Other approaches centre on the reality of evil and suffering, and seek to remove their causes rather than understand their significance.

To what extent does the experience of evil and suffering count against the existence of God?

The 'inconsistent triad' stated by **Epicurus**, and later by **St Augustine**, states that God is either all-powerful but not all-loving, or all-loving but not all-powerful, in view of the presence of evil and suffering. In either case God is deficient, which is a contradiction, and therefore He cannot exist. The two forms of evil that constitute the so-called problem of evil are moral evil and natural evil. Moral evil is that which originates from human wickedness, such as murder, rape, arson, theft and of course war. Natural evil is that which results from natural causes, such as earthquakes, floods, drought, disease and the like.

Moral evil is perhaps the easiest to deal with, since it is noticeably linked to human action, which presupposes free will. This is the basis of the so-called **free will defence**, which says that evil is ultimately rooted in the misuse of human free will. This is a theory that looks to the past, present and future.

It looks to the *past* to the misuse of the free will of Adam and Eve, which St Augustine believed led to the 'Fall' of mankind into sin, and of all creation into a state of disorder. The effect was the weakening of human will, and the emergence of disorder in the workings of nature. In turn, both led to evil and suffering.

It looks to the *present* because it is in the here and now that free will is being misused, and causing untold suffering and evil. This can be seen in the field of criminal violence, drug addiction and the exploitation and enslavement of the weak.

Another aspect of the theory, popularised by **Richard Swinburne** and **John Hick**, looks to the *future*. Here free will is seen as a necessary prerequisite for leading a truly moral life. We live in a world at an **epistemic** distance from God (God's presence is not easily seen), but through faith we believe that the moral struggle against pain and suffering is somehow worthwhile. This implies that part of the answer to the problem of evil is to face it courageously, and aim to live the moral life so as to root out evil and its effects. A possible philosophical argument for this view lies in the idea that although God could theoretically remove evil and suffering, by doing so He would prevent the moral good that is possible by the good use of free will. This implies that the possibility of good being freely done is enough to outweigh the possible harm and evil caused by the bad use of free will.

A criticism of this theory is that it appears to overlook the way in which evil is so unevenly spread in the world, and how it can appear so random and often so overbearingly cruel. In addition, great numbers of innocent people are often disproportionately victimised by the evil and perverse misuse of the free will of a few. This is exemplified in cases such as the Holocaust, and by repressive, cruel and unjust regimes such as Stalinist Russia. In these cases, the fate of whole populations was often decided by one individual. This makes it difficult to see how such injustice could make any moral sense, and why, if God existed, He allowed it to happen.

A further objection has been put forward by **J. L. Mackie**, that God could have avoided the free will problem by creating 'free' creatures that would always do good. But this is hardly possible if moral freedom is taken to presuppose the ability to *choose* between good and evil. The idea of people being 'programmed' not to do evil only seems possible through the sacrifice of free choice, and therefore free will.

An additional difficulty created by the free will theory is that God is seen as being responsible for the evil that has resulted from its misuse. If God is **omniscient**, then He cannot be exonerated from all responsibility for letting things happen as they did. Ironically, this view has led to some believers being so angry with God as to 'lose faith' in Him. This was famously exemplified by the character of Ivan in **Fyodor Dostoyevsky's** novel *The Brothers Karamazov*, who refused to believe in a God who would let innocent children suffer. This shows that if evil and suffering can be a problem for believers, it cannot be surprising that unbelievers, like **Jean-Paul Sartre** or **Albert Camus**, should see such evils as evidence that no God exists.

Natural evil is somewhat different, in that it can be explained as the inevitable working out of natural laws. Fixed natural laws, it is argued, are necessary for a dependable world, and without them science would not be possible. The unbeliever may reply to this by saying that if God is responsible for natural laws He cannot escape responsibility for the sufferings they bring. Besides, if God existed surely He could at least intervene in certain situations to avert disasters that cause large-scale suffering to the innocent and the poverty-stricken.

The believer's reply is that although God does not directly intervene in the world, this does not mean that He does nothing. **Jurgen Moltmann** sees the Christian faith as an important source of inspiration for overcoming those evils that cause suffering. Besides, human reason and enterprise can reasonably be seen as a God-given power by which we are enabled to predict or ward off such misfortunes, and take the necessary measures to minimise their effects. For Moltmann, it is the overcoming and elimination of evil, not its acceptance, that is the essence of faith.

Richard Swinburne's argument is that only in a world in which people are at risk of such suffering can moral virtue be attained. Thus if no suffering took place there would be no Good Samaritans; if there was no risk of danger there would be no courage. One problem with this is the fact that the distribution of suffering is so erratic. This makes it difficult to see any pattern that would justify seeing any 'good' in it. Besides, it suggests that evil is somehow necessary in order to do good. This is difficult to square with the traditional view that unavoidable suffering may be a blessing, but suffering itself is an evil that should be fought against.

Another objection, mentioned by **Maurice Wiles**, is that if God sometimes performs miracles, especially miracles of healing, why then is He so selective as to help some but not others, and then not always those in greatest need? Wiles' conclusion is to question the traditional understanding of miracles, and to argue that God does not act directly by way of miracles, but shows His concern indirectly by inspiring human intervention.

Antony Flew has claimed that evil and suffering disprove, or falsify, belief in a loving God. The fact that believers are not prepared to allow anything, including so much evil in the world, to count against their belief in God, says Flew, shows that their belief in a loving God is meaningless.

Flew's point here is weakened by the difficulty of actually falsifying love. A parent's love for a child may theoretically be falsified if the parent deliberately harms the child, but surely not if the parent chastises the child, or allows it the normal risk of coming to harm. Many parents believe, and their children agree, that it is a healthy part of their growing up to be allowed to face some hardship, danger and risk. The real question, though, is whether the balance of evil over good in the world is such that the believer is left with no reasonable choice but to lose faith in God.

D. Z. Phillips attempts to bypass Flew's objection by ruling it a mistake for believers to even attempt to explain evil. He believes that Job in the Bible gives the clue to why this is. We cannot rationalise a problem that involves a transcendent God. We have to accept that there are some things that are beyond human understanding. Theodicies, he believes, either minimise evil or minimise God. Evil and suffering must simply be accepted as part of the mystery of faith in a God of grace. Moltmann has suggested that the way in which people recover from great disasters is evidence of God's grace. After great suffering and misery caused by floods, earthquakes, accidents, war or terrorism, there is a shared sense of either the misfortune or injustice of such episodes. This in turn becomes the launch-pad for bringing about a better world in which there is less injustice and less suffering. Whether the vision of a better world can be put down to human sensibilities alone, or something inspired by divine grace is, in the end, a question not easily settled by rational argument.

A final approach is suggested by what is called **process theology**. In this view, outlined by **Charles Hartshorne**, God is really more like the person revealed in the Bible than the figure outlined by **classical theism**. The logic of this is that God is not omnipotent at all, but is dependent on the way in which people use their free will. This implies, in turn, that evil and suffering are not caused by God, and that God is powerless to remove them. The most He can do is influence and persuade human beings to fight against suffering and remove its causes. This is called **process theodicy**. The solution that it offers is an attractive one, but it fails to deal with what has always been an assumed truth – namely, God's omnipotence. To surrender this attribute of God looks like solving the theodicy problem at an enormous price. After all, if God is not omnipotent there can be no guarantee of any future redress for undeserved suffering and, worse, the evidence could well point to the contrary.

Related questions:

1 How far is the problem of evil a challenge to religious belief?

2 How convincing or satisfactory is the free will defence?

3 Discuss the view that the problem of evil will never be resolved between believers and atheists.

Theodicy and the Problem of Evil

(a) How successful are the theodicies of Irenaeus and Augustine in explaining the problem of evil? (b) To what extent are they likely to help those who are suffering?

(a) The traditional attempt to explain evil as consistent with the existence and goodness of God is called **theodicy** (literally, justifying God). Since God is both infinitely good and just (righteous), it is necessary for believers to see evil as in some way part of God's plan, and not a reflection on His goodness. The earliest theodicy was that of **Irenaeus**, a second-century bishop of Lyon. He put forward the idea that Adam and Eve fell from grace because of their *immaturity*. They were made in God's *image*, but had not yet passed the test to share God's *likeness*. Their failure was a prefigurement of the fate of future human beings. Everyone would have to be tested, for without a **moral test** none of the great human **virtues** – such as love, courage, honesty, self-sacrifice and so on – could be attained.

Life is therefore a battleground for the struggle from immaturity to moral virtue, a 'vale of soul-making', in the words of **John Hick**. Jesus Christ was sent by God to show human beings the way of moral courage. By His redemptive death, the moral leadership He provided, and the spiritual grace He gives to those who follow Him in the moral struggle, He reveals that God is on the side of those who suffer.

Both Hick and **Richard Swinburne** argue that a world containing evil and suffering, including exposure to the misfortunes and tragedies of life, provides the conditions for true human moral growth. Critics of the theodicy will point to the erratic nature of evil and suffering. It seems to occur at random, is no respecter of persons and shows no evidence of any guiding hand. Some may profit from it, but many are also crushed by it. Some instances, such as the Holocaust, appear overwhelming and pointless. Besides, the view that moral virtue needs excessive suffering for its attainment is questionable. In its favour, the theodicy is consistent with the evolutionary view of the human being as a creature of development, but it fails to show that evil and suffering are willed by God for any good reason.

The theodicy of **St Augustine** is based on the writings of **St Paul**. When Adam sinned he lost God's grace, and threw the whole of creation, including the world of nature, into a state of disorder not willed by God. But from chaos came the redemption brought by Jesus Christ. The cause of the world's evil therefore is not God but us sinful humans. But God sympathises with our plight and offers help and grace now, through the agency of others, as classically exemplified by Jesus.

The weakness of this theodicy is that it seems at odds with the evolutionary facts of the world. Evil appears to have preceded our arrival, so the Fall cannot be used to explain all evil. Yet this is not a fatal objection. If the Fall is seen as the mythical representation of a universal test of our ethical integrity before God and the reality of our failure, its significance can be retained. The theodicy can then remain valid as an attempt to explain suffering as something ultimately traceable to human **egoism** (self-will).

There are some elements of the theodicy that are attractive. Evil is permitted but not willed by God, and God is not indifferent to our suffering, as is evident from the life of Jesus Christ. It also makes a place for the legitimate relief of suffering as exemplified by Christ, and as increasingly made possible by the advances of modern medicine. It also places a strong emphasis on redemption, and the promise of future justice in a life to come. This total vision of the world with its mixture of good and evil led **Gottfried Leibniz** to declare that God created the 'best of all possible worlds' for the realisation of His purposes. Significantly, of course, only within the perspective of faith could this be credible, since the world is clearly not the best that can be conceived.

(b) Both of the above theodicies have been criticised for being too theoretical. Both attempt to justify God in terms of events that are distant from the present day. Irenaeus could be said to look more to the future, and Augustine more to the past. For those who may be burdened with suffering, the idea of 'having to suffer' as the result of some historical accident is hardly likely to be of much comfort. The notion that suffering will bring moral maturity, or will help to create the great moral character, sounds patronising and question begging.

For this reason, modern thinkers such as **John Habgood**, **Richard Harries**, **D. Z. Phillips**, **Jurgen Moltmann** and others see suffering as part of the mystery of the Christian faith, the response to which may best be one of silence. Within this somewhat blurred vision, suffering is seen from two perspectives. First, it is an evil, and so cannot be directly willed by God. Therefore it is good not only to avoid suffering by all legitimate means, but to help others to overcome it or accept it, as exemplified by the Gospels. Alternatively, if it cannot be avoided, prevented or alleviated there is the scriptural promise that future (**eschatological**) happiness will outweigh all temporal misery (confirmed by Jesus in the Beatitudes, and by St Paul). This means that those who suffer unfairly are blessed now, and will be rewarded in the future.

This faith-based approach meets head-on the atheistic challenge that, on the evidence of the world, God can only be perceived as powerless or heartless. It also puts into a religious perspective the challenge of **Albert Camus** and others, that nothing can justify the torture of innocent children. Nothing humanly can, but within the wider vision offered by religious faith it is possible to see things differently.

Related questions: _____

1 Assess the view that the problem of evil is 'the rock of atheism'.

2 How satisfactory a solution to the problem of evil is the view that this world is meant to be 'a vale of soul-making'?

3 Assess the claim that 'God loves us' is made meaningless by evil and suffering.

4 *Religion and Science*

The Conflict between Religion and Science

It is common today to talk of the conflict between religion and science. In many people's minds, such conflict is an evitable part of their relationship. But this was not always the case, and even today there are serious attempts to show that a reconciliation between the two is quite possible. Up to medieval times, science and religion were in relative harmony. This was achieved by both sides showing sympathy for each other's findings. **Isaac Newton** represented the humble attitude of the religious scientist. The world that he saw could be explained according to scientific laws, but behind the world lay its Creator, whose will was decisive for the way in which scientific laws operated. This outlook is not too far removed from that of many modern theologians of science. In this view, a place is made for both religious faith and scientific knowledge, since both are seen to contribute to an overall vision of how the world is and how it works.

SIR ISAAC NEWTON

Isaac Newton was the first great champion of scientific law to explain the world

Today, such a tolerant view often appears to be more the exception than the rule. This is partly the result of antagonisms built up on both sides since the days of Copernicus and Galileo. One source of antagonism was reluctance by the Church to give ready support to scientific advances that appeared to conflict with the Bible. This led scientists to regard religion as intolerant of any scientific truth that caused difficulties for religious faith, and to adopt the more aggressive attitude that religion was the enemy of science. This attitude was further fuelled by the growth of more extremist religious positions such as fundamentalism. Fundamentalists saw the Bible as the source of fixed truths, such as those recorded in Genesis about the Creation of the world, and the Fall of mankind. This led to their absolute rejection of scientific findings about the origins of the world, and especially about human life.

However, fundamentalists correctly observed that science was having the effect of appearing godless. The claim of many scientists that everything can be explained without God carries the implication that human life has no real religious or moral significance. Some modern scientists show no hesitation in saying this, or show no awareness that such a claim makes them competitors with religion in the field of **metaphysics**. This means, ironically, that the conflict between religion and science is more about differences in beliefs than about differences in facts. Where differences are about facts, there is always hope of reconciliation. Where differences are about beliefs, the same hope does not exist.

Evaluate the conflict between religion and science.

The relationship between religion and science has more often than not been marked by conflict and disagreement. In principle, there should be no conflict if each side sticks to its proper role. Science deals with fact, religion with faith; science with physics, religion with metaphysics. According to this view, both should be able to coexist on the agreement that each has its own special contribution to make to the understanding of reality. The problem is, though, that not all scientists are prepared to allow religion any place in the understanding of 'reality'. They claim that 'reality' is what science investigates, and that beyond that there is nothing else. Religion therefore has nothing to offer and its claims are false. This deeply entrenched view has hardly been calculated to make religious leaders sympathetic towards an enterprise perceived as openly hostile to the claims of religious faith.

From medieval times, both sides have had difficulty in accepting the neat distinction between faith and fact, physics and metaphysics. Historically, as in the case of **Galileo**, religion objected to the apparent destruction of faith by science when it claimed to disprove truths from the Bible. Equally, science has objected to the claim of religion to speak with authority on matters of metaphysics (things beyond the empirical world), on the grounds that the only reality is that which is empirical, and which only science can investigate.

Science's boast of being able to support its truth-claims with evidence and verifiable proof merely adds salt to the wounds of religion, which by comparison has been cast as a purveyor of myth and mystery because its truth-claims cannot be proved. From this, it is a short step to eliminate from the realm of reality anything that cannot be verified by experimentation and proof. In this way, scientists from **August Comte** to **Richard Dawkins** have claimed to be in possession of the 'high ground' of what is ultimately real, and to look with scorn at religion's claim that reality has other dimensions, and that it possesses an 'ultimate truth' that is not accessible by the methods of science.

While most believers would readily admit that the claims of faith are not as open to empirical proof as the claims of science, this does not mean that religious faith has no empirical grounding whatever. The rise of Christianity was itself an extraordinary empirical phenomenon that poses the question of its origin. Christianity gives its origin as being the Resurrection, an event that can be dismissed as mere myth or mystery. The historical truth of the Resurrection has been defended by **Wolfhart Pannenberg**, who has argued that it was a phenomenon open to, and confirmed by, the normal methods of historico-empirical investigation.

Believers can also point to the testimony of history, which shows that religious faith has been a significant aspect in shaping civilisation. Believers can also claim that some of the greatest works of art of Western civilisation, from the frescoes of Michelangelo to the stones and glass of Chartres, have not only been masterpieces of scientific engineering but, equally, empirical expressions of a level of spiritual awareness that points beyond science.

Believers can also argue that the Five Ways of **St Thomas Aquinas** are arguments that support the claims of faith based on empirical facts about the world. Equally, for **Immanuel Kant**, the empirical fact of our moral awareness as human beings raised the question of the existence of a divine power, without whom no ultimate sense can be made of our moral awareness. For **Ludwig Wittgenstein**, the sheer fact of the world's existence was an empirical fact that constituted the mystical, a sense of wonder that is real, but eludes proper expression in empirical terms. In a similar vein, **Gottfried Leibniz** had wondered why there is something, and not just nothing – a natural philosophical question, but one ruled out by science, not because it is not a proper scientific question, but because it is not a proper question at all!

For others, it is the reality of our inner spiritual nature that defies scientific explanation, and that raises stubborn metaphysical questions. These are questions that arise from our spiritual capacity for artistic creation and appreciation, moral conviction and religious faith. **William James** has also observed that our insatiable thirst for truth inevitably leads beyond the limits of what science can offer. It was this that made Wittgenstein declare 'when all possible questions of science have been answered, the problems of life remain completely untouched'. A similar recognition of science's limits seems to lie behind **Albert Einstein's** remark that 'religion without science is lame, science without religion is blind'.

Historically, it has seemed that the religion–science conflict has been mainly caused by empirical disputes that religion should not have been involved in. A case in point has been its too rigid attachment to the perceived empirical claims of the Bible in respect of the origins of life and the world. Today, it is widely accepted that scientific explanations of the origins of the world and life can hardly be questioned. Yet these explanations have not made religious faith redundant. Is this because scientific explanations are never *ultimate* but merely causal? Religious explanations, on the other hand, are always ultimate but never causal in an empirical sense. Such explanations can neither be verified nor falsified by empirical claims of any kind, simply because faith is not so much about how the world is, but why it is.

Ultimately, therefore, the real conflict between religion and science will continue to revolve around beliefs about what constitutes reality. As long as science insists on its belief that reality is only what can be investigated by scientific methods, religion will represent a rival belief that reality has a wider reach. From this perspective, there can be logically no more agreement between religion and science than between religion and atheism.

How far are the findings of modern science compatible, or incompatible, with religious faith?

The two big areas in which science and religion appear to be in conflict are questions to do with the beginning of the world and the beginning of life. In broad terms, the disagreement may be stated as follows: one side says that the question is a scientific one, while the other side says that it is also a religious one. We begin with the origin of the world.

The **Steady State** theory of **Fred Hoyle**, in which matter was considered to be constant in a universe that had existed forever, has now been discarded both on scientific and philosophical grounds. In 1965, the discovery of background radiation confirmed the Big Bang theory and the formation of the first atoms. Philosophically, the notion of infinite time or eternal matter has been argued as intellectually absurd without the notion of a metaphysically necessary being to provide an ontological starting point. This was the position put forward by **St Thomas Aquinas**, and it now finds renewed support from some modern philosophers.

The **Big Bang** theory developed by **Edwin Hubble**, on the other hand, supposes that billion years ago an explosion of cosmic gases from a point of great density (known as space–time singularity), started the series of events that resulted in the physical universe that we know today. In this theory, the world is recognised as having a beginning in time and, by and large, scientists are happy that all of the evidence supports this.

Scientists, as scientists, are naturally confined to the empirical world of cause and effect, but even scientists find it impossible to avoid getting involved in metaphysical questions, and even suggesting metaphysical answers. The atheistic scientist **Quentin Smith** argues that the Big Bang had no cause whatsoever, a supposition that runs counter to all experience. But as **William Lane Craig** has shown, Big Bang cosmology is an emperor without clothes if it supposes that something can really come from nothing, a long recognised absurdity in medieval thought. For this reason, he thinks that science might after all have to reckon with the idea of a creator God.

Admittedly, the Big Bang does raise the question of why God, if He existed, did not begin with life rather than prime matter; or why humankind, claimed by faith to be made in God's image, should only emerge later, after a long time, by such a zigzag route and seemingly almost by accident. While to a believer these may seem to be mysteries, to a non-believing scientist they raise questions that seem to cast doubt on the claims of religious faith.

Perhaps the most threatening development in the relationship between science and religion came with **Charles Darwin's** theory of evolution. This was because evolution had serious implications for the understanding of the Bible, the foundation document of the Christian faith. The account of the origin of the world and the creation of man in Genesis was, for centuries, regarded as factually accurate. When scientific discoveries began to undermine the Genesis account, a reaction was provoked among religious leaders, which led many to oppose such findings because it was thought that they contradicted the Bible. In some cases the perception was justified, with scientists claiming that 'religion had been disproved', 'the Bible is shown to be untrue' and the like.

Many religious thinkers (with the exception of fundamentalists) are now able to reconcile the findings of science with their faith. Yet atheistic scientists reject religious claims, insisting that evolution is a purely natural process. This theory, known as **naturalism**, is actually a metaphysical theory, one that cannot claim to be based on any positive empirical evidence. Many could claim that such a theory has all the characteristics that make scientists critical of religion: it lacks supporting *evidence*, and it can neither be verified nor falsified.

The scientific attack on Genesis soon led many theologians to recognise that a book belonging to a pre-scientific age could only be expected to contain poor science. Genesis therefore came to be seen as a religious document, the product of a time when the inspired writer's aim was not to provide scientific knowledge about the natural world but to offer an insight, based on faith, into the ultimate origin of the world. This was the insight that the world ultimately came about by the personal will of a creator God. When this was taken into account it became possible to concede many of the perceived empirical claims (including the instant creation of everything) that had conflicted with the findings of science.

This apparent phenomenon of religion being put to flight by science has created the impression that the real issue between religion and science is one of causality, or explanatory theory. This is the notion that what was once explained by religion can now be perfectly well explained by science. This idea once gave rise to the infamous **God of the gaps**. This was the 'god' who was used as an instrumental explanation for things that couldn't otherwise be explained, a role now fulfilled by science. The more science is able to explain, the less room is left for God, who gradually becomes evicted from the gaps now filled by science, in much the same way as light dispels the mysteries of the dark.

It is this kind of thinking that is displayed by crusading atheistic scientists such as **Richard Dawkins** and **Peter Atkins**. They explicitly attack any form of religious interpretation of the origin of the world or of life. The argument of such theorists is that everything began by chance, and that evolution is determined exclusively by impersonal forces, and can be explained exclusively in terms of the needs and genetic characteristics of evolving organisms, given sufficient time. Both aggressively challenge the religious view of the origin of life as naive and childish, lacking credible evidence, and claim it to be irrational because it is unscientific.

A world that is somehow 'unscientific' even though part of the physical world has become a source of discomfort, if not embarrassment, to scientists. This is the world of **quantum physics** and **chaos theory**. In the former, elementary particles such as electrons exist but cannot be observed, give light either as waves or particles, and are impossible to track either with regard to position or momentum. This is an unusual world for science to deal with, a world full of everyday impossibilities. Some religious thinkers have noticed how here scientists think nothing of using the unobservable to explain the observable, yet hotly protest at the religious idea of seeing God as the factor by which the whole observable world is understood.

In chaos theory, the Newtonian world of fixed mechanical systems has had to be abandoned, to be replaced by a world of fluctuating and unpredictable possibilities created by the existence of life. Thus weather systems depend on delicate changes in what birds or butterflies might do. However, these discoveries can lend no support to the idea of causality 'out of nothing'. As **John Polkinghorne** has pointed out, the quantum world already exists as a condition of the events happening within it.

While these discoveries have caused science to revise its claims for clear knowledge, supposedly in contrast to religion, they do not affect the issue of primal origins. Chance happening in an existing world is not the same as chance happening to *cause* the world. Many, like **Aquinas**, reject a pure chance theory of origins as intellectually untenable. This is because it flies in the face of the what to many is simply a self-evident truth; namely, that ultimately nothing can come from nothing (*ex nihilo nihil fit*), even by chance!

The alternative is the idea of a *personal* causality. This is an idea that was already implicit in **Plato's** theory of a World Soul, one that has recently received compelling rational support from the philosopher of science **William Lane Craig**. Drawing on the thought of Aquinas, he argues that nothing can go from potency to actuality without a cause, and within a given scenario of 'empty space' or 'eternal matter' there could be no point at which things could begin to happen without a *reason* for their happening, as **Gottfried Leibniz** had already held. The only ultimate plausible reason could be the intervention of a Creator by a personal **act of will**. This would make the Big Bang (before which there was nothing) the possible scientific counterpart of the Genesis creation story.

To settle for the 'brute factuality' view of the universe is seen by many believers as opting out of the natural search for meaning in the universe. Religion, as **William James** pointed out, is partly the result of the human mind's relentless search for ultimate meaning and truth and, as he put it, 'to date its most satisfying answer to this search'. A world of 'brute fact', or one generated by 'blind chance', is a world of unpredictable chaos, a world without aim, purpose or end, and therefore without ultimate meaning. For most of us, it seems, the idea of a universe without any ultimate meaning or value is difficult to accept.

It is probably for this reason that the religious view of reality is so deeply ingrained in human history, human culture and human experience.

Sigmund Freud may dismiss religious faith by theorising about the mind's tendency towards wishful thinking, and 'inventing' a feel-good factor in the form of religion. But there are other explanations of religion that take into account far more of the dimensions of religious faith than Freud was either able, or willing, to do.

It could well be argued, against Freud, that a faith that makes existential demands in terms of morally responsible behaviour is less likely to be an illusion than one that advocates narcissistic self-indulgence. An outlook that advocates the freedom to satisfy selfish, emotional and physical drives may be closer to wishful thinking than one that advocates restraint, self-denial and selfless concern for others. It could therefore be argued that the Oedipal origins of religion that were so dear to Freud could also be the same origins of the modern wish to see the so-called **death of God** initiated by **Friedrich Nietzsche**. In the end, as **Anthony Flew** noted but for a different reason, nothing in the empirical world has been able to falsify religious faith.

In conclusion, we have seen that the findings of modern science have led some to replace religious beliefs about the origins of the world, and of life, with a belief in the higher credibility of scientific explanations. We have shown that this reveals a mistaken understanding of the claims of religion, and of how religious faith works. From the believer's viewpoint, religious faith is far from being incompatible with, much less undermined by, the findings of modern science.

 Can religion and science ever be reconciled?

The possibility of science and religion being reconciled will depend on an agreed understanding that both can contribute to a total vision of reality.

Alvin Plantinga calls religious faith a basic belief that has the capacity to offer a credible understanding (not explanation) of reality. Such a belief is well grounded because, first, we have a natural tendency to hold such belief; and, secondly, it is consistent with sufficient evidence from the world as to be properly credible. This means it is possible to incorporate the best scientific information into any religious vision.

For believers (including many scientists) religion is seen as necessary, not for adding to scientific knowledge, but for putting scientific knowledge into the context of an overall view of reality. The need for such a context, or overall view, is denied by science, which sees reality as having originated from the action of blind impersonal forces that have no coherent future or ultimate destiny.

This is a serious division of opinion, with implications not only at the level of conceptual thought but also at the level of attitude to life. The latter has further implications for human values and moral living. For this reason, so-called fundamentalist believers continue to resist the findings of science because they perceive them to be a threat to cherished beliefs about God as Creator, and Christ as Redeemer. They reject the 'godless' implications of the scientific world-view, which they see as morally threatening because it is morally empty. They believe what **Jean-Paul Sartre** said, that in a world without God 'everything would be permitted', and would lead to moral chaos.

This suggests that a threatened takeover by science may have more implications in the moral realm than was previously thought. This may explain why some liberal theologians today, such as **Keith Ward**, are beginning to adopt a more confrontational approach to science by suggesting that theism is a more probable explanation of the world than pure chance. This approach, however, runs the risk of making theism appear to be an explanatory rival to science in a causal sense. Theologians such as **John Habgood** deny that religion can be put in competition with science at the level of causal explanations, and insist that to do so is a mistake. But while a religious belief cannot be used directly to challenge a properly scientific explanation, it can challenge an impersonal vision of reality, and seek to replace it with a vision that is moral and personal.

Furthermore, in view of the restricted notion of truth that is characteristic of the scientific world-view, it is not surprising that religion should insist, for its part, that science cannot be a competitor in the area 'beyond physics'; that is, **metaphysics**. The most common objection from the **positivist** (scientific) side is that religion is a system of beliefs without supporting evidence. Believers may reply that in few areas of life are any of our beliefs backed up by the kind of evidence demanded, say, by a scientific theory or a court of law. **William James** said that if the demand for empirical evidence were carried too far, no trust between human beings would ever be possible. Believers claim that **trust** is the essence of religious faith, and that such trust is properly grounded by a combination of reason, history and human experience.

Believers, for their part, can argue that scientists are often reluctant to admit their own reliance on what can be called **metaphysical faith**, and the beliefs and trust that such faith entails. The reliance of all human knowledge on some kind of faith can be seen, for instance, in the metaphysics of **René Descartes**. He was keenly aware that something beyond human reason and experience

(God) was needed to make it possible to trust that human claims to truth are not deceptions. Scientists often appear to pretend that no such reliance on metaphysical faith is needed, but it is a basic presupposition for scientists to trust the reliability of their findings.

This is possible only because scientists place an unquestioned faith in the objectivity and consistency of experience. They believe in the regularity of nature, the predictibility of its laws, the reliability of observation and the consistency of things such as time, space and measurement (all unproved metaphysical assumptions). It is also interesting to note that **Gottfried Leibniz** and **Isaac Newton**, like Descartes, saw the need to postulate the idea of God to guarantee the reliability of their experiences and calculations. This is only to confirm that, despite denials, science as much as religion has its own kind of basic beliefs.

In conclusion, we have seen that science and religion are in a serious state of conflict over the meaning and nature of reality. Religion claims that reality goes beyond the empirical and the verifiable, while science denies this. But we have also seen that, for many believers, the findings of modern science are not necessarily incompatible with religious faith. Even despite differences among believers, exemplified especially by fundamentalists, all agree that the findings of science make no necessary impact on the essentials of religious faith. As long as this is denied by scientists, no reconciliation will ever be possible, and the view of **Albert Einstein**, that one side needs the other for a total vision of reality, will be denied.

Related questions:

1 Explain and evaluate the extent to which it is important for religious believers to challenge 'scientific' views of the world.

2 Evaluate the statement that 'religion without science is lame, science without religion is blind'.

3 How far is fundamentalism a valid reaction to modern science?

Science and Theology

If science is the study of empirical reality, theology is the study of faith and its relation to empirical knowledge. The many conflicts between religion and science have given theologians a busy time. From the time of **Copernicus** and **Galileo**, when scientific investigation began to have uncomfortable implications for the credibility of the Bible and faith, theologians have been busy trying to work out how faith can be harmonised with the facts of science. They have done this in the main through a greater awareness of the human nature of documents such as the Bible, and by allowing for human errors and mistakes in the understanding of what was essential to religious faith.

This has resulted in a general acceptance of the probability of evolution and the findings of modern scientific cosmology, both of which have had important implications both for the understanding of the Bible and for religious beliefs based on certain texts. It has been the task of theologians to see how faith can be harmonised with the latest scientific advances. In this section, the work of a number of theologians will be examined. It will be seen that science has brought about significant changes in how we understand the world and its origin. It has been the task of theologians to show that any advance in human knowledge of the world is to be welcomed, because it is a legitimate source of revelation about the workings of God, who is the source of all truth. But theologians have also been concerned to insist that any attempt by science to exclude religion from an overall view of reality is neither legitimate nor scientific.

Q (a) **What impact have advances in modern science had on theology?**
(b) **How successfully have theologians responded to these advances?**

(a) The advances in modern science that have caused particular problems for theology come under two main headings. Advances in the science of **biology** that have uncovered facts about the evolution of life have created problems for the understanding of the Bible. Evolutionary science sees life as the outcome of a process that began with single-cell life forms, that developed in ever increasing degrees of complexity to the arrival of *Homo sapiens*, us humans.

Advances in the science of **cosmology** have, equally, created problems in the understanding of the Bible. The evidence shows that the universe began with the Big Bang, an event that took place around 15 billion years ago. The outstanding discovery in both of these related areas is the significance of time. Science has shown that the world is immeasurably older than was previously thought possible, and that time-lapse is an integral part of the explanation of our present world.

Advances in both fields have led to a serious rethinking among scholars about the meaning and nature of the Bible, in particular the Genesis account of the origin of the world and human life, which was long held to be factually reliable. If Genesis is taken literally, the timescale of creation is very short (six days), animals are created directly, separately and completely, and they enter an environment that is ready for their arrival. The calculations of **Bishop Ussher** in the seventeenth century, that the universe was some 6000 years old, went largely unquestioned for a century.

However, under the impact of modern science, Genesis is no longer seen as a scientific guide to the origin of the world and living things. Scientists today talk of time-spans of hundreds of millions, not thousands, of years. Contrary to a literal reading of Genesis, life is seen as originating as a single-cell organism from which all later forms emerged, and the human being is also a product of this same process, not a unique creature with some separate origin outside the evolutionary system. This has had obvious implications for the understanding of mankind as a special creation of God, made in the *imago Dei*.

The Bible has also been challenged by another important scientific fact. Genesis gives no hint of the brutal struggle for survival against a hostile environment which animals – including our own ancestors – underwent, some perishing to extinction long before *Homo sapiens* arrived. The Genesis statement that God saw what He had created, 'and saw that it was good' is therefore, in the light of this, a serious oversimplification, and difficult to reconcile with the traditional belief that God rules everything with His providence (loving care). However, the Bible story has proved to be remarkable consistent with modern science in one important respect, to which we shall return below.

Another important challenge to the Bible and theology came from the newly developed science of history, partly as a result of new archaeological findings and the discovery of ancient texts such as the Dead Sea Scrolls. Traditionally, the Bible was regarded as a sacred book that was free from error because it was written under divine inspiration. But the study of some ancient documents has led to a new understanding of the influences under which they were created. This was to bring about a radical revision in the understanding of the nature of the Bible. Like all other ancient documents, the Bible too was subject to human, cultural and time-bound influences. No longer could it be regarded as a book that 'came down from heaven' – rather, it began to be seen as a book written by human beings who were subject to the cultural influences of their time.

A recognition of these discoveries made it necessary to understand 'divine inspiration' in a new way. It also made possible a more relaxed and more liberal conception of how the Bible was really meant to be understood. If its contents were somehow culturally conditioned, it would not be surprising to find that the knowledge of its authors would reflect the limitations of all pre-scientific societies. Hence, ironically, the science of history was to provide the tools for an understanding of the Bible that would make it resistant to scientific criticism! A book that was understandably weak on scientific knowledge could now be treated as a religious book, with a religious message that was not dependent on scientific accuracy.

However, it would be wrong to conclude that theology was somehow destined to end up in the shadow of science. The initial result of the conflict was a win for science on empirical issues, but also a renewed determination on the part of theology to fight for a wider vision of life, extending beyond the horizon of science. New theological developments therefore put the spotlight on new ways of understanding faith that would establish its continuing relevance to human life.

In broad terms, there was a move away from simplified, or picturesque, ideas of God that were vulnerable to scientific criticism. These were influenced by the transcendent, objectified and anthropomorphic (human) tendencies both of classical theism and the biblical picture. A new understanding of God would have to stress His more enigmatic spiritual nature, and put a new focus on the meaning of divine faith for the understanding not so much of the world but, as **Immanuel Kant** argued, of human life seen as the arena of a moral struggle in the midst of a material world.

Paul Tillich is a representative of this new approach to theology. He has put forward ideas of God that are meant to find an echo in the self-awareness of human beings about themselves. Life in the scientific age is a moral challenge rooted in the question of its meaning. Therefore, no longer can God be considered as some being on the same level as other beings, or a being distant from the world but, rather, as the source of all being, **Being Itself**. God is no longer just the highest Good, but our 'ultimate concern', the focus of all moral values. God is no longer a distant Creator, but 'the ground of our being'. In this view, faith is an essential component in making sense of life. Without faith life is meaningless, and human life has no ultimate aim or purpose. Such an emphasis on faith as necessary for a more adequate account of the meaning of life is without doubt a clear reflection of the impact of an understanding of the world, and of human life, which eliminates the moral and the spiritual. Where this happens, human beings begin to experience what **Roger Scruton** has called a sense of 'estrangement' from the world, which he calls 'the poisoned gift of science'.

(b) It has been the task of modern theologians to face up to the challenges of modern science, and to face the discrepancies that have been uncovered between the truths of faith and the empirical findings of science. A number of them have vigorously taken up this task.

We begin with **Pierre Teilhard de Chardin**. Perhaps the most outstanding of the earlier theologians of science, Teilhard tried to join the findings of science and the insights of religion into a single vision of the world. What seems a blind process, evolution, was to him infused with the Spirit of God, driving it towards greater and greater complexity, from inert matter to animal instinct, to human consciousness, and upward still to the realisation of a community of ethical awareness and brotherly **agape love**, supremely exemplified by Jesus Christ.

Teilhard's theory is fideistic to the extent that it is a religious vision based on faith, and is therefore unlikely to make any impact outside a believing community. But it offers a moral vision of life that is logically coherent, and shows at least that evolutionary science can be seen with religious, as well as with non-religious, eyes.

A more recent theologian, **Adam Ford**, concedes that the findings of modern science call for a new understanding of God's creative role in the world. Although he accepts Einstein's claim that God *played dice* with evolution – by which he meant that a lot was left to chance – Ford insists that limits were set within which purpose could be achieved, making impossible an ultimately random, or chance, outcome. He insists that it is the function of faith to provide a coherent interpretation of all scientific facts about the world.

Arthur Peacocke grants that we must bow to science for knowledge of how the world works. But he sees religion as providing an important perspective on reality, one that plays a crucial role in providing humans with a sense of ethical responsibility, and promoting a Kantian respect for life as a central value. This is to imply that the scientific notion of truth leads to a vision of life that is limited to material and physical processes, a vision that lacks the capacity to account for our complex nature as spiritual beings endowed with a sense of ethical and aesthetic appreciation. As **William James** has argued, a world that consists of 'armies of molecules' is unlikely to define the limits of the human mind's 'thirst for truth'.

The scientist–theologian **John Polkinghorne** has devoted much of his writing to processes such as **quantum physics** and the **anthropic principle**. In the former, the complexity of matter is beginning to humble scientists, because they can neither describe it with accuracy, nor predict its outcomes; while the latter is providing a route to a new natural theology based on the mystical wonder of what **Ludwig Wittgenstein** called the sheer fact of the world's existence. However, theism cannot be used as a cause of the world in the old sense, because God is a *Thou* who can only be addressed, not an object for inspection (an *It*), and cannot be invoked as a cause in any scientific sense. But a purposeful personal intelligence, he maintains, provides a far more satisfactory account of how the universe evolved than some theory of blind chance. The odds against mankind arriving out of the chaos of the Big Bang are so improbable that a theistic interpretation (that is, a guiding intelligence) has the greater ring of truth.

Keith Ward agrees with Polkinghorne, but responds more directly to criticisms brought by modern science writers such as **Richard Dawkins** and **Peter Atkins**, both of whom attack religion as naive and irrational, because it lacks supporting scientific evidence. Ward insists that chance is a less 'likely' or less 'probable' explanation of the universe than God. However, in his effort to take on his adversaries in this way he risks get stuck in a special pleading position, as when he appeals to the 'beauty and elegance of the evolutionary process' and insists on the more likely explanation of a 'cosmic mind of infinite wisdom'. The danger of this approach is that in treating God as a rival hypothesis to a scientific theory, it reduces God to the realm of one possibility among many. As **Pierre Laplace** famously declared, science has no need for such an hypothesis.

A far more uncompromising approach is taken by the scientist–theologian **William Lane Craig**. Craig puts forward the daring argument that any theory based on the principle that something can come from nothing without the intervention of a personal deity is conceptually absurd. In this approach, God is a necessary, not merely possible, part of any understanding of reality.

We have seen, therefore, that the findings of modern science have raised serious questions for theologians in respect to traditional beliefs based on the Bible. We have seen that many theologians have responded to these challenges in a positive way. Most have accepted the factual findings of science, but have maintained a firm position regarding the legitimacy of the religious perspective on the world in general, and human life in particular. All have in some way drawn out the implications of Einstein's remark that 'religion without science is lame, science without religion is blind'.

In advancing this insight, the modern theologians we have seen have all in their several ways shown that faith, far from being undermined by science, can continue to live with it, and provide a credible perspective to understanding the whole of reality in a way that adequately takes account of the many dimensions of our complex and mysterious nature. In the end, how far theologians have successfully answered the challenges of modern science will no doubt continue to provide the material for a continuing debate.

Related questions:

1 How successfully has religious faith coped with the challenge of modern science?

2 How far is it necessary 'to deny the Bible to make room for science'?

3 How persuasive is the view that science only offers a partial understanding of human life?

Evolution, Cosmology and Religion

How far can religious beliefs be reconciled with (a) the discoveries of Charles Darwin and (b) Big Bang cosmology?

(a) Although it has been modified over time, **Charles Darwin's** theory of evolution remains the accepted understanding of how life developed on earth. A life form with a very basic structure – a single cell – was the beginning of a process that we call evolution, in which life developed from primitive to more complex forms over a period of millions of years. This process was influenced both by environmental factors (such as the accessibility of food) and by random mutations (changes) in the evolving organism, all of which took place over an extremely long time-span. Those organisms that adapted best to their surroundings were the most likely to survive and propagate the species further. This is called natural selection.

The process reached a certain high point of complexity with the arrival of animals, known as primates. A fork in the road of evolution was reached at this point, some 300 million years ago. One continued to develop within non-rational limits as apes, leading to chimpanzees, baboons, gorillas and the like. Another group of primates developed differently, for reasons that appear to be related to geography and climate. They evolved along a different road, passing through different stages of greater complexity. Today, this group of animals is considered to be the ancestors of the human race.

This theory of human development is strictly scientific, built up on the basis of the available evidence – historical, biological, archaeological and physical. The implication of this view for religion is that it appears to conflict with the centuries old account of the Creation and Fall contained in the Bible. Besides contradicting the Genesis account that all animals were created separately, it seems to undermine the sacred belief that mankind was a special creation of God, showing us instead to be merely products of the evolutionary process. From a scientific viewpoint, this is of course what we are.

The immediate reaction of some religious leaders to Darwin's discoveries showed that they were unprepared for the new revelations of biological science. This was famously exemplified by **Bishop Wilberforce** in his debate with Darwin's spokesman, **Thomas Huxley**. The debate centred on the implications of evolution for the truth of the Bible. While the debate appeared to expose the bishop as naive and reactionary with regard to science, it did nothing of the sort with regard to his understanding of religious faith. Wilberforce was predictably concerned to defend some key biblical beliefs that he saw as crucial: the uniqueness of humans 'made in the image of God', mankind's fall from grace as symbolised by Adam and Eve, and the need for the Redemption brought by Jesus Christ. What the bishop correctly recognised was the threat that evolution posed for the credibility of these beliefs, a threat that his agnostic opponent did nothing to play down. Later, it would be shown that the Bible was not as vulnerable to scientific attack as was earlier feared, but in the meantime some religious leaders felt that they had to choose between faith and science.

The need to make such a choice led to the rise of so-called **fundamentalism** in America, the driving force of which was to make no concessions to science, and specifically to evolution. Fundamentalists were particularly sensitive to what they perceived as the 'godless' implications of purely natural explanations of human origins. They believed that once one cherished belief from the Bible was challenged, all related beliefs would come under threat, like the fall of dominoes, or of a house of cards. Especially alarming was the perceived threat to the moral authority of the Bible. For these reasons fundamentalism became, and has remained, a powerful reactionary force in defence of religious faith and the truth of the Bible.

However, many feel that fundamentalists pay an unnecessarily high price for the defence of their faith. Their claim that the Bible is correct about the earth being relatively *young* flies in the face of compelling geological and archaeological evidence to the contrary. To get over this by saying that God *miraculously* gave the world a 'superficial appearance of age' is, even for many believers, to test credulity to the limit.

But not all religious leaders refused to accept evolution. **Bishop William Temple**, a contemporary of Darwin, recognised that religious faith had to be reconciled with biological fact. In his view, all truth was sacred whether religious or scientific, since it had God as its guarantor. While the Bible does not mention evolution, it does not rule it out either. Yes, science had forced a rethink of many biblical assumptions about how life began, but it did not necessarily undermine the *essence* of the biblical story.

The stories of Creation and of the Fall, for instance, are today seen as a mythical–religious account of three basic realities central to human experience; namely, the reality of the world, the mysterious nature of human life, and the reality of good and evil. The story of Redemption is seen as the revelation that good can overcome evil only by the aid of a spiritual power given by God. The precise mechanisms by which life arrived in the world are now seen as an inessential part of the biblical message.

When the smoke of the initial explosion caused by Darwin had cleared away, theologians began to see the real issues for religion in a clearer light. One was that no merely scientific account of reality – one that fails to take account of the complex, mysterious and spiritual nature of human life – can be accepted as adequate. They pointed to the capacity of human beings to appreciate and create the beautiful, our sense of the profound, or as **Ludwig Wittgenstein** said the mystical, and our nature as characterised by will and ethical awareness. These, they said, cannot be accounted for by scientific, causal explanations. As **Immanuel Kant** had highlighted, mankind cannot be explained as merely the product of the evolutionary process. By our ethical will we are able to transcend our world and establish our freedom over it. With arguments such as these, theologians began to reassert the validity of the Bible's religious message.

Allowing, therefore, for the function of religion to contribute to an overall understanding of reality, it can be reconciled with evolution. Yet, it remains to Darwin's credit that he indirectly brought about a new understanding of biblical truth, and of how a world that has undergone a process of evolution can also be a world created by God. To this extent his contribution has not only been to science but also to religion. But, for many, his findings remain an enduring challenge to the claims of faith.

(b) Recent studies by philosophers such as **William Lane Craig** have begun to reverse some of the earlier claims of scientists that the Big Bang cosmology had disproved creationist beliefs that had looked to Genesis for their inspiration.

Creationism, which is the belief that ultimately reality had a divine origin, is directly denied by scientific materialism. Craig believes that the Genesis version that the world had a beginning in time has been remarkably borne out by recent scientific cosmology. It is now more or less scientifically certain that the world that we know did have a beginning in time. This puts to rest the **Steady State** theory, which **Fred Hoyle** is said to have developed in order to rule out any 'beginning' in time, with its possible religious implications.

Craig argues that the notion of an **infinite regress** (a chain of events going backwards with no beginning) is an absurdity. For one thing, an infinite regress makes it impossible to conceive how anything along an infinite time-line could ever get started, since there could be no point along such a line from which reference could be made. Thus infinite time makes the notion of a time lapse impossible and 'an infinite time entails infinitely distant events', another concept that is impossible to conceive, says Craig.

But we know from science that there was a start. Craig concludes that the only credible explanation is an uncaused cause, what religion calls God. This point is one of the salient features of the *kalam* cosmological argument. It also restores to prominence the First Cause argument of **St Thomas Aquinas**, and gives philosophical support to the historical testimony of believers. Craig discounts the objections of Kant that causality only applies to the world of space and time. He argues that causality can rightly apply to the objective world as a condition of all experience, and not just, as Kant said, to the operations of the mind in relation to phenomena (events or things in the empirical world). This makes it possible to see how causality could apply outside the world of space and time. Otherwise, Kant couldn't have ruled out metaphysics, because to do so is already to go beyond space and time!

Craig concludes that the most plausible theory is one involving the operation of a personal will, a conclusion that finds support in **Plato's** World Soul theory. The scientific alternative that something came from nothing, as the Big Bang supposes, is not only intellectually unsatisfactory but is impossible to imagine. It fails to answer the famous question posed by **Gottfried Leibniz**: *Why is there something, and not just nothing?* The objection that the cosmological argument begs the question 'What caused God?' is to overlook the claim that God is by nature uncaused, and posited by Leibniz as the *efficient* cause of the world, not its *material* (that is, empirical) cause. Suggesting material causes of events is the province of science, not religion.

Craig's conclusion, therefore, is that Big Bang cosmology not only fails to challenge faith, but offers the surprising possibility of a religious conclusion derived from philosophy. For Craig, this is a more satisfactory conclusion than that of the atheist **Quentin Smith**, who describes the universe as 'inexplicably and stunningly actual', but says that it exists 'for no reason at all'!

Related questions:

1 Assess whether evolutionary theory is a genuine threat to religious belief.

2 Explain and evaluate the view that 'science has replaced the Bible in explaining the origin of the world'.

3 For believers, how far is the Big Bang a satisfactory, or unsatisfactory, explanation of the universe?

Science and Miracles

The question of miracles has brought into particularly sharp focus the differing perspectives of religion and science. At the centre of the conflict has been the understanding of miracles as violations of the laws of nature, to use **David Hume's** definition. The issue of miracles has not been unconnected to the rising confidence of science to explain everything, including the extraordinary. In many instances, what used to be seen as extraordinary is now explained by science in terms of natural laws. The idea of storms once being seen as evidence of the anger of the gods can serve as an example. Today, it is normal to look to science for causal explanations of events, rather than to religion for supernatural explanation.

For believers, however, this is not the end of the miraculous. There are many testimonies of things happening that are credited to some form of supernatural agency. But it is the precise nature of this agency that is now at issue. If God exists, His power must in some way be operative in everything that happens, either directly or indirectly. The preference today is to see the miraculous as that which may be credited to the hand of God, but seen as working indirectly through the laws of nature. This means a shift away from seeing miracles as synonymous with the abnormal and spectacular, in favour of the view that more ordinary events can be seen as miracles within the perspective of faith.

Evaluate the view that there is no place for miracles in a scientific age.

In order to answer this question, it is necessary to clarify what is mean by 'miracle'. The traditional understanding was classically expressed by

David Hume, who defined a miracle as a 'transgression of the law of nature by a particular volition of the deity'. This will be contrasted with modern understandings of 'miracle' that do not necessarily presuppose any transgression of natural laws.

Hume's criticism of miracles was based on empirical probabilities. Wise men, he said, proportion their belief to the evidence. Quite simply, there will always be more evidence for an event having a natural explanation than a miraculous one, and so claims of miracles will always be open to doubt and suspicion. From this standpoint, Hume is of course right, and one might say that he does the service of showing that **empiricism** is an unwise and fragile basis for believing in the miraculous. For this reason, many religious thinkers have preferred to see the miraculous in ways that permit a greater convergence between the laws of nature and the action of God.

Hume's understanding of miracle reflects the traditional 'divine intervention' view, in which God is supposed to interfere with or suspend the laws of nature to bring about cures and other wonders, such as those reported in the Gospels. The empiricist **John Locke** had assumed that such 'signs and wonders' surrounding the life of Jesus could be used as empirical evidence to prove the truth of the Christian faith. It was to show the limitations of this confident assumption that lay behind Hume's later attack on miracles.

But many believers today would concede that the Gospel miracles may not necessarily provide evidence of the direct intervention of God. It is conceivable that Jesus could have been the focus of God's power by having special gifts. **A. N. Wilson** has suggested that Jesus had a large following because he was a remarkable *healer*. This would still make it possible to attribute His healing powers to God and for others to see them, or not see them, as such. Some scholars have seen significance in the fact that all of the Gospel miracles involve some human agency. Thus what is reported as divine agency may not necessarily be as direct (or miraculous in the traditional sense) as is often supposed.

Even the special case of the Resurrection is subject to different interpretations by scholars. **Wolfhart Pannenberg** has argued strongly for its credibility as an *historical* event on the grounds that: (1) such an event was forecast within the biblical tradition; (2) it was sufficiently confirmed by the reported evidence of the empty tomb to convince the apostles; and (3) from the point of view of human existence, it is something that makes immediate sense as an answer to the question of what happens to the virtuous after death. But many believers leave the question about the precise nature of the Resurrection event open. They see its acceptance as part of the trust in the significance of Jesus as testified by the apostles. What is important in the end is that some events can be given a *religious* significance within the perspective of faith.

There is no contradiction of course, as **Richard Swinburne** has pointed out, in the author of nature intervening to change water into wine, or causing the dead to rise. However, the interventionist view of miracles raises some *moral* questions. **Maurice Wiles** asks why, if God chooses to intervene in the world, should He appear to work in such odd ways, often intervening to help an individual, while letting evils such as Auschwitz run their course.

To the sceptic, this is further evidence to support the claim that no God exists, but believers do not see it like this. For many, although the question can only be answered within the perspective of faith, there is the recognition that God still acts in the fight against evil. This is seen in what can be called the principle of **human agency**. God may not intervene directly, but He can be seen to give others the inspiration to act on his behalf. He can do this at the moral level of inspiring human kindness and giving assistance to others. But as **John Habgood** has argued, He can also be seen as the source of the wisdom that brings human help through the agency of science (especially medical science) and technology.

In reply to Wiles, it could be argued that private miracles, or miracles benefiting a single individual, may reflect the possibility of personal faith playing a part. Seen in this way, the miracle becomes something of a powerful subjective experience under the influence of faith, an experience that may sometimes bring about some remarkable physical effect. As a result, the recipient rightly thanks God, but any divine involvement remains invisible from the outside and is not directly, but indirectly from God.

For this reason, many theologians have favoured an interpretation of miracles as ordinary events, but *seen as* miracles within the field-vision of faith. This view has been popularised by **John Hick**, who took it from **Ludwig Wittgenstein**. Just as something in the world can be seen as, say, a misfortune to one or good fortune to another, so an event can be seen as having religious significance to one person and not to another. Significantly, Wittgenstein had argued that religious faith was a way of seeing the world.

Talk of miracles, he believed, was part of the 'language game' of faith. To contest a claim of a miracle therefore is futile. There can be no possible evidence to refute the claim, because only the believer is in the commanding position to see the event as *religiously* significant. Wittgenstein's thought here bears some similarity to that of **Rudolf Bultmann**, who rejected the old 'divine intervention' view of miracles, and refused to regard even the Resurrection as an event that could be confirmed or refuted by science.

For Wittgenstein, the language game of faith cannot communicate on the same level with the language game of science. Each side needs to understand that both language games operate on fundamentally different levels, one side concerned with provable facts, and the other with matters of meaning and significance on a cosmic level. Religion has to do with matters of 'absolute value' as he put it, such as the belief that you are dealing with God. For this reason, he claimed that religious belief in something like the Resurrection involved a more total involvement of the person by way of **love** and **trust** than would a mere scientific fact.

The modern view of miracles, therefore, shared by Habgood, Wiles, Hick and others, is to see God's intervention as indirect, acting through or in accordance with, but not against, nature. This represents a shift away from the traditional view that a miracle was something that was located in an objective fact: Did this happen, or didn't it? Was this caused by God, or could it have a natural explanation? The new approach is to locate a miracle more properly within the faith perspective of the believer. This makes claims for miracles part of faith as a way of seeing the world, and shifts the focus from the objective to the subjective, from concern with fact to concern with meaning.

An obvious philosophical objection to this view is that it appears to reduce a miracle to the subjective judgement of the claimant. Since there are no **objective** grounds to warrant the claim of divine involvement, does this not empty the word 'miracle' of its usual meaning? This objection falls within the wider field of difficulty raised by religious faith. Why is a claim of a miracle any different from the believer's claim that God exists? In either case, there is the problem of objective verification, which leads the non-believer to conclude that faith is illusory. In the end, the understanding of miracle is closely bound up with the understanding of faith. Miracles are only impossible if God does not exist.

Dietrich Bonhoeffer has added his own moral objection to the traditional understanding of miracles. He considered the traditional belief in, and indeed expectation of, miracles as a sign of a dependence mentality. Instead, we should follow the example of Jesus in the Gospels and take responsibility for our own lives in the midst of a secular world. 'Man come of age' does not look for divine intervention, he said.

Atheists might reply to this by claiming that it fails to meet the challenge of why, if God exists, humans are often left at the mercy of evil. Bonhoeffer would no doubt reply with his own provocative vision of faith, but that would hardly answer the question. But his call for more direct human involvement in the fight against evil (as shown by his own costly example in opposing Hitler), which he saw against a wider, **eschatological** (other-worldly) perspective, shows the sincerity of his conviction.

In conclusion, while science cannot be allowed to determine what is possible or not possible for God to do, the weight of evidence seems to point to God's normal action in the world being indirect, working either through natural laws, human wisdom or the love of fellow human beings. The interpretation of natural events as showing the hand of God has now replaced the traditional understanding of 'miracle'. The miraculous is now what faith sees it to be, not necessarily some spectacular display of divine power that overrides the laws of nature.

This leads to an abandonment of the traditional understanding held by Locke and Hume, and gives way to a concept of 'miracle' as an event perceived by faith as divinely inspired, but still consistent with the same event being explained naturally. Taking this changed understanding of miracles into account, it is still possible to make room for the miraculous in a scientific age.

Related questions:

1 Discuss the view that 'after Auschwitz, miracles are impossible to believe in'.

2 Evaluate the view that the advances of modern science have destroyed belief in the miraculous.

3 Discuss the claim that miracles do not have to mean violations of the laws of nature.

Life after Death

Perhaps the greatest miracle of all, from a theoretical and religious point of view, is the possibility of life after death. Since death could be called one of the most puzzling aspects of life, a possible life after death would undoubtedly be of universal interest. The earliest burial sites show indications that the disposal of the body was not regarded as the end of the matter. One of the arguments for the appeal, if not the intelligibility, of some religions is that they offer the promise of life after death. **St Paul** made it clear that faith in Jesus would be without foundation had He not risen from the dead.

While the Resurrection has been interpreted by some as a non-historical (in the 'experience' of the apostles) event – in contrast, say, to the Battle of Hastings – the earlier claim that it was an *historical* event has been defended in modern times by the respected theologian **Wolfhart Pannenberg**. He sees the historical evidence, such as the empty tomb and the convictions of the apostles, as forming sufficient evidence for an event that was then expected to happen, an event that is of immediate significance for every human being. The idea of bodily resurrection is only one possible form of life after death, the other being the immortality of the soul. However, the one can be seen to depend on the other. If the soul is not immortal, there can be no continuity between the person living now and the same person in the after-life. This would make a bodily resurrection impossible.

 What are the philosophical problems associated with belief in life after death?

In any discussion of life after death, the relationship between body and soul is crucial. According to one view the soul is active in, but ultimately independent of, the body, and survives after the body perishes. In the other view, soul and body are made for each other, and eventually become reunited by way of bodily resurrection. The latter view is more true to the biblical tradition, which saw body and soul forming a single unity, and is confirmed for believers in the Resurrection of Jesus. Both views are challenged by atheistic materialism, which holds that body and soul are two sides of a single coin, one merely the life principle of the other, and that both perish together on the death of the individual.

What is called a dualistic account, in which body and soul are two separate entities, was put forward by **Plato**. Although they combine in a human life, the soul lives on in immortality after the death of the body. Plato's dualism is consistent with his understanding of reality. He gave an illustration of this in his famous **allegory of the cave**. The majority of us are like prisoners in a cave, where shadows cast by a fire are seen projected on a wall. The prisoners in the cave think that the shadows are the full reality, all there is. Only by making the effort can one escape from the cave and discover the truth. Then one can see by the light of the sun, and realise the difference between *shadow* and *reality*. It is like this, says Plato, in our everyday existence. We are surrounded by shadows that we take for reality. The true reality is different, and exists in a spiritual realm of **ideal forms**.

The ideal forms are spiritual realities that have always existed and never change. Earthly life is only a shadowy world in which everything is merely a dim reflection of these ideal forms. Thus we can only know earthly forms of beauty, truth, goodness, justice and so on, we cannot know their ideal form as the 'Good', the 'True', the 'Beautiful', the 'Just' and so forth. The human soul (or life principle) belongs to the world of ideal forms, where it once existed. Its reality is manifested in our ability to show spiritual powers such as free will, self-consciousness, memory and understanding. In fact, Plato attributed to the soul the ability to do the really important things, such as acts of good and evil, justice and injustice, and so on. Besides, argues Plato, the soul's power is confirmed in the ability of the individual to rise above earthly pleasures and contemplate the higher things of the intellect. This view was highly influential in early Christianity, but is today seen as too metaphysical and speculative to be taken seriously.

The separate existence of the soul was assumed in some of the pronouncements of Jesus, and was later supported by **René Descartes**, and again later by **Immanuel Kant**. Descartes made a firm distinction between the world of the soul (or mind) and the physical world of the body. This appeared to conform to common sense, which shows that the mind is able, by rational thought, to be independent of the body and, as psychology shows, to be able to exercise a certain power over the body. Kant argued for the immortality of the soul as a condition of the ***summum bonum*** (the 'highest good'), the rewarding of virtue with happiness, which required a continuous life after death. However, difficulties have been raised about an independently existing soul.

To begin with, there is no evidence that an independent soul exists. This was the view of **Aristotle** who, unlike **Plato**, took an empirical approach. Experience shows that soul and body exist together, and that they both work together to create conscious human life. This makes the concept of a soul without a body as incoherent as a body without a soul. For Aristotle, the soul was the 'form' of the body, that which makes the individual unique in personality and character, and accounts for individual human thought and action. Aristotle also distinguished between 'vegetable', 'animal' and 'human' souls in ascending order, but insisted that the existence of a soul without a body was impossible. Alleged reports of ghosts and spirits, of apparitions and hauntings, are therefore literally without substance. The so-called workings of the soul are seen as an abstraction, with no evidence to support the view that a human being is some 'ghost in a machine', as **Gilbert Ryle** famously put it.

Such a view, however, would not necessarily undermine the notion of an independently existing soul. Descartes felt that his thinking was more reliable than his experience, making it possible to imagine a soul without a body. Its weakness is that it refers to something outside experience, but the notion of the spirit or personality of an individual being held in existence by an all-powerful God is not logically incoherent. Indeed, it is this belief that is central to the eschatology (beliefs about the after-life) of Christianity, in which the deeds of an individual are believed to be held on account by God. But this view is less about the immortality of the soul than the future bodily resurrection of the individual.

The model for this belief is the Resurrection of Jesus as testified by the New Testament. The belief depends on the power of an omnipotent God who is able to bring it about. Again, this belief is challenged, on two grounds. The first challenge is on the grounds of lack of empirical evidence. The historical claim of believers for the Resurrection of Jesus is seen as being offset by the absence of any such happening since. Secondly, on logical grounds, if death is the end of life, there could be no way to coherently say that someone 'rose from the dead'. The believer will reply that, philosophically, the idea of survival beyond death by divine power is not incoherent, and that its truth is uniquely confirmed by the New Testament in regard to Jesus. As **St Thomas Aquinas** held, the human wish to survive after death is a sign of **transcendence** over all earthly things: as he said, 'it is impossible for a human appetite to be in vain'. Since this idea could never be confirmed or denied by reason, it must be left as a matter of faith.

Related questions:

1 Assess the evidence for and against life after death.

2 How might a religious believer defend objections against the idea of life after death?

3 Compare and contrast the ideas of Plato and Aristotle on the immortality of the soul.

5 Religion and Language

Religious Language

Modern interest in the meaning and use of language has its roots in the scientific understanding of reality traceable to **David Hume** and **August Comte**. If reality in its totality can be confined to the material and the physical, then if follows that the only legitimate use of language is in expressing what comes under those headings. Thus religion and metaphysics can be dismissed as meaningless nonsense. It is precisely this charge that was brought by the movement called **logical positivism**. In this section, we shall examine the questions that the logical positivists raised, and how believers have responded to their challenge. Religious language will be seen to have its own grammar and logic, but will also be seen to suffer the weakness of not being either verifiable or falsifiable by empirical methods.

As we shall see, a key figure in the philosophy of language is **Ludwig Wittgenstein**, who was also one of the founding fathers of logical positivism. But he would later adopt an understanding of language in which the priority was placed on its *use* rather than on its *meaning*. This had the effect of shifting the debate away from the supposed limitations of, say, religious language, to a practical understanding of how such language was used by believers. Wittgenstein's inspiration for this approach was said to have come from watching a soccer match, from which he got the idea of **language games**.

Although Wittgenstein remained neutral about the truth of religious language, he did provide insights into how it could be a valid area for expression. His insights into what he called the 'mystical' showed that he recognised certain transcendent aspects of human life and experience (similar to what religion speaks about), but which were difficult to put into words. In the final section, the way in which language has traditionally been used to express religious beliefs will be examined.

 Assess the view that religious language is meaningless.

The charge that religious language is meaningless arose from the thinking of **Ludwig Wittgenstein**, and was further developed by **A. J. Ayer** and the logical positivists in the 1930s. **Logical positivism** was the verbal correlate of the philosophy of positivism, started by **Auguste Comte** in the nineteenth century, but was also derived from the eighteenth-century empiricism of **David Hume**. Positivism held that the only real truth was scientific, that which can be posited (clearly shown) by empirical observation and confirmed by experimental proof.

Applying positivism to language, the logical positivists claimed that only two types of statement are meaningful. First, there are analytical statements such as 'all husbands are married men' (considered meaningful, but trivial). Secondly, and more important, there are synthetic statements. These are statements of purported fact (they could be true or false), and they are meaningful precisely because they can be empirically verified. Since religious statements (for example, God exists) can never be verified by empirical evidence, such statements have to be classed as meaningless. This is known as the **verification principle**, the new measuring stick of meaning, the ultimate test of whether a statement is informative or cognitive.

Although Ayer made several amendments to the verification principle which made it more flexible in its application (for example, the idea of verification in principle, rather than in fact), it still ruled out religious statements because they were beyond any form of verification. Later, by using a method that is common in science, **Anthony Flew** introduced the principle of **falsification** to argue that religious language was meaningless. According to Flew, religious beliefs have no cognitive meaning because the believer allows nothing to count against them. Take the belief that God loves us. No matter what happens in the world, says Flew, it will make no difference to the believer's fixed belief that God loves us. This immunity from any kind of falsification makes the belief meaningless. However, Flew fails to show that the believer has no basis for saying that God loves us.

Responses to the logical positivist challenge have revolved around the claim that religious statements are cognitive; that is, that they are statements about reality in the fullest sense. The verification principle had confined 'reality' to what can be empirically observed and tested. This, it was argued, was a masked statement of metaphysics; that is, about the ultimate nature of reality. Because this could not be verified, it ironically left the verification principle itself in no man's land, since it was neither analytical nor synthetic (neither factual nor informative).

As **James Richmond** pointed out, reality must also include other areas that are part of human life: moral conscience, aesthetic awareness, existential concern, and the well-attested historical testimony to the truth of faith. All of these carry knowledge about reality, and have therefore cognitive significance even though they resist the kind of empirical verification demanded by the logical positivists.

The aim of religious language was seen to be that of expressing a perception of reality that had God at its centre. While it was accepted that empirical evidence was insufficient absolutely to confirm this perception beyond all doubt, there was nevertheless sufficient evidence to justify it. This became the main point of a series of **parables** that were used to support the meaningfulness of religious language.

John Wisdom's parable of the gardener (Flew later used a more slanted version), attempts to show that, like a long-neglected garden containing weeds and plants, it is possible to see patterns of the world that appear to show evidence of a gardener (God), as well as other patterns that appear to show lack of such evidence. For the believer there is sufficient, if not conclusive, evidence in the world (the garden) to support faith.

Basil Mitchell's parable is of a resistance fighter, asked to place absolute trust in a stranger who is on the side of the resistance, but is also a double agent. Sometimes the stranger is seen to act one way, then another. The parable is meant to show how religious faith is constantly tested by events in the world, but it remains possible to hold on to it because in the end nothing counts *decisively* against faith. Both parables illustrate how religious faith is based on aspects of the world, seen from experience, which justify faith. Thus religion is shown not to ignore such patterns, but to be a legitimate interpretation of them.

The claim that religious faith is meaningful because it is based on trust has been made by **John Hick** in his theory of **eschatological verification**, by which it is meant that religious statements will be verified in the hereafter. The claim is illustrated by a parable, taken from John Bunyan's *Pilgrim's Progress*, about two travellers on a road, one of whom believes that it leads to the celestial city, while the other, an unbeliever, thinks that it leads nowhere. Only at the end of the journey will the truth be finally known.

In this view, the truth or otherwise of religious language will only be settled in the hereafter, but there are good grounds for trusting in its truth now. The parable's stress on the significant possibility of a positive result recalls **Pascal's Wager**. While Hick's parable, like the others, raises the question of whether such trust is justified, the answer of course is that which divides the theist from the atheist. In the end, the strength of the parable may not depend on how well it answers this question, but on how well it illustrates the everyday faith of the believer, which looks to the future and depends on trust. Like the other parables, it illustrates how religious faith is a valid interpretation of certain aspects of human experience along the road of life.

Other responses have been developed along the lines that religious statements can be reduced to moral statements to make them verifiable. **R. B. Braithwaite** suggested that the statement 'God is love' amounts to a commitment to live an agapeistic way of life. The move fails because only the sincerity, not the truth, of religious beliefs can be made dependent on ethical living. Besides, such an account of religious beliefs, which leaves out the question of their claim to truth, would not be accepted by most believers.

Ludwig Wittgenstein's approach was to examine the peculiar nature of religious language. He saw religion to be a distinct 'language game', tied up with profound feelings about the *meaning* of the world. By contrast, science was a different language game, concerned with discovering and stating *facts* about the world. The claims of religious language therefore cannot be contradicted by the unbeliever, who plays a different language game. Religious belief is about 'matters that are outside space and time', and is not belief about facts additional to 'facts about the world'. It is therefore somehow 'inexpressible,' less a matter of factual truth than of 'absolute value'.

Yet the believer, as Wittgenstein well knew, could not possibly 'see the world' through religious eyes without having an underlying conviction about the reality of God, regardless of the unique nature of such a reality. For this reason, accounts of the nature of religious language that fail to address the critical question of their objective truth are somewhat inadequate. In other words, if God does not exist outside the mind of the believer, fact-supposing religious statements cannot be what they claim to be. Thus any attempt to salvage the meaning of religious language by focusing on its psychological effects can only be incomplete.

This is the approach taken by **D. Z. Phillips**, who agrees with Wittgenstein that the peculiar nature of religious language is to express attitudes and beliefs. He agrees that it is not about 'reality' in the empirical sense, and that its 'grammar' does not fit the language that we use for speaking about everyday facts about the 'real' world. Therefore Phillips' understanding of God is called **non-realist**, because he denies God any objective reality, leaving the word 'God' to function as something that has meaning only within the mind of the believer. Like **Don Cupitt**, Phillips appears to put *belief* in God as more important than the possible *existence* of God. Clearly, this would appear to many believers as reducing faith to a mere mind-game, with no reference to reason and experience. This would make it an unfaithful representation of what religious language means. Quite simply, if God has no objective existence, it makes no sense to believe in Him or speak about Him.

The removal, therefore, of religious language from any claims to objective truth cannot be satisfactory to believers. At the very least, it would fail to do justice to the rational as well as the empirical grounding of many religious beliefs. It would dispense with the value of the traditional arguments of **St Anselm**, **St Thomas Aquinas**, **Friedrich Schleiermacher**, **Rudolf Otto** and others. While such an approach does do justice to the existential, or life-meaning, of faith, it begs the question of its ultimate foundation.

In conclusion, therefore, we have seen that the logical positivist theory of meaning amounted to a metaphysical claim of its own. It was a case of the kettle calling the pot black! This exposed its failure to pose a conclusive challenge to the meaningfulness of religious language. It ignored the illegitimacy of limiting knowledge to what can be verified by the methods of science. It failed to allow for the reality of certain aspects of life that do not easily lend themselves to empirical verification, but which raise significant questions. These include the moral, the aesthetic and the religious. While the challenge of logical positivism has called attention to the non-scientific, non-verifiable nature of religious language, it has certainly not shown that such language is meaningless.

Related questions:

1 How valid is the claim that religious language uses the insights of both faith and reason?

2 How important for religious language was Wittgenstein's theory of 'language games'?

3 Evaluate the various attempts that have been made in response to the logical positivist challenge that religious language is meaningless.

Wittgenstein and Religious Language

Ludwig Wittgenstein, whose towering intellect made him one of the most famous of modern philosophers, was an Austrian who studied in Cambridge, where he came under the influence of **Bertrand Russell** and his ideas on language. Wittgenstein went on to teach at Cambridge, after making his name in a book called *The Tractatus*, written in 1921. In effect, the book was to become the bible of **logical positivism**, a movement that was then taking shape in Wittgenstein's home town of Vienna. The book's main idea was that 'language mirrors the world', making the language of science and everyday things the only valid language. The language of religion was seen as meaningless, unable to express anything about reality. Wittgenstein's disciple, **A. J. Ayer**, publicised these ideas in England in an influential book called *Language, Truth and Logic* in 1936.

Bertrand Russell, a philosopher who influenced Wittgenstein

The trouble was that Wittgenstein later wrote another book called *Philosophical Investigations*, published in 1951, in which he introduced the idea of **language games**. This was a recognition that language could not be confined to facts about the empirical world. Instead, language was a tool for expressing meaning, and meaning was found in the way in which language was actually used. This appeared to breathe new life into religious language. But Wittgenstein did not go so far as to say that religious language was factually true, only that it had meaning for those who used it.

Wittgenstein's ideas opened up a new debate about the way in which language was used, how its meaning could be identified and how certain kinds, such as religious language, could be understood. Wittgenstein also acknowledged that there was a dimension of reality that could not be clearly spoken about, called the **mystical**. This appeared to have some affinity to the roots of religious language, and seemed to offer the possibility of justifying its use.

(a) **Explain the significance for religion of Wittgenstein's views on language.**
(b) **How far did his influence contribute to showing that religious language was meaningful?**

(a) One of the most profound philosophers of the twentieth century, **Ludwig Wittgenstein** was a leading figure in the study of language. In his earlier phase (represented by *The Tractatus*), he held the view that language mirrors the empirical world investigated by science. Truth was the correspondence between a statement and its object, and the model of truth was the descriptive language of science. The Vienna Circle, logical positivism and the verification principle were products of his influence. Against this criterion, religious statements (such as 'God made the world', 'God loves us', 'Jesus was the Son of God' and so on) were dismissed as non-cognitive, nonsensical and meaningless, because such assertions could not be verified empirically.

However, Wittgenstein underwent a change of opinion about language in a later work (*Philosophical Investigations*), published shortly after his death. His new vision was that language could not be confined to mirroring the world. Language was a tool that could be used for different purposes. To understand its meaning, one must examine the specific context or '**form of life**' to which it belongs, and within which it is intelligible. The language of the sports centre will be different to the language of the lecture room, the language of the theatre different from the language of the law court; and religious language will be different from the language of science.

Wittgenstein is said to have seen the parallel between different 'language games' and different ball and board games, each with its different rules and thought patterns. So, to understand a particular language game one must enter the 'form of life' to which it belongs. It is then as meaningless to question a form of life as to ask why people play football. This seemed to give a new lease of life to religious language, which many had dismissed as meaningless.

The insights of Wittgenstein have been taken up by modern thinkers such as **D. Z. Phillips**, who has used them to show that religious language is meaningful within the contextual vision or 'form of life' shared by religious believers. The down side of this move is to make religious language look as if it is immune to criticism from outside. But, in a true sense, this is actually the case, argues Phillips. Believers play a 'language game' that cannot be contradicted or criticised by unbelievers for reasons that are quite logical. Unbelievers cannot understand a form of belief that believers consider to be about what is ultimate, and a matter of 'absolute commitment'. God is not some 'reality' over and above, or additional to, all other realities (an insight central to the ontological argument of Anselm, and the cosmological argument of Aquinas).

God is a unique concept, and cannot be thought of as some 'real object' which might or might not exist. Such a view would not do justice to the true nature of God as a necessary being, or indeed to the true nature of religious faith. This is not to say that the 'religious language game' is some private language played by believers in some special reservation removed from the real world. As Phillips points out, believers are constantly applying their faith to the realities and circumstances of everyday life, enabling them to interpret life in the light of their faith. In fact, the function of faith is to provide a vision of life, one that is logically coherent and personally satisfying to its adherents.

To understand this is to comprehend how the 'grammar' of religious language is radically different from the grammar of ordinary language about things in the world. This leads Phillips to support a so-called **non-realist** understanding of God. This means seeing God more as a key to understanding the world than as some objective being. It means a shift from concern with the *existence* of God to the *meaning* of God to the believer. Such a view bears some similarity to the views of **Paul Tillich** and **John Macquarrie**, who distinguish God not as some particular being, but as the **Ground**, or **Being**, underlying the being of all contingent things. All of this means that God is radically different from any single being that 'exists' in the world, and cannot be spoken of in the same 'realist' terms.

The non-realist view of religious language is also held by **Don Cupitt**. Like Phillips, Cupitt sees religious assertions as statements about the way in which the believer *views* the world. If classical theism is 'theology from above', where the priority is given to what 'God is like', non-realism is ' theology from below', where the priority is to decode religious terms and translate them into a language of everyday life. So it is a 'mistake' to speak of God's 'objective existence', but not to speak about what 'God' means for the everyday life of the believer. Thus to believe in 'God' is to mean that I believe in all the ideals and values associated with that word. To say that God is Creator, for instance, is to believe in goodness and creativity, or to say that God is 'good' is to be committed to goodness, honesty, justice, love and virtuous living.

But many problems follow from this attempt to make the language of religion immune to criticism. To many people, non-realism is theologically sailing so close to the wind that it effectively empties the traditional understanding of God of all its content. For all its efforts to reinstate God as a meaningful idea in today's atheistic culture, it seems very vulnerable to **Ludwig Feuerbach's** atheistic theory that God is a psychological **projection** upwards of a human reality on to an imaginary 'divine' reality. If non-realism were taken as the norm, there would seem to be no way to criticise faith or question its truth, since faith has become simply what the believer says it is.

This runs counter to all traditional theological language which, despite the questions it may raise, has favoured the biblical view that faith means the acceptance of God as real, and unfaith the refusal to accept Him as real. Therefore, this attempt to rescue religious faith, and the language used to express it, is likely to appear as a slippery evasion to those who challenge the traditional claims inherent in religious language. The challenge is not that such language lacks any meaning for those with faith, but quite simply that its claims are false.

The non-realist understanding of the language of faith seems therefore in danger of missing the point. The big question for most people is whether its claims to truth about ultimate reality, God, have any credibility. Ironically, it was Wittgenstein himself who recognised that there were things that were transcendent over everyday facts about the world of which we are sometimes aware, and which, significantly, are difficult to express in everyday language. If this is true, then religion might claim to have a legitimate authority to speak of such things.

Wittgenstein called this area of experience the **mystical**. The mystical is a dimension of experience which, he said, cannot be 'expressed', but can be 'contained' in the empirical. The mystical is that which is gained from a profound sense of the significance of things, but which can never be clearly put into words. The mystical 'shows itself' when we kiss a photograph, kneel at a grave or take part in worship (which, he believed, was 'a great gesture').

When people ask 'Why am I here?' or 'How did the world come about?', or when they 'lift their eyes to heaven', they are asking mystical questions, not questions that have causal answers. Such questions suggest the irrelevance of the causal explanations of science, and point to something more profound, something that gives rise to the kind of feelings that are commonly evoked by art, music, nostalgia or religion.

The mystical may also be perceived in the sheer fact of the world's existence. As Wittgenstein famously put it: 'It is not *how* the world is that is mystical, but *that* it is'. The mystical may also be perceived in the limitations of scientific knowledge. As he put it, 'we feel that when all possible scientific questions have been answered, the problems of life remain completely untouched'.

Wittgenstein was strongly impressed by the difference in outlook between someone only concerned with scientific 'facts' or 'reasons' and someone with a deeper awareness of things, such as their significance, or their ultimate origin. It was this insight that led to some of his more enigmatic statements, such as 'the solution of the riddle of space and time is outside space and time'. This was the mystical, which could be felt and perceived, but never properly expressed. Yet it is always 'contained in the empirical' in the sense that it manifests itself, or arises as a more profound aspect of it. Wittgenstein's views of language, therefore, began by allowing that religious language was meaningful within the circle of believers. But he also recognised the possibility that language can point beyond the empirical, to reach a deeper level of awareness about the world. If this is what religious language claims to do, then it cannot be dismissed as meaningless.

(b) The validity of the mystical as a true aspect of experience suggests the validity of language that attempts to reach beyond the purely empirical. This would appear to justify religious language. A problem remains, however, in justifying talk about the mystical; namely, the problem of showing that something real is being talked about. For Wittgenstein, the mystical is not just the product of the subjective imagination: it is something 'nonsensical' (that is, non-empirical), yes, but it is nevertheless real and meaningful. Wittgenstein himself recognised this and, unlike many of his followers, had great respect for people's personal religious beliefs, something that **Fergus Kerr** said reflected his life-long interest in religion.

By calling attention to the human capacity for deep levels of awareness of life which lie beyond the empirical (and the legitimacy of speaking about them), Wittgenstein made a place for speaking about what he called 'what is higher' and 'uttering the unutterable'. In this way, he made a place for language about things that reach beyond the realm of science, and why the language of religious faith might have a legitimate place in human discourse, just as legitimate as other 'mystical' forms of life, such as aesthetics, ethics, music and perhaps even philosophy.

It is therefore surprising that writers on Wittgenstein, such as **Brian Clack**, have concluded that his views on religion tend more towards atheism than theism. The reason he gives is that Wittgenstein saw religion as alien to an atheistic culture, which of course it is. But Wittgenstein made it clear that he was no defender of the scientific world-view, which he saw as having led to 'the darkness of our time' and having 'sent our wondering spirit to sleep'. The extent to which, through his insights into the mystical, he opened the door to giving credibility to the meaning of religious language remains an intriguing question.

Related questions:

1 How far does Wittgenstein provide a basis for justifying religious language?

2 Evaluate the strengths and weaknesses of the view that religious language merely expresses the convictions of its users.

3 Assess the view that religious language is an expression of a non-realist understanding of God.

Forms of Religious Language

The problem of religious language is the problem of speaking of *transcendent* realities – such as God, creation, redemption, forgiveness and so on – in language that we use in speaking of *everyday* realities. In the latter case the truth of what we say is open to verification or falsification, while in the former it is not. Another way of stating the problem is to say that the language of religion is *grammatically* similar to ordinary language, but *logically* different. The similarity and difference is easily seen in the two statements 'the books are in the library' and 'God is in heaven'. One is verifiable, while the other is not.

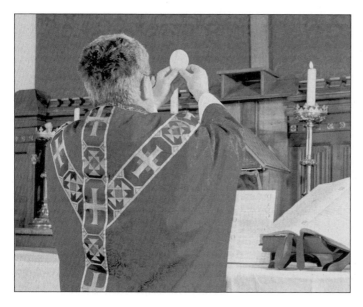

Christian symbolism is supremely represented by the communion host/cup, where the visual (bread and wine) is held to have a metaphysical and cosmic significance

The claim, therefore, that religious language employs grammatical devices such as analogy and metaphor begs the question as to whether such devices refer to anything at all. When the comparison is to something within the observable world, there is no question that analogy and simile work. But the situation is somewhat different when the comparison is to something outside the observable world.

Putting these difficulties aside, we shall be looking in this section at the way in which religious faith has been expressed in language, and how various linguistic devices such as symbols, simile, metaphor, myth and analogy have functioned to express transcendent truths.

Assess the use of analogy, metaphor, symbols and myth in religious language.

When we examine religious language we can see that it employs various figures of speech for describing its subject matter. These include techniques and literary devices such as **analogy**, **metaphor**, **symbols**, **models** and **myth**. Theologians have always recognised that language about religion is not used literally, but analogically. Analogy means comparison. **St Thomas Aquinas** said that language about God presupposes some point of similarity with human language since, theologically, we are made in God's image and likeness. Hence the Bible refers to God as a person – often portraying Him like a human person, with feelings and emotions – but this is not literally, but analogically, true. Aquinas saw analogy falling halfway between the univocal and the equivocal. 'Univocal' means using language about God in the same sense as we use it about ourselves, while 'equivocal' means using such language in a completely different sense.

Analogy allows for some similarity and some difference between ourselves and God. This is generally to recognise that all positive things that we say about God need to be qualified. So, when we speak of God as good, wise, loving, powerful, forgiving, merciful and so on, we apply these terms to God with qualification. This is the purpose of the *corrective* device known as the *via negativa*, or the **apophatic way**, a principle of speaking about God recognised by mystical writers such as **St Augustine**, **Dionysius** or **Meister Eckhart**. Every positive quality attributed to God (the *via positiva*, or *via affirmitiva*) – for example, God is loving, wise, just and so on – must always be balanced by the recognition that God is also not these things in the same sense as we might apply these qualities to ourselves. In the words of **Karl Barth**, this is to recognise that God's nature is 'wholly other' than ours.

Ian Ramsey has developed the use of analogy by identifying how **models** and **qualifiers** have been used to speak of God. For instance, to speak of God's omnipotence is to use the model of power. The important qualifier 'omnipotence' (*all* powerful) singles God out as unique. Likewise, in using the models of wisdom or mercy, we add the qualifier 'infinitely'. Ramsey proposes the need for a range of models to be used together, to provide a fuller and more adequate description of the reality of God.

For Ramsey, however, the main function of religious language is not so much to describe religious 'facts' but to express the existential significance of God for mankind. Thus the important thing is to create an understanding of God that brings about a moment of religious enlightenment. Learning that God is almighty father, heavenly king, everlasting love and so on, evokes a 'disclosure' that leads to a faith 'commitment'. Ramsey's main aim is to show that the language used in religion is less descriptive than dynamic, and that its main purpose is not so much to achieve accuracy of description as to arouse religious and moral awareness. How far his models are meant to express the underlying objective truth of religion appears to be of secondary importance.

Metaphors and symbols are other ways in which language can be used to speak of God. **Metaphors** are figures of speech by which one thing is explained in terms of another; for example, 'a camel is the ship of the desert'. The traditional metaphors used to describe God are taken from the scriptures, where God is variously spoken of as *father*, *king*, *fortress*, *rock*, *shield*, *shepherd* and so on. Each metaphor highlights some aspect of God's character, such as His loving care, His authority, His power to protect, His constancy, His eternity and so on.

The need for metaphor, as **J. M. Soskice** has pointed out, is also found in science, with its descriptions of black *holes*, magnetic *fields*, light *beams* (or *particles*), sound *pulses*, radio *waves* and so forth. Metaphors in science may also take the form of models to illustrate the unobservable. The activity of gas atoms may be described as 'colliding billiard balls' or elastic spheres. In quantum physics, **Neils Bohr** suggested the need for a 'complementarity' of metaphors to describe certain realities. Confusingly, light can sometimes be a *wave* and sometimes a *particle*. In the same way that science reaches out to metaphors to express itself, religion uses a complementarity of metaphors to speak of God.

However, as we saw above, the legitimacy of scientific metaphors is less open to question than that of religious ones, since the scientific ones are subject to verification. The believer insists nevertheless that this does not render them meaningless, because they are an attempt to express insights that **Ludwig Wittgenstein** might have called 'mystical', 'of absolute value' and 'beyond space and time'. Such insights, it is claimed, have a proper validity, but they can only be expressed in empirical language with the help of metaphors. In the end, the legitimacy of this reasoning is logically dependent on the existence of God. If, and only if, God exists, language about Him is valid.

Symbols also play an important role as sources of meaning within believing communities. Examples are the cross, the sacred book (the Bible, Qur'an and so on), the sacred cup, and icons of Christ or the saints, as well as the great life symbols of earth, fire, light, water and bread. Religious writings abound with such symbols, which are meant to convey images and ideas that bring about insights into transcendent realities.

Paul Tillich stressed the importance of recognising that human comparisons with God are always symbolic, because they are always drawn from everyday life. This is to alert the believer to the fact that God is transcendent, and that His reality cannot be captured in simple images. Thus God may be spoken of as a 'person', but not at the expense of forgetting that God is not an individual 'being' but 'Being Itself'.

While Tillich's point is valid, there can be no doubt about the power of symbols in everyday life. Sometimes symbols are drawn from one area and applied in another to powerful effect. For example, the Nazis made astute use of Christian symbols – such as the Cross (swastika), the messiah figure (Hitler) and the Ayran blood myth (the grail) – to justify their own perverted ideals.

The psychological power of symbols was an important theme in the works of **Carl Gustav Jung**. He believed that symbols exercise great power over the mind because they enable us to get in touch with the archetypes of the **collective unconscious**. Since one of these archetypes is the '**God image**' imprinted on the soul, religious symbols have a special importance. Symbols such as the cross, the virgin birth, bread, wine, water or the images from the parables are more effective in communicating truth and meaning than descriptive language. However, the question as to whether religious symbols have an objective signif-icance over and above being meaningful to the believer is typically not dealt with by Jung, who is only concerned with their psychological power. This gives them the value of being 'psychologically true' for the believer.

For Jung, this was enough to justify their importance. He saw any concern with their 'objective truth' as a legacy of scientific thinking. Certain symbols, partic-ularly religious ones, had the spiritual power to penetrate the soul and transform the psyche. This was enough to qualify them as objectively real forces that worked for the individual. For Jung, recognising the power of symbols was part of that deeper human 'wisdom' that lay beyond the reach of science.

Myth, the last of our categories, takes the form of *stories*, which may at the same time contain symbols or metaphors. In myth, God is given a human-like role and made to appear as an actor on the stage of history in the company of humans. The creation story of Genesis is generally regarded as a classic example of myth. The problem with myth is the way in which God is portrayed with human-like qualities, and the way events in which He takes part are portrayed as human events under His guidance or control.

This *pictorial* way of expressing God's action, typical of myth, is open to challenge on the grounds of distortion. Although myth can be said to describe events that 'didn't happen', for the believer they still convey truthful and valid insights. Concern with factuality (as in the creation myth) is said to lead to a loss of vision of what the myth is trying to convey. Within religious traditions, myths are seen as vehicles of spiritual truth, regardless of their factual credibility. The creation and redemption myths, for instance, are seen as expressing the truth of God's creative and personal involvement in our origins, salvation and ultimate destiny.

This was the view of **Rudolf Bultmann**, who stressed the **existential** meaning (the meaning for human life) of religious myths. But many feel that he did this at the expense of overlooking their claims to factual truth. Bultmann held that myths were important for the *meaning* that they contain, but that their actual form can be dispensed with. God acting as a human in the space of six days, Christ descending to earth, or rising to the heavens, wonders happening by divine intervention, time coming to an end – all of these he saw as pictorial ways of expressing the ultimate significance of God for mankind, and the urgency of deciding to live an 'authentic' life of moral integrity before God.

The ordinary believer, however, may feel short-changed if only the significance of a myth is held to be valid. Many of the great myths are believed to contain a hard core of truth about things that have happened and are true, and their meaning is usually taken to depend on their 'factual' side. They feel that faith means making a decisive choice – not just about the way we in which live, but about the truths of life.

Either God did create the world, or He didn't. Either Christ was the redeemer of the world, or he wasn't. Either time will end with God's judgement, or it won't. To the ordinary person, therefore, myths have at least a core of significant fact that cannot be ignored. But just as a strip cartoon is full of distortions justified by artistic licence, so perhaps can myths continue to carry the story of salvation in a way that combines truths of religious and moral significance with basic truths about reality told in story form.

However, it is the claims of myth to express truths about reality that attract the most criticism from non-believers. For this reason, the problems of myth typify the problems of religious language in general. Some have argued that it is itself a myth that we ever 'apportion belief according to the evidence available', as **David Hume** said we should. Many disagreements in science and in human affairs are about beliefs and opinions that are not supported by the kind of evidence, say, demanded in a law court. Why, then, single out religious beliefs, asks **Peter van Inwagen**? He claims that a double standard exists when it comes to criticisms that religious language lacks a foundation of evidence and proof. He says that 'this double standard consists in setting religious belief a test that it could not possibly pass, and in studiously ignoring the fact that almost none of our beliefs on any subject could possibly pass this test'.

In conclusion, we have seen that different figures of speech are employed in religious language, and that believers find them useful as expressions of the truths of their faith. But religious language will always be open to challenge as long as its claims to truth lack empirical verification. Believers may reply that religious language does have a cumulative empirical grounding – in historical events, in the coherence of its perspective on life and in the experience of believers over centuries, and that it expresses what **St Augustine** called 'the truth that matters'. But whether this reply will satisfy those who insist that religious claims are only based on faith, or who insist, like **A. J. Ayer**, that such claims are meaningless because there is no method for their verification, will remain open to question.

Related questions:

1 Explain the meaning of the '*via positiva*' and the '*via negativa*' in speaking about God.

2 Explain what is meant by saying that religious language is 'grammatically similar' to ordinary language but 'logically different'.

3 Evaluate the claim that religious metaphors, and other statements of religious language, are meaningless because they cannot be verified.

Religion and Ethics

Like *meta*physics, **metaethics** refers to areas not directly related to but somehow beyond (meta)the main subject-matter. It is therefore not concerned with *right* and *wrong*, but with questions that in some way arise from them. This means that metaethics has little to do with the real business of ethics, which is concerned with the ancient question 'What is the good life?', or 'What is the good?' or, in more modern terms, 'How should I live my life?' or 'How should I solve this moral dilemma?' Metaethics gives no answers to any of those questions.

In metaethics, a different set of questions are asked: questions about the *nature* of ethical thinking and ethical language; about what is meant by such things as free will, and whether we can be said to possess it; about what is meant by terms such as 'relative' and 'absolute'; and so on. Metaethics questions whether we can legitimately speak of objective ethical truth, or whether ethical convictions are merely the expressions of the individual's inner feelings. The latter is called **emotivism**, which is the view that ethical convictions can only be expressed in terms of one's feelings or attitudes, but cannot possibly be explained or justified. The former is called **intuitionism**, because it holds that ethical convictions can be directly intuited, sensed or grasped, but again not explained. However, unlike emotivism, intuitionism at least opens the debate about what in the objective world makes us intuit goodness and evil, right and wrong.

Questions about whether we are *free*, or whether our actions are already *determined*, have an important bearing on ethical behaviour. If we are free we can be held fully responsible for our actions, and are deserving of praise or blame as the case may be. If we are not free, we are in danger of being reduced to robots, driven by pre-existing forces that are assumed to determine and explain how we behave. On the other hand, there is a universal recognition that we are often caught between temptation and rational choice. This is indeed a sense of being free, but not from the constraints of what we call conscience. To what extent this is a purely **rational** faculty, unhampered by upbringing, religious beliefs or other influences, and to what extent we are bound by its dictates, remain key questions.

6 Metaethics: Ethical Language, Concepts and Ideas

Emotivism

 How satisfactory is emotivism as an account of ethical claims?

Emotivism is an offshoot, or by-product, of the logical positivist restriction of meaning to what is either tautological, or empirically verifiable. Either a statement is true by definition, or true or false if verifiable. The claims of religion and metaphysics were said to be unverifiable (impossible to tell whether they were true or false), and so were classed as meaningless. Into this category came statements or ethics such as 'stealing is wrong', 'honesty is good' and so on.

For this reason, ethical language is said to be non-cognitive; that is, it gives us no information about the real world. But in an attempt to rescue some meaning for ethical claims, defenders of logical positivism and its empiricist theory of meaning came up with the so-called **emotivist** theory of meaning, originally attributed to **A. J. Ayer**. According to this theory statements, or claims, of ethics about what is right or wrong are merely expressions of one's feeling about them. So the claim that stealing is wrong is an expression of disapproval about stealing. Equally, the claim that honesty is right is merely an expression of approval about honesty (the so-called 'hurrah–boo' theory).

This rather shallow account of ethical statements is the result of the logical positivist restriction of meaning to what lies within the range of empirical verification. It is as if someone was prepared to admit the existence of the tip of the iceberg, but not what lies below the water. In this 'iceberg syndrome' analogy, ethical statements are the tip of the iceberg; that is, they the outer expression of inner emotion or feeling. Going below the surface of ethical feelings is ruled out because it is seen to go beyond the range of what is verifiable, and hence meaningful. As a result, emotivism is seen as a superficial, if not impoverished, account of ethical claims. The question 'What could account for ethical beliefs or feelings in the first place?' is simply outside the range of what is 'meaningful'. But to the ordinary person, ethical convictions are more than one's approval or disapproval of something.

An exception to this, of course, is where 'right' and 'wrong' are empirically testable. Here the emotivist is allowed to recognise, at a descriptive level, the empirical base that underlies a moral claim. So when a statement such as 'stealing is wrong' is made, the emotivist will accept that if 'wrong' stands for something that is verifiable in terms of, say, being convicted and sent to prison, then it is meaningful.

Defenders of religious ethics, natural law theory and **Kantian ethics**, as well as those who claim that the ethical sense of right and wrong is a matter of intuition, see emotivism as both inadequate and reductionist. No common-sense view of ethical claims can allow them to be reduced to the expression of subjective feelings. There is an agreed sense that ethical statements about right and wrong arise from a level of awareness that goes deeper than the merely emotional, and is properly called moral awareness, or moral conviction. Because emotivism ignores this reality, it is unable to distinguish moral feelings from any other kinds of feelings. Thus, disapproving of television is on the same level as disapproving of murder.

Emotivism, therefore, is unable to recognise the peculiar nature of ethical convictions. Such convictions are reduced to 'expressions of feeling' regardless of their foundations. As a consequence, it is blind to the differences between the standard ethical theories. In religious ethics there is the belief that right and wrong are matters of objective moral truth, and behaving morally is considered decisive for our ultimate destiny. In Kantian ethics there is the belief in an unqualified rational sense of duty, the categorical imperative. In a similar vein, writers such as **Bernard Williams** speak of an inner sense of right and wrong that is decisive for everyone's personal integrity, and one's sense of self-worth, which people reveal when they speak of 'having to live with their conscience'. The agreement across societies and cultures that some things are 'right' and some 'wrong' raises important questions for a theory that reduces morality to personal subjective attitudes or feelings.

Another inadequacy of the emotivist theory was later exposed by **R. M. Hare**, who nevertheless defended the non-cognitive character of ethical claims. Hare agreed with **C. L. Stevenson** that ethical statements were more than just expressions of feeling: in particular, they were also meant to *persuade* the hearer. Hare believed that they were best described as expressions of an intention to lay down, or prescribe (literally 'write down beforehand'), behaviour for others. Thus when I say that 'stealing is wrong' I am not just expressing my feelings, but also wanting to lay down for others the rule that stealing is wrong. This is known as **prescriptivism.**

However, like emotivism, prescriptivism overlooks two important questions. First, 'Does anything at all underlie the feeling I express that makes me want to influence the behaviour of others?' It is only human to expect that one's own feelings, or the feelings of others, have some rational or cognitive basis. Secondly, 'Why should an obligation be applied to others on the basis of my personal feeling?' This would clearly be an instance of the '**naturalistic fallacy**' highlighted by **G. E. Moore** (see under intuitionism below). Why should a fact (my feeling) be converted into an obligation for others to do or not do something? Why should this 'is' logically imply an 'ought'? For this reason so-called prescriptivism is only a trivial addition to emotivism, and fatally rests on the same moral void, refusing to offer any reasons for prescribing behaviour to others. But at least it goes beyond emotivism by recognising that moral feelings are quite unlike other kinds of feelings. To say that beating women is wrong is not quite like saying that the team's attacking policy is wrong. The former can be a subject for moral prescription, while the latter cannot. For this reason, Hare called moral prescriptions those that can be **universalised**; that is, applied to everyone in all circumstances.

In conclusion, we have seen that emotivism is a restricted account of ethical claims, and because it is reductionist, is unacceptable to those who hold that such claims arise from a sense that right and wrong are more than a matter of someone's personal feeling. The addition made by Hare merely emphasises the view that ethics touches on a significant aspect of reality that emotivism on its own cannot account for.

In either case the question remains, 'What underlies the need to express ethical feelings and prescriptions, and the claim that they are universally binding?' Since emotivism is not prepared to delve so deep as to inquire into these questions, it remains – like prescriptivism – bound by the empiricist limitations of its starting point, and thus offers an account that only touches the surface of ethical claims.

Related questions:

1 How satisfactory is the emotivist view that ethical judgements are merely expressions of opinion?

2 Evaluate the view that 'good' and 'bad', 'right' and 'wrong' are expressions of feeling.

3 How fair is the criticism that prescriptivism is only a trivial addition to emotivism?

Intuitionism

How far is intuitionism an adequate account of ethical claims?

Intuitionism is said to be the oldest ethical tradition, going back to **Aristotle**, who taught that human beings had an intuitive notion (inner sense) of the 'Good'. The modern theory of intuitionism was put forward by **G. E. Moore**, who argued that our sense of right and wrong, good and evil, derives from a non-natural quality that something possesses, which can only be directly intuited, but not explained in terms of something else. Therefore, to say that murder is wrong cannot be explained either by reference to the *social* effects that might follow if it was permitted, or by the *religious* claim that it is against the 'will of God'. Moore accepted that certain things were good, such as love and friendship, but nothing outside such things can explain why they are good. To do so is to commit the **naturalistic fallacy**; that is, to look for an **extrinsic** reason to explain what is a self-evident, or intuited, reality. What is good is good, and no reason can underpin why it is good, said Moore. Friendship may be good, but good is not friendship.

To explain his theory, Moore takes the example of the colour yellow. We can recognise or intuit yellow when we see it, as in a lemon, but yellow cannot be explained in terms other than itself. An attempt to do this would involve a scientific examination of light rays and wavelengths, but would not necessarily lead back to the colour yellow. For Moore, it is an *open question* whether good can ever be identified with something else.

Likewise, good can be recognised in things such as art, nature, friendship and so on, but none of these things can be identified with good. Yet the important thing is the ability to intuit goodness in such things, and to be able to create goodness in the world.

We have an obligation or duty to 'maximise' the good wherever we can. **H. A. Pritchard** and **W. D. Ross** held that **duty** was as much a matter of intuition as good, as Kant had claimed, especially '***prima facie* duties**' to such things as justice and truth, duties that most people would agree with. Kant, however, subjected his theory of moral intuition to the test of reason, both in relation to the individual and society. So he cannot strictly be called an intuitionist. It is difficult, however, to see any real difference between duty and goodness, since one implies the other.

There is a certain strength to Moore's claim about the objective quality of goodness, but many have found the idea of self-evident moral truths somehow unsatisfactory. While goodness is not difficult to recognise, does his theory not open the door to spurious intuitions? What if someone claimed an intuition that to kill, say, prostitutes was the right thing to do? Moore accepted that people could be mistaken in this way, but used this to argue, rather lamely, for better judgement. In the end, it appears that some objective point of reference is needed for understanding good and evil, right and wrong.

In other words, we need to submit in some way to the court of reason in assessing moral values. But provided that such reasons are not based on empirical evidence, it seems that the naturalistic fallacy can be avoided. Moore himself avoided it when he went from a metaphysical, or non-empirical, fact (good) to an 'ought' (maximise the good). It should also be possible therefore to go from the 'fact' of what reason declares good to the obligation of universalising it (**Kant**), and from the sense of what God declares right or wrong to a similar obligation, as in religious ethics, without committing the naturalistic fallacy.

The fallacy of naturalism goes back to **David Hume**, who argued that our sense of right and wrong derives from our natural feelings of sympathy with others. As an empiricist, Hume refused to recognise any non-empirical basis for ethical judgements. He said, rightly, that we cannot perceive the 'wrongness' of murder or theft. So ethics becomes a matter of shared feelings about things, and can have no deeper basis. This, he held, rules out any form of reasoning from empirical facts to moral oughts. Ethics is simply about facts.

Yet Hume admitted that ethics was not just about feelings, but that it revealed some 'universal principle': it could 'touch a string to which all mankind have an accord and sympathy'. In these words, Hume appears to be committing the naturalistic fallacy himself, of deriving an 'ought' (*value*) from an 'is' (*fact*), the very thing that he condemned! Here, a universal principle recognised by all people (fact) leads to the moral awareness of what is right or wrong (ought).

Naturalism, then, is basing an 'ought' on an empirical fact. All ethical theories go from a statement of fact to a statement of obligation, but not all go from an **empirical** fact to a moral ought. So, if the moral law exists we ought to keep it (Kant); if happiness is what we all desire, we ought to aim for it (**John Stuart Mill**); if God exists, we ought to obey His law; if all mankind sees this as harmful, we ought not to do it (Hume); if what we see is good, we ought to maximise it (Moore). We can see from this that only the empiricists Mill and Hume appeal to empirical facts, and so commit the naturalistic fallacy.

This shows that there are grounds for making a distinction between natural, or empirical, reasons for making ethical judgements, and non-natural or metaphysical reasons for doing so. **Christian ethics** claims that morality has a metaphysical basis in the will of God. The **natural law ethics** that underlies much of Christian morality claims that human nature is itself an indication of a metaphysical reality, which conveys a sense of obligation. This is very close to Kantian ethics, which is based on the claim that ethical obligations arise from the metaphysical reality of the moral law, leading to the categorical imperative. Utilitarianism, although empirical, at least raises (but doesn't answer) the metaphysical question of why, if we all value happiness, we ought to value it.

With this distinction, it becomes possible to see that linking morality to empirical facts is indeed a fallacy, but not linking morality to metaphysical facts. If morality is seen as essentially a *metaphysical* enterprise, then it becomes possible to see that metaphysical claims lie at the heart of ethical discussion. Even the appeal to reason, let alone any appeal to religious belief, is itself an appeal to a metaphysical reality.

Critics of intuitionism claim that pushed too far, it leaves the question of ethical judgements within the minds or feelings of the individual. To do so is to make ethics irrational, and makes it impossible to find any basis in reason for arriving at ethical values. Under intuitionism, the rationale behind all the traditional ethical theories would collapse, because it refuses to allow any ethical *reason* to support an ethical *judgement*.

103

All ethical systems, on the other hand, have appealed to some form of reasoning. Natural law ethics is based on the theory that nature, especially human nature, provides the clues to how we should act. Utilitarianism is based on the theory that happiness is what we all value, and so our actions should aim to create this value. Kantian ethics is based on the notion that reason can perceive what is in accordance with the moral law, not intuitively, but by submitting it to the test of how morality works in the affairs of mankind. Religious ethics is based on the belief that ethical values reflect the will of God, a cosmic claim but one consistent with reason and confirmed by religious revelation. All these theories are operating on the assumption that an 'ought' does indeed follow from an 'is'. Put another way, they are attempting to ground their **ethical principles** on a basis of reason. Intuitionism fails to do this beyond saying that we ought to maximise the good.

For these reasons, intuitionism is not considered to be an adequate account of ethical claims. It fails to account for why ethical perceptions of right and wrong, good and evil, arise in the first place, and is therefore unable to contribute to any rationalising of ethical judgements. But, unlike emotivism, it has the strength of grounding ethical awareness in something more than subjective feelings. It does this by putting the focus on a more profound level of moral awareness in which some objectivity is recognised. Intuitionism is therefore more likely than not to lead to ethical judgements that coincide with what most people would recognise as ethically right or wrong, but as an account of ethical awareness it is noticeably question-begging and incomplete.

Related questions:

1 Discuss the view that intuitionism makes ethical debate impossible.

2 Assess the strengths and weakness of intuitionism as a theory of ethical knowledge.

3 Evaluate the claim that intuitionism produces more satisfactory ethical judgements than emotivism.

Free Will and Determinism

The dispute about whether we are truly free or are subject to forces outside our control that interfere with our *freedom* is part of the standard diet of ethical discussion. There is no doubt that some circumstances do interfere with human freedom, such as the influence of force or the threat of force. Besides, there is religious and philosophical backing for the claim that our nature is sufficiently morally flawed to make us less free on occasions than we might suppose.

The claim that we have no freedom and are driven to act as we do is called **determinism**. If this view is correct, we can never be held accountable for our actions. In this case, no legal system could operate. For this reason out and out determinism has serious weaknesses, and has little support from common sense. At the same time, the idea that circumstances can alter one's freedom of behaviour is unquestioned.

Assess the claim that human beings are not really free to make moral choices.

It is a common-sense assumption that when we act in the moral sphere without any obvious external coercion we are considered free. The question 'Could I have acted other than I did had I chosen to do so?' is taken as the litmus test of moral freedom. Those who believe that we are always absolutely free are sometimes called **voluntarists**, or **libertarians**.

In Christian ethics there are two problems that are seen to impinge on the question of human freedom. One has to do with the nature of God, and the other with the nature of human beings. If God is omniscient, and has full knowledge of how we are going to act, then it becomes questionable whether our freedom is real or illusory. If we take **St Thomas Aquinas'** claim that God's foreknowledge only sees how we *freely* act, or that of **Richard Swinburne** that God shuts off His foreknowledge in order to leave us free, or **Maurice Wiles**, who believes that our freedom is beyond God's foreknowledge, then according to all these views our freedom is not affected by God's omniscience. Aquinas' claim that God only foresees what human beings freely choose to do renders invalid the excuse that 'I was not free because God knew anyway how I was going to act'.

With regard to human nature, there is widespread recognition that a number of factors do influence the level of our actual freedom in the world. These factors are more interlocking than separate, and fall under the headings of temptation and upbringing. Under the effects of temptation, the human will is said to be weakened sufficiently to leave people less than fully responsible for their actions. **David Hume** said that when reason and the passions are in conflict, the passions always win. This has been recognised in religious terms by the doctrine of **original sin**, and philosophically by **Martin Heidegger**, who has argued that humans are naturally 'fallen'. This results in a fundamental state of human weakness that works against our freedom to act rationally.

A second factor that may limit freedom is that of upbringing. This can include the influence of parental values and control, peer-group pressure, and the effects of the social and moral environment in which one grows up. Living in an area in which **crime** may be common, drug addiction rife and so on will have a predictable effect in terms of moral attitudes, especially among the young and vulnerable. In these situations, it is difficult to argue the case for moral freedom.

Immanuel Kant, showing little awareness of these factors, made freedom a fundamental assumption of the moral life. Having outlined the categorical imperative as an absolute sense of duty, he said 'ought' implies 'can'. Thus we are not mere products of the evolutionary process like the lower animals. Not driven by instinct, and not a prisoners of our environment, we are able to transcend it by the freedom of our will. We are able to detect the moral law of reason, and we are free to act on it, or not. Whether Kant made enough allowance for the depravity of reason, as stressed by **Martin Luther**, or the weakness of the will, as recognised both by religion and by philosophy, is not so clear – in which case his claim for the absolute freedom of the individual in facing moral choices is open to serious question.

Opposite to the Kantian view that we are free in our moral choices, there is the view that of all our actions are determined in advance. In this view, all our choices are already decided by a series of causes and effects that make us what we are and determine how we behave. Determinism is of course easy to apply in the physical realm, where events in nature follow physical laws. The process of evolution is one example, but we can see determinism in everyday events where effects are known to follow from prior causes. But in the *moral* realm a theory of determinism seems difficult to justify.

Determinists are divided into two camps: so-called 'hard' determinists and 'soft' determinists. The former deny free will altogether, and argue that our notions of responsibility, blame, praise, credit and so on are invalid because we are not masters of our will. This means that we can never be held responsible for what we do. This group is also called *incompatibilists*, because they hold that human freedom is incompatible with the determining factors that make us act as we do.

One challenge to the determinist view is that it runs counter to our common-sense awareness that we feel ourselves responsible for our actions, and feel entitled to praise or blame for how we decide to act. To deny human freedom would pose a serious threat to human dignity. Personal autonomy (the capacity for personal decision-making) presupposes free will and is an essential aspect of being fully human.

Soft determinists, sometimes called *compatibilists*, take a more common-sense view recognising that our freedom is somewhat hampered by the way we are made and by the circumstances in which we act. This view makes allowance for such factors as genetic make-up, human weakness, the influence of upbringing and so on. It also recognises that there are extreme circumstances that can determine how we behave. Examples of these would include being 'forced' to behave in a certain way under threat of injury, loss or death. However, even voluntarists would accept that there is a serious loss of freedom in these cases.

Serious doubts about the extent of human freedom arose from the findings of Freudian psychology. By uncovering the role of the unconscious in human motivation, Freud also uncovered the complexity of knowing why we act at the conscious level, thereby casting doubt on our actual freedom. When we do something we are only as free as we consciously think we are. Freud's contribution here has been informative, but hardly significant. To most people, unless we are externally constrained, or suffering from a psychotic illness, we consider ourselves to be free whatever unconscious motives lie behind our actions.

Another supposed limitation to human freedom has been raised in connection with religious ethics. The idea of being obedient to an external power such as God, it is argued, is inconsistent with true inner freedom, because the individual is not acting with autonomy (self-directed) but through heteronomy (other-directed). This objection is based on the idea that such obedience is imposed from outside the individual, resulting in behaviour that cannot be truly free. On closer inspection, however, this can be questioned.

While allowance can be made for some forms of faith where 'fear of hell' may have an exaggerated influence over behaviour, obedience to God, many believers would insist – and as **Søren Kierkegaard** made clear – is in principle a free religious and moral choice made from the *heart*. This follows from the belief that God exists, and is the supreme reality over everything. It is therefore a rational decision, an act of maturity and a true exercise of autonomy freely to choose to obey the will of God. Many believers would consider the idea that they are forced or coerced by God into making a religious or moral response to Him as patronising and undignified. It would also be to overlook **John Hick's** claim that we are at an 'epistemic' distance from God, which ensures that we are not coerced by an overbearing deity.

Neither does this criticism of religious ethics allow for the perceived rationality of divine law, or allow for the moral nature of faith. As **Aquinas** has pointed out, if God's nature is identical with Goodness, then it is right to trust that the divine will and the values it directs are also good. But it is a responsible exercise of free will to adhere to such values not only because they come from God, but because they can also be defended on rational grounds as well.

While religion is claimed to hamper freedom, the reality of human free will has been a clear assumption of existentialist writers such as **Friedrich Nietzsche** and **Jean-Paul Sartre**. Both have seen moral behaviour as essentially free and autonomous. Nietzsche's 'overman' (superman) is one who freely challenges inherited beliefs, and freely creates his own values as he goes along. Why new values should inevitably overthrow old ones is not made clear by Nietzsche, who refuses to grant any autonomy to religious faith. Sartre sees moral values as being too closely tied to belief in God, and calls for a new morality in which 'everything is permitted' if God does not exist. Again, why it is necessary to prove one's freedom by overthrowing established values is difficult to see, especially if such values have a rational foundation?

In conclusion, we have seen that there are different views of human freedom. One is that we are free for all practical purposes, but that circumstances can sometimes diminish our freedom. The other view is that freedom and free will are only illusions, because we are in fact determined in how we act by factors outside our control.

The weakness of the latter view is that it accords badly with our common-sense understanding that we possess free will. It also entails an undignified view of human nature, because it disallows any entitlement to blame or satisfaction from how we act. This in turn would mean having to renounce any claim of autonomy over our lives. Full-blown determinism would therefore undercut a basic premise of both the Christian faith and our common understanding as human beings, that we possess enough freedom to be held responsible for what we do.

Related questions:

1 'Our freedom to make ethical choices is only an apparent freedom.' Discuss.

2 Evaluate the view that acting out of obedience to God makes ethical freedom an illusion.

3 Assess the view that determinism makes ethical behaviour an impossibility.

Absolutism and Relativism

While the terms **absolutism** and **relativism** are central concepts in ethics, it would be safe to say that they interrelate rather than exist independently of each other. Whereas, for instance, the sanctity of human life is seen as an 'absolute' value, in practice its application becomes quite relative to particular circumstances, such as war and self-defence. From this, it can be seen that the relative becomes a factor in the application of the absolute. In the realm of ethical theory, relativism is often linked to consequentialism, and absolutism to deontology.

Consequentialism is the view that actions should be judged on their effects or consequences. So utilitarianism and **situation ethics** are typical examples of consequentialism. Ethical systems that are based on deontology, or duty, see ethical acts differently. **Deontological ethics** is based on the view that certain actions are absolutely 'right' or absolutely 'wrong' regardless of situations or circumstances. Typical examples are the Ten Commandments, natural law theory (and the ethics of the Catholic Church to which it is closely linked) and Kantian ethics.

Deontologists stress 'laws' and 'rules' and see the absolute character of moral obligation as being closely linked to the absolute character of a supposed moral law. Thus actions such as stealing and murder are absolutely wrong. However, as we suggested above, the application of deontological ethics is often complicated by relativist considerations. Stealing, say, from a rich person to save someone's life is generally regarded as morally permissible on the grounds that two conflicting obligations are impossible to fulfil at once. An example may also be taken from everyday life. The rule of law is that red traffic lights must be obeyed absolutely. The fact that ambulances, police vehicles and fire engines sometimes 'break' the rule for a good reason does not invalidate the absolute character of the rule. For this reason, many deontologists argue that respect for absolute rules is not inconsistent with sometimes breaking them.

A Nazi rally – a reminder that cultural relativism has many dangers

Assess the problems associated with absolutism and relativism in ethics.

Relativism in ethics is the view that all moral values and principles are *relative* to times, places, cultures or specific individuals. It is opposed to the view that certain moral values or principles are absolute; in other words, that they admit of no exceptions and are valid in all circumstances. This means that certain actions are right or always wrong, regardless of time, place, culture or individual. There are problems with either view. Extreme relativism would make moral discourse impossible, because if all values were relative it would be impossible to discuss them or evaluate them. This would be the most bizarre form of autonomy, in which everyone would be literally a law unto him- or herself.

Plato suggested the reality of absolute standards of such things as goodness, beauty, truth and justice, but held that these existed only in another realm as **ideal forms**. In his *fourth way*, **St Thomas Aquinas** argued that our limited notions of goodness, courage, love and so on, and the varying degrees to which they are realised, pointed to an absolute standard of all moral values, which is God. While both recognise the difference between the real and the ideal world, they would not rule out the existence of absolute ideals in this life. Plato famously said 'let justice be done though the heavens fall', suggesting the need to strive for an absolute ideal in moral matters even if it is impossible to realise absolute perfection in this life.

Those who deny the reality of absolute ethical ideals appeal to the supposed existence of so-called **cultural relativism**. This is the view that some cultures have values that are different from those of others, either at the same or at different times. To make sense of cultural relativism, however, it is necessary to distinguish between **descriptive relativism** and **normative relativism**. The former is merely an observation that some cultures appear to have values that are different from those of others. The ancient Greeks believed that they could kill weak babies, and the Nazis that they could kill Jews, homosexuals and other 'undesirables'. Descriptive relativism therefore has played its part in the scandals of history, but can make no contribution to morality except by exposing the risk of attempting to be judge in one's own case.

Normative relativism, on the other hand, is the view that different cultures are *entitled* to have their own values. This view would make it impossible to pass moral judgements on the behaviour of others, and would undermine all ethical debate. Just because babies are killed in one culture cannot be a basis for saying that people of that culture are entitled to do so. International law is based on the moral idea that all cultures have to conform to a shared belief in certain *absolute moral* values that are seen as basic to civilised living everywhere. The Nuremberg trials and modern war-crimes tribunals confirm this.

The notion of relativism, though, still retains validity when it comes to realising moral ideals. This may be called **practical** or **subjective relativism**, which is implied in some ethical theories, such as utilitarianism and **situation ethics**. In utilitarianism, moral acts are always relative to how far they achieve the utilitarian ideal of happiness, so there is never any 'absolutely' right way to act. Similarly, in situation ethics the absolute value of love is recognised, but the morality of an action is relative to how well that love is shown. This is something of a hidden agenda in **Joseph Fletcher's** system: although love is an absolute value, the goodness of an action is relative to how far its benefits are practically extended.

Relativism is also entailed in some theories about the meaning of ethics. Since **emotivism** reduces ethical claims to the personal feelings of the individual, ethical judgement is relative to the mind of the individual person. The same seems to go for **intuitionism**. In this theory, values are confined to the perception of the individual. Each person is sovereign over his or her own convictions, and can claim to know right from wrong intuitively. However, since many moral intuitions about what is good or bad, right or wrong, find agreement across cultures, intuitionism implicitly encourages the view that moral values are in some way absolute. This is also the case with **prescriptivism**. This view implies that moral values are not confined to the speaker but should be applied to everyone; that is, *universalised*. This suggests that some values are independent of persons or circumstances, and therefore cannot be relative to the individual.

Support for the absolutist character of ethical values is found in both Kantian and Christian ethics. In Kantian ethics the moral law is seen as making an absolute demand in the categorical imperative. Yet, in practice, if the demands of the moral law are not as clear to reason as Kant supposed, how the content of the moral law is perceived is bound to be relative to each individual. This is seen especially when an individual has to decide between conflicts of duties. It may be said, therefore, that from a subjective viewpoint your duty to the moral law is relative to your perception of it, yet the moral law itself is absolute, making an absolute demand in principle.

In Christian ethics there is also a belief in the absolute character of certain ethical values. General principles such as goodness, truth, honesty or love are seen to have an absolute character; but also certain practices such as divorce, adultery, extramarital sex, abortion and euthanasia are still ruled as absolutely wrong by the Catholic Church. However, as in Kantian ethics, there is a recognised gulf between what is wrong in principle and what is perceived to be so in practice. This leads to the distinction between subjective guilt and objective wrongdoing. Thus a unifying factor in both systems is the absolute character of the subjective **good will**. Both for Kant and the religious believer, the subjective intention to do what is right or not what is wrong is the necessary precondition of any moral act, and therefore has an absolute moral value.

A philosophical underpinning to an absolutist understanding of Christian morality was later provided by Aquinas, with his theory of **natural law**. According to this theory, there can be no exceptions to acting in accordance with the laws of nature. These laws are said to be known through the natural functioning of things, perceived through reason and common sense. Thus it is absolutely wrong to prefer evil to good, to betray, torture or take away an innocent human life, or to knowingly pursue one's own interests at the expense of others. Aquinas also included the natural bond of marriage to rule out adultery, the natural purposes of sex to rule out artificial contraception, and the natural bond of family relationships to rule out behaviour that would undermine such relationships.

In conclusion, we have seen that absolutism and relativism are terms used in ethical debate, but that there are problems in the application of both of those terms. Extreme relativism would make ethical debate impossible, while extreme absolutism creates difficulties in ethical practice. In particular, there is the difficulty of matching **objective** demands of an absolute kind with a **subjective** awareness that is always relative to each person. Perhaps, therefore, it should be left to personal **conscience** (with some qualifications) to bridge this gap and claim for itself to be the only real absolute in all moral decision-making.

Related questions:

1 Assess the view that relativism allows humans to alter the moral law to suit themselves.

2 How far is absolutism or relativism a factor in different ethical theories?

3 How valid is the distinction between subjective and objective in the discussion about relativism and absolutism?

The Meaning of Conscience

If **conscience** is the perception of what we feel we ought to do in a situation then, in theory, everyone has a conscience. In practice, however, it is possible to describe some behaviour as showing a 'lack of conscience', or some people as having 'no conscience'. These expressions point to some objective, or universal, reference point by which it is possible to pass judgement on the behaviour of others. This presupposes some universal sense of right and wrong in relation to certain things. The reality of such a universal sense is revealed in judgements of international law, such as 'gratuitous evil', 'inhuman and degrading treatment' or 'crimes against humanity'.

In less clear situations there may be a theoretical conflict between different forms of conscience. A religious conscience will be influenced by the **will of God**, and a utilitarian conscience by the **principle of utility**. But a Kantian conscience seems to have its own dynamic if, as he claims, the sense of **duty** is 'categorical', or absolute. In Kant's view the individual is confronted by conscience, and has no moral choice but to follow its dictates. This is a more significant view than is often realised, emerging especially in the supposed conflict between reason and faith in moral decision-making. That is, of course, in the case of those who can be said to have a conscience.

Explain and evaluate the role of conscience in moral decision-making.

St Thomas Aquinas gave a simple definition of **conscience** when he called it 'the faculty of reason making moral judgements'. From this, conscience is simply a rational faculty that enables us to understand right from wrong. The faculty works on the basis of knowledge, first a knowledge of moral first principles as enshrined in natural law, and ideally a knowledge of divine law as revealed in the Bible. But Aquinas recognised that conscience is by no means an infallible voice. We can have a mistaken, erroneous or uninformed conscience, and it is a moral obligation in itself to have an informed conscience. Aquinas, like **Joseph Butler**, believed that we have a capacity to grasp at a basic level the moral principles that should govern the right ordering of our lives.

Such principles include the pursuance of good and the avoidance of evil, and the treatment of others as one would like to be treated by them. Other principles are contained in the four **cardinal virtues** (**prudence**, **justice**, **fortitude** and **temperance**), which can be understood by reason as fundamental to the moral life. Justice combats selfishness and self-interest at the expense of others. Fortitude moves the will to recognise the needs of others and follow the good. Temperance helps to combat the excesses of the emotions and passions, such as anger, lust, pride and so on. Prudence is the correct use of reason, leading to a right knowledge about what is good and evil, right and wrong.

At the moral level, one can speak of a conscience that needs 'arousing', the subject of Holman Hunt's *The Awakening of Conscience*. More extreme is the dead conscience, sometimes referred to as 'no' conscience. In such cases the actions done fail to stand up to reason or justice. The Nazi leadership were accused of having no conscience, but culpably so, in contrast to psychopaths and schizophrenics, who are generally held to have no conscience, but are morally inculpable.

The views on conscience held by **Joseph Butler** show much agreement with those of Aquinas. Conscience is one of the components that belong to our nature, by which we are able to arrive at moral awareness and make critical moral judgements. Judgements of right and wrong should not be based on external consequences, but follow from an examination of how our nature responds to how we act. As with **Aristotle**, the good leads to happiness, and evil to unhappiness.

Butler held that by nature we are capable of acting with **benevolence** (good will) on the one hand, or **self-love** (selfishness) on the other. Whenever these get 'out of proportion' we act wrongly. The more we act out of self-love, the more we go against our nature; for example, by anger, hatred, revenge or pride. The result is a sense that we have acted wrongly, a sense of dissatisfaction with ourselves (guilt). For Butler, unhappiness or dissatisfaction with our moral life is the clue that we have acted against our nature.

Benevolence, or behaviour that is unselfish and is other-regarding, leads to happiness, both now and in the hereafter. *Happiness* is the reward of duty, and is the natural '*telos*' (aim) of moral behaviour, but it is not to be identified with the sensation of being 'happy'. A doctor is happy when his patients get better, but such happiness is *indirect* and resides in a sense of personal fulfilment. It is the function of conscience to lead us to fulfilment by helping us to keep the balance between other-regarding and self-regarding behaviour. The result for Butler is an intuition of the 'rule of right', which will be clear to the conscience of all 'plain and honest men'.

So far, the emphasis has been on conscience as a rational faculty. In Aquinas and Butler reason is its essence, our nature is its guide and the cardinal virtues are its ideal foundation. In ethical theories, conscience is also directed by rational considerations. A 'utilitarian' conscience will be one that is sensitive to how far we bring benefits to others. A 'Kantian' conscience will be one that is sensitive to the fulfilment of duty and the moral law. A religious conscience will be one that is sensitive to doing, or not doing, the will of God.

But conscience is not just about reason. It also has a significant *emotional* and one might say *non-rational* aspect. Conscience, especially a bad conscience, can make us feel guilty and fill us with anxiety. Butler spoke of how 'conscience magisterially exerts itself', referring to the force of its authority and its capacity to be a reproachful voice impossible to ignore. The torments of guilt suffered by Macbeth after the murder of Duncan, provide a classic example of how 'conscience doth make cowards of us all'. Here Macbeth seems torn by guilt for doing something that he intuitively knew to be wrong. But this function of conscience can be given other explanations. Perhaps conscience is something that we pick up from others, and is simply a socially conditioned faculty.

Such was the belief of **Sigmund Freud**, whose theory of conscience also promised the means of its removal as a centre of mental and moral disturbance. Freud argued that conscience is really the functioning of the superego, the store of information about right and wrong derived from social attitudes, parental wishes and other authority figures that contributes to our conditioning when we are young and impressionable. As a result, we are prone to anxiety and guilt from fear of disapproval, and loss of the love of others. Once we break free from the restraints of the superego, we become masters of our own destiny and able to live with autonomy, with no conscience to fear.

If Freud is right, conscience is only a temporary restraint that remains tied to our dependence on the superego. Reality, however, shows that conscience is not so easily got rid of, and the force of its voice is such that it has to be reckoned with at the moral, not just the emotional, level. The breakdown of the relationships that form the superego does not mean the disappearance of moral values. We continue to feel the voice of conscience long after we have outgrown the parental or social values that we originally inherited.

Aquinas and Butler would of course accept that conscience has an important *social* dimension, but would see this as following from the fact that human nature is also social. For Aquinas, the social aspect of conscience is one of its essential aspects, since the common good is an important ethical consideration. To this extent both would agree with Freud. But they would insist that the values sensed by conscience are more profoundly based than by merely socially imposed conventions. For them, conscience is the faculty that alerts us, through nature and reason, to the moral values that shape our moral identity as human beings. If this is the case, Freud's theory dissolves into superficiality.

For **J. H. Newman**, conscience was much more than a socially conditioned moral response system. Conscience was the voice of reason and nature, but it was also the voice of God. Newman held that the insistent force of conscience suggests that there is someone to whom we feel answerable and responsible, someone who is the personal source of the moral law, God. In this way, Newman carries the natural law a step further, by linking it directly to its source in a divine law-giver. Newman believed that the personal nature of morality, and more especially of guilt, is better explained not in terms of breaking a law, but of offending against a person. Freud's observation that guilt arises from fear of a loss of *love* has an ironic echo with the religious view.

While the *religious* understanding of conscience is of course confirmed for the believer in God's revelation in the Bible, Aquinas, Butler and Newman were not content to rely on this. Each was concerned to show that God's law is in accordance with our natural lights, and can therefore be rightly perceived through conscience. This idea goes back to **St Paul**, who taught that God's law is 'written in the heart', a suggestion that there is no inconsistency between the voice of conscience and the voice of God. This explains why, for believers, an understanding of conscience as the voice of God, especially an informed or educated conscience, gives it a sacred authority.

In conclusion, we have seen that conscience has been understood as a rational voice that informs us what is right and wrong, and when, or whether or not, we are living up to its dictates. We have also seen that conscience itself needs to be corrected, revised or awakened, as the case may be. It can be either informed or in a state of ignorance. The implication of this is that while it is the moral aspect of reason, it is still subject to reason in terms of how reasonable our conscience is. We have also seen that in its correct functioning it can also be regarded as the voice of God.

Yet we have also seen that attempts have been made to reduce conscience to an inconvenient and troublesome socially conditioned voice, something that can be put right through a process of psychological adjustment. This is in contrast to the views of other thinkers, and if Aquinas, Butler and Newman are right, conscience remains an insistent inner voice that can only be stilled when its moral dictates are obeyed.

Related questions:

1 Explain how different thinkers have understood the nature of conscience.

2 Assess the view that conscience is part of our nature, and its workings are the result of our conditioning in society.

3 Evaluate the view of some thinkers that conscience is the voice of God.

7 Ethical Theories

The Relationship between Religion and Ethics

It is generally accepted, especially since **Immanuel Kant**, that ethics can stand on its own feet and has no need for religion. But historically, ethical awareness has been greatly influenced by religious beliefs. In this section, we shall look at the extent of this influence, and examine how far it has been for good or ill. A key question will be the relationship between **faith** and **reason**, and the extent to which they overlap, complement each other or conflict. A related question is the relationship between faith and conscience.

If faith were to override conscience, there might be a risk of taking away the individual's **autonomy**, the ability to act out of personal conviction. If, on the other hand, conscience were to override faith, the latter would risk being discredited as irrational. Does the individual often have to choose between the two? And if not, what is the special contribution of faith to ethics? The concept of divine law theory, therefore, and its relationship to reason will be a key consideration.

 Evaluate the contribution of one religion to ethical understanding.

The Christian religion makes a special contribution to ethical understanding in three ways: (1) by its claim that morality is an integral part of human life, that it is the ultimate measure of its worthiness, and is subject to the judgement of God; (2) by specifying certain rules and principles that should govern human life; and (3) by providing the context and inspiration to make possible a higher level of morality based on agape love, the altruistic (unselfish) love of other human beings.

In the Bible, God's will for the way in which life is to be lived is revealed in various ways, but may be seen as condensed in the **Decalogue** (the Ten Commandments). Further revelations are given by Jesus, who called for a higher ethic in terms of tolerance, generosity, forgiveness, non-retaliation and compassion towards others. An understanding of our relationship to God is the necessary setting within which biblical ethics makes sense. What is morally required is not primarily a matter of 'principles' or 'consequences', but the fulfilment of a duty of *personal* respect and obedience towards God, who is seen as protector, saviour and judge. This makes biblical ethics quite different from other systems such as utilitarian or Kantian ethics, which are noticeably *rational* and *impersonal* by comparison.

At the same time, biblical ethics has a lot in common with both utilitarian and Kantian systems, not only in approach, but also in content. All of the accepted moral principles governing the behaviour of human beings towards each other that can be defended either on consequentialist and deontological grounds are found in the Bible. That we should relate to others on the basis of reason and justice is central to biblical ethics. This gives biblical ethics a claim to be both true to reason and guaranteed to promote the greatest happiness of the greatest number. At the same time, it would be a mistake to try to confuse biblical ethics with any other system. The biblical perspective has the uniqueness of making human beings at the same time subordinate to the demands of reason and to the law of God. However, its stress on personal responsibility to a personal Creator gives biblical ethics a far more relational, or personalist, dimension than purely secular systems.

A number of philosophical issues arise from these considerations. How can I be sure about knowing God's will? Can it be trusted to conform to the insights of reason? What if my good *intentions* lead me to do actions that, unknown to me, are against God's will? The first two questions were dealt with by **St Thomas Aquinas**, when he pointed out that God's will is revealed in special revelation (the Bible) and general revelation (reason and conscience).

Aquinas argued that not only would a wise deity be in the best position to determine questions of right and wrong, but since God's essence is Goodness, there could be no question of God laying down moral principles that are independent of God's nature. This immediately rules out the idea of God laying down *arbitrary* moral rules that go against reason. It would therefore rule out any possibility of a believer losing his or her moral autonomy, or having to sacrifice reason to faith. In the light of this, the so-called **Eurypthro dilemma** (Is an act right because God wills it, or does God will it because it is right?) becomes a false one.

The sovereignty of **conscience** as judged by critical reason is a keynote of Christian ethics as shown by Aquinas. This means that ultimately it is a good intention that is a necessary prerequisite for all moral acts, since the intention is consistent with the dictates of conscience. This makes the objective 'rightness' or 'wrongness' of an act less decisive than the subjective intention. For most people, a bad motive or intention means a bad act. A good motive or intention is not enough for a completely good moral act, as Kant held, but in religious ethics it is the most crucial aspect. An unsatisfactory aspect of utilitarianism is that an action is judged by its effects, and thus the intention of the agent is irrelevant to the worthiness of the act.

At the same time, the search for objective moral truth was seen by Aquinas as an important responsibility. He believed that this was possible because of the existence of **natural law**, a rational principle of guidance built into nature. **St Paul** had stated that non-believers had the law of God written on their hearts. This meant that it was possible to arrive at a knowledge of right and wrong by looking at the way we are made, at the moral sense provided by our conscience, and by taking into account the purpose for which we exist. In this view, the laws of nature and reason are a correct pointer to the laws of the author of nature and reason, God. Laws and principles, such as not killing the innocent, not violating the person or property of others, not bearing false witness or not breaking solemn vows such as marriage, are as much against reason as against any explicit divine prohibitions that we might find in the Bible.

There are difficulties, however, with the notion of natural law. Many claim that there is no such thing – that morality is essentially about social living rather than following some supposed law built into nature. Aquinas, like **Immanuel Kant**, however, insisted that reason shows that we are bound by some objective moral law, a law that is essential for ethical and social living. The similarity between biblical laws and the main outlines of the moral law as put forward by Aquinas and Kant suggest that they are two sides of the same coin. This leaves the question: What is special about the Bible's contribution to ethical understanding?

Most scholars point out that the Bible is more concerned to offer an inspiration for living a moral life than to lay down a set of rules for doing so. The motivation is the personal relationship between human beings and God (called a covenant), which is encouraged to exist between our neighbours and ourselves. The key religious and ethical background of biblical ethics is the fatherhood of God and the brotherhood of mankind. This is a principle that is meant to promote a better world by means of agape, selfless love. All ethical guidelines in the Bible must therefore be understood against this religious background.

In conclusion, we have seen that the contribution of Christianity to ethical understanding has both a religious and a rational dimension. Its belief in the sovereignty of God's will over all human behaviour, and its concept of the brotherhood of mankind that follows from it, provide an important context for understanding the moral life, and may be seen to offer a special motivation for living it. This is implied in the perspective of faith, which sees ethical obligation as a response to a *personal relationship* between human being and God.

Related questions:

1 Evaluate the criticism that religion interferes with the rationality of ethical decision-making.

2 Compare and contrast religious ethics with one other ethical theory.

3 Assess the view that religion provides a greater motivation for living the moral life than secular ethical systems.

Ethics and Religion

To what extent should ethics be independent of religion?

All religions have an ethical dimension, but ethics need not have any religious dimension. Where the latter is the case, ethics is said to be autonomous; that is, self-governing, based on reason alone. The ethical theory most notable for its stress on autonomy is that of **Immanuel Kant**. Kant strongly rejected the dependence of ethics on religion or any other ulterior motive, such as creating benefits for others, a view central to utilitarianism. Ethics was a matter of reason alone, the faculty by which we come to know the moral law. Our duty is to follow the moral law as a categorical imperative, something to which we are all bound in virtue of our rationality. Although Kant introduced the idea of religion as something that was required to make better sense of the moral law, he did not in any way wish to imply that ethics was dependent on religion.

Secular dissatisfaction with religious ethics is linked to the criticism that only an autonomous morality is consistent with human dignity. Living in obedience to some external power such as God, it is claimed, robs us of our autonomy and dignity. Believers might reply that if God is the supreme power over everything, and is Goodness itself, it is far from immature not to recognise this. This would entail ordering one's life in accordance with the will of such a God, in the belief that this is facing up to reality, the mark of maturity and a true exercise of autonomy.

Moral maturity means taking responsibility for our convictions, which is also the mark of autonomy. The claim, therefore, that religion interferes with our natural autonomy conceals a hidden assumption about what constitutes autonomy and maturity. A corollary of this is that a God who is perceived as some external authority, divorced from the true nature of right and wrong, would undermine autonomy. Such a God would be seen by many as a caricature of the God of religious faith. To combat this idea, **St Thomas Aquinas** set out to show that the ethics implied in religious faith was an extension of our natural moral sense.

Secular (non-religious) ethical systems such as utilitarianism claim to be autonomous by being based exclusively on rational considerations, such as the here-and-now happiness of others. The system encourages a dispassionate assessment of how an action can be judged right or best, wrong or worst, by looking at the benefits or otherwise that it brings. Yet both **Jeremy Bentham** and **John Stuart Mill** tried to show how utilitarianism was consistent with the Gospel ethics of Jesus, especially the **Golden Rule**, 'Do unto others as you would have them do unto you'. In this way, they confirmed the rational transparency of basic Christian principles and, by implication, their autonomy.

The so-called **existentialist ethics** contained in the writings of **Friedrich Nietzsche**, **Martin Heidegger**, **Jean-Paul Sartre** and **Albert Camus** claim to be autonomous because they are free of religious influences. Human existence, these thinkers argue, is characterised by freedom, and each person must decide for him- or herself how to exist in a world of no fixed moral laws. The task of the human will is to forge a set of values by which the individual is going to live, even if the process of living itself is absurd and pointless. In existentialist ethics, it seems that conformity with others is the greatest sin.

Whether existentialist systems are as autonomous as they claim is something that has been questioned by some religious writers. Our 'natural' transcendence, revealed in the endless search find the truth, do what is right or seek after justice, has been seen as an indication of a natural spirituality, which can only be ultimately satisfied by God. This view, held by **Augustine** and **Aquinas**, has been proposed by modern religious thinkers such as **Wolfhart Pannenberg** and **Karl Rahner**. From this religious perspective, human nature is seen as 'elevated' or 'driven' by a divine inspiration, or grace. If this is true, the idea of a rationally autonomous ethics would be an illusion. Yet, as **James Mackey** has pointed out, modern atheism has defiantly insisted on the independence of humanistic values, and has seen the pursuit of such values as not requiring any further explanation. If this is true, the claim that human transcendence is evidence of a religious dimension is not necessarily accepted.

Some religious writers have insisted that a merely rational approach to ethics leaves the individual stranded on a second highest level of moral attainment, because it lacks the dynamism to motivate the individual to seek the most heroic values (such as self-sacrifice for others). Ironically, this stands in direct opposition to the claim of **Nietzsche** that only a non-religious rational ethics could be truly elevating, and capable of rescuing the human race from ultimate decline.

Søren Kierkegaard believed that religion was needed to complete our ethical sense, and transform it into a higher order of living. He argued that the 'religious' stage is a step higher than the 'ethical' stage. Abraham's readiness to sacrifice his son in response to God's call was heroic and right, even though it would not appear so from a purely ethical point of view. However, such a view is very individualistic and has many practical dangers. The spectacle of the modern cult leader driven by the belief that 'God told me do it' has become sadly familiar.

Rudolf Bultmann has argued that the pursuit of authentic values (goodness) is only made possible under special inspiration, such as that provided by Christ's death and Resurrection. Here, religion is seen as a necessary support to enable the ethical will to seek the good and resist the evil. This may seem a brash claim, and it seems to ignore the possibility that human beings are naturally capable of doing what is good. In any case, it would be vigorously rejected by non-religious humanists, and is frequently undermined by so-called religious believers whose lives show little evidence of the religious inspiration claimed by Bultmann.

But is mankind without religion as likely to create the values of Nietzsche's superman as mankind with religion? This remains an interesting question in the light of the claim that biblical agape love is a richer source of motivation than less personalist secular systems, such as utilitarianism or Kantianism. It is a matter of record that Mill saw religion as one of the most important sources of character formation, and the source of important utilitarian benefits for society. At the same time, at the practical level, believers have to answer for some spectacular moral failings, and for the fact that religious inspiration can be turned to evil as well as good.

In conclusion, we have seen that religion has played a key part in the history of human behaviour, and that a code of ethics is central to all religious systems. Yet we have also seen that a claim for the autonomy of ethics has been a feature of modern thinking since Kant. This implies that ethics should be based on reason, and should owe nothing to religion. Taking into account the secular nature of modern society, and the decline in popularity of religiously based ethical guidelines, it is perhaps good that this should be so. Yet given the fact that religious ethics are more autonomous than is often recognised, and are a recognised source of inspiration for ethical behaviour, it is perhaps also good that ethics should have some connection with religion.

Related questions:

1 Evaluate the view that religion undermines the autonomy of ethics.

2 Assess the claim that Kantian ethics is a mixture of faith and reason.

3 How convincing is the view that ethics is better off without religion?

The Ethics of Immanuel Kant

Kantian ethics is called **deontological** (from the Greek *deon*, duty) because it sees the ethical enterprise in terms of law and duty. The two key ideas for Kant are the moral law on the one hand, and the absolute duty (categorical imperative) to obey it on the other. Kant's ethical system stands somewhat in contrast to utilitarianism, because the one stresses fixed rules while the other stresses the consequences of actions. Kant believed that some things were right or wrong regardless of the consequences. At the same time, it must be remembered that there is a clear overlap between the two systems. Kant justified his theory partly with reference to social consequences ('What if everyone did this?'), while utilitarians such as **John Stuart Mill** saw respect for traditional moral rules (rule utilitarianism), and the character that they were likely to produce, as the best hope for the greatest social utility.

One great strength of Kant's theory is its independence of religion. This makes it accessible to all human beings because it appeals to **reason** alone. A second strength is its positive support for justice, and respect for persons. Kant's theory may be said to be the forerunner of international charters of human rights. A third strength is its openness and honesty, and its refusal to make any compromises that might encourage hypocrisy and special pleading. Nobody can be exempt from the obligations of the moral law.

At the same time, the theory is not without its weaknesses. Kant's assumption that the morally good will would always coincide with a correct knowledge of the moral law has not proved to be well-founded. Differences in moral perception show that this is rarely the case. Kant's clear-sighted vision of objective morality has not been so clear to others, as moral disputes always show. Secondly, Kant's laudable stress on duty leaves behind the problem of *what* duty. Thus Kant is no help where duty is difficult to discern, or where conflicts of duty arise. But it is the *sense of duty itself* that remains a provocative aspect of Kant's ethical theory.

 Assess the strengths and weaknesses of Kant's ethical theory.

Immanuel Kant's ethical theory (what we call **Kantian ethics**), is a combination of a **subjective** good will and an **objective** moral law. The two components are essential in Kant's ethics for the performance of a morally good act. If only a good will is present, the act might still be against the moral law, whereas if the moral law is observed it might be done for an unworthy motive, thus lacking the good will.

The first important difficulty with Kantian ethics is his notion of a **moral law**. Kant assumed that an **objective** moral law existed, one that would be as clear to others as it was to him. Unfortunately, many of the principles that were clear to Kant have been questioned by other thinkers. One example often taken is Kant's insistence on telling the truth. According to Kant, we are obliged to tell the truth as an absolute moral requirement, for without truth-telling social life between human beings would become impossible. The standard example is that of a maniac wielding a knife, in pursuit of a fugitive: if he should ask, Kant is alleged to have said that he should be told the truth about the fugitive's whereabouts. But to believe this is to give little credit to Kant's intelligence. Kant did not say he should be told the truth, but merely that he should not be lied to. This allows for silence, or the *refusal* to tell the truth (ideally by disappearing quickly), an option that makes far more sense of Kant's reasoning, and shows that his argument is quite compelling.

A further objection centres on the nature of the moral law. Kant argued that moral laws were those that could without contradiction be **universalised**; that is, made binding on everyone in all similar circumstances. The technique of 'universalising' an action is a test to see if, as a law, it would have a positive or negative effect on human life. But is this test a sure way of proving the existence of a moral law? Many would argue that so-called moral laws are at most social conventions, drawn up over the course of civilised history to make life tolerable and just. This, it is argued, partly explains why 'morality' is not the same everywhere, because conventions are made to meet particular needs and circumstances.

If this is the case, and all laws are human laws, then the idea of a moral law is a mistake. But how strong is this objection? It does seem that there is a big difference between seeing an action or prohibition as an agreed convention, and seeing it as a matter of morality. A sense of morality touches on our inner sense of integrity, our sense of what our conscience permits, while a convention is simply seen as a practical social requirement that a good citizen should observe. It is widely accepted that many laws are not mere conventions, but reflect a deep and universal awareness of what is 'right' and 'wrong'. International law, for instance, is based on fundamental principles of reasoned morality that say that we should value life and respect others for their own sake. An important test of Kantian ethics, therefore, might be to see how far his moral law accords with such fundamental principles. Many would say that in its broad outlines it does indeed pass this test.

Kant's rigid attachment to the idea that morality was based on an objective moral law put him on collision course with the utilitarianism of **Jeremy Bentham** and **John Stuart Mill**, which he described a 'calculating' and 'serpentine way' to do morality. Kant saw his deontological ethics, based on objectively fixed principles, as a more authentic alternative to a consequentialist theory that only looked to material results. This could mean, and Kant was right to say so, that an act that was widely seen as wrong could be made right if it created social utility, the 'greatest happiness of the greatest number'. Killing an innocent suspect of a murder could be justified if it helped to ward off, say, social unrest. While utilitarianism may be more complex than this, Kant saw it as sanctioning the *morally repugnant* if the results justified it.

The second important element in Kant's ethical theory is the **subjective** aspect of the moral act, the **good will**. For Kant, the motive behind an act was crucial for its moral worthiness. This amounted to the doing of *duty for duty's sake*; that is, acting not for reasons of selfishness or out of inclination, but strictly from a sense that this was one's duty. Kant has been criticised for putting so much weight on duty that other motives, such as love or compassion, are cast aside. But this may not be so.

A sense of duty is often consistent with acting out of love or compassion, or from a sense of justice. Kant specified that the categorical imperative should include treating others not as means only but always as ends in themselves, and that others should be treated in a way that would promote a community in which people treated each other as members entitled to dignity and respect ('a kingdom of ends'). In this, Kant called for the elimination of acts that lead to the exploitation and unjust treatment of others, and for the practice of those positive acts that promote the decent and dignified treatment of others as part of the human community. In this lay the essence and material content of the good will.

123

For this reason, the *strength* of Kant's ethics lies in its support for actions that are usually recognised as noble, virtuous and other-regarding. The individual who speaks up for the truth despite the cost to life or limb finds support from Kantian ethics. The individual who dies for a cause because he or she believes in moral integrity – that is, in being true to him- or herself – or who is prepared to sacrifice self for love of others, is a true Kantian. Those who might have the Faustian temptation to 'sell their souls to the devil' will not find support from Kant. Above all, Kantian ethics has been seen as a bulwark against any *degradation* of the individual person. His dictum 'never treat others only as a means, but always as an end' sets a standard for *human relations* and the proper treatment of people everywhere, regardless or colour, race or creed.

In conclusion, Kant's system of ethics has some weaknesses that follow from his insistence on the rigidity of the moral law. But these, I believe, are outweighed by the strengths of a theory that advocates the development of an *inner* sense of right and wrong. As a result, Kant's theory encourages a high degree of personal integrity. By following the dictates of your personal **conscience**, combined with a sense of what is demanded by your own dignity and that of others, you are not likely to go far off the path of the moral law as conceived by Kant. But whether his theory on its own is the answer to all moral questions remains disputed.

Related questions:

1 To what extent does Kant's theory support human rights and duties?

2 How fair is the criticism that the main weakness of Kant's theory is his claim about an objective moral law?

3 Assess the view that Kant's theory is incomplete without religious faith.

The Ethics of Utilitarianism

Utilitarianism is said to be one of the most influential ethical systems of modern times. However, it must be remembered that all ethical systems have an important utilitarian dimension. Kantian ethics is seriously orientated towards benefiting (or being useful) to others. Codes of religious ethics such as the Ten Commandments are clearly orientated to have a utilitarian effect through their emphasis on respect for the life, property and rights of others. In both of these systems, there is an assured place for the value of creating happiness and minimising pain.

It is somewhat ironic, therefore, that utilitarianism proper should be partly a reaction to both Kantianism and religious ethics. Bentham was strongly opposed to the idea of fixed rules, which to him brought no benefits to others. He was equally opposed to a

John Stuart Mill improved on the thought of Jeremy Bentham, but was described as a wayward utilitarian

religious lifestyle that appeared to put a premium on practices such as self-denial and asceticism, which he thought could have no conceivable use. It is again ironic that such practices are usually carried out because they are seen as useful, both to the ascetic and to others. The problem of course is that only within a religious outlook is this vision possible. Within a religious perspective all virtuous (good) behaviour has a utilitarian consequence but not a utilitarian motive. So while the good may go to heaven, it is neither dignified nor meritorious to be good in order to go to heaven. Such an attitude would amount to moral and religious hypocrisy. For this reason, there are good reasons for calling religious ethics a form of theological utilitarianism.

Utilitarianism properly so-called is a system that judges actions in terms of their **consequences**. It encourages the maximisation of happiness and the minimisation of pain. On the face of it, this is an attractive idea. It is hard to disagree with the aim of making the world a better place. The problem, though, is how this is achieved without having to sacrifice other values and principles. It would conceivably be possible to clean up a city of crime by rounding up and eliminating all possible suspects. The *result* might be good from a utilitarian viewpoint, but the *means* used would keep lawyers busy for some time. It is the problem of *means* and *ends* that utilitarianism has to deal with.

 Explain and evaluate utilitarianism as an ethical system.

Utilitarianism is an ethical system based on the principle that happiness is the most sought after – and therefore the highest – good, and that the opposite applies to pain. The philosophical weakness of the system is its inability to say why the most sought-after good should logically be the highest good. Such a claim is challenged by a tradition of philosophical ethics on the one hand and the tradition of religious ethics on the other.

Plato argued that the highest good was an ideal form that existed outside all its empirical manifestations. A beautiful girl is really only an earthly shadow of ideal beauty, while a good person is only a shadowy manifestation of ideal goodness. Thus goodness belongs to the realm of objective reality, and, as **G. E. Moore** held, cannot be identified with what people might think is desirable or preferable. Equally, the Judeo-Christian tradition holds that what is morally good is that which conforms to the will of God. In the end it leads to happiness, but with two qualifications.

One is that happiness is not measurable exclusively in terms of here-and-now sensations, but must also make allowance for the hereafter. Next, good acts are not directly, or necessarily, linked to happiness. Some may be, but others may still be seen as good even if no observable happiness results. In **Kantian ethics** what is good is what is in accordance with the moral law. The idea, therefore, that the pursuit of worldly happiness or the avoidance of worldly pain should determine what is right or wrong is contrary to both Kantian and religious ethics.

But this is what the utilitarian theory founded by **Jeremy Bentham**, and further developed, although along different lines, by **John Stuart Mill**, sets out as its basic principle. Bentham rejected all so-called deontological, or rule-centred, theories, such as the ethics of **Immanuel Kant** or traditional Christian ethics. He believed that all actions should lead to the increase of happiness and the reduction of pain. The rightness or wrongness of an action is judged by its **consequences**, and the act that produces the greatest balance of happiness over pain is the best action to perform in the circumstances. 'The greatest happiness of the greatest number' became the slogan of utilitarianism.

R. M. Hare has suggested (probably in a tongue-in-cheek way) that utilitarianism is the philosophical counterpart of the Christian virtue of agape (selfless) love, by which we should seek the good of others impartially. This, I believe, is to overlook the fact that agape, properly understood, depends on the acceptance of certain religious and moral principles. A utilitarian form of agape would inevitably see actions as good that traditional Christian ethics would not. The reason is that the utilitarian idea of happiness is immediate, while the Christian one is **eschatological** (related to the hereafter). So 'helping' a fellow human being would not necessarily be the same under both systems. However, as Mill claimed, the Golden Rule, 'Do unto others as you would have them do unto you', was the nearest thing to the principle of utility.

The puzzle as to why we should act in such a way as to think of our fellow humans' happiness or pain is raised by utilitarianism. One possible answer is in terms of selfish interests. If everyone adopted the utilitarian principle of promoting the greatest happiness of the greatest number then, it is claimed, everyone would benefit equally. In this sense, the principle of utility can be seen as a theory that is both **egoistic** and **hedonistic**, geared ultimately to the promotion of one's own happiness. However, this is not necessarily a criticism of utilitarianism. The driving force behind all ethical behaviour involves some form of self-interest, otherwise moral behaviour would require a heroic level of **altruism** (concern for others) that is normally beyond the capacity of most people.

Other supporters of the utility principle say that its truth is self-evident. If the promotion of happiness and the lessening of pain is what we all value, then all human actions should have these aims and effects. Bentham went so far as to produce a **hedonic calculus** by which the utility value of an action could be empirically judged. Good actions should be judged by the extent to which they are capable of producing a balance of pleasure over pain.

126

It is difficult to see how a scientific system of happiness calculation could suitably be applied to what is a human thought system (morality). Moral acts are normally taken to involve the heart as well as the will, and are difficult to judge by a scientific method. A gladiatorial contest against lions, for instance, could by the use of the calculus be justified on the grounds that the pleasure of the audience would outweigh the pain of the gladiator, a conclusion seen as laughable to most people. This is a short step from justifying public hangings of innocent prisoners to instil respect for the law for utilitarian reasons.

As far as *personal morality* is concerned, the hedonic calculus would seem to be of little relevance. Even if it were possible to work out what happiness an act might create, it would still be necessary to wait for the lapse of time before its consequences could be fully assessed. This led to the suggestion that the prediction of consequences is enough to justify a utilitarian act. In a modern refinement of utilitarianism, 'happiness' has been replaced with 'the satisfaction of preferences', on the grounds that different things make different people happy.

Mill is remembered for counting 'higher', more cultural, pleasures as more important than 'lower', more physical, pleasures, thus introducing a judgmental element into the utilitarian calculus (but see below). A further refinement has produced so-called *liberal utilitarianism*, which moves away from the Benthamite calculus by allowing for a hierarchy of needs and preferences. One person's need for life cannot be offset against another's need for happiness.

As far as *public* or *social morality* goes, the calculus may have some relevance. Bentham was a social reformer who believed that good laws were the ones that produced good social benefits and vice versa. This gives grounds for saying that the natural *home* of utilitarianism may be in the field of *social reform*. The enactment of laws based on the principle of utility aims for the 'greatest happiness of the greatest number' (the essence of democratic government). The principle of utility has probably provided the greatest impetus to modern social reforms in the UK, such as the Divorce and Abortion Acts of the 1960s. These were reforms that reflected a typical utilitarian concern with maximising certain freedoms in order to minimise certain social evils, but by means of utilitarian *compromise* with 'something for everyone'. The Abortion Act, for instance, gave some recognition to the 'sanctity of life' principle.

Recent debates in **medical ethics** are also highly influenced by utilitarian considerations of social benefits. However, the danger with the excessive use of utilitarianism is that it risks dominating all moral debate – only, in the end, making it serve non-moral purposes. So we get something like 'whatever the ethics of euthanasia, there are at least the utilitarian benefits of saving beds and money'. Or, more notoriously, 'whatever the ethics of war there are good utilitarian benefits from having one, like controlling the population'. Not so long ago, utilitarianism was the overwhelming 'moral' justification for ridding certain societies of Jews and other 'undesirables'. For this reason, utilitarianism often appears linked more to the word *justify* than to the word *just*.

This becomes apparent when it comes to *personal morality*, the arena in which personal ethical dilemmas are fought out. The attempt to apply strict **utilitarian** considerations to moral issues that affect individuals, such as abortion and divorce, make it look as if ethics was a matter of cold calculation of costs and benefits. This is the so-called *critical* thinking lauded by **R. M. Hare**, by which the 'maximising of the preferences of all concerned' becomes the important criterion.

To adopt a more *human* approach, which might touch on a Kantian, or religious, *inner sense* of what is right or wrong, is dismissed by Hare as *instinctual* thinking, with the implication that this is in some way inferior. Thus a major weakness of utilitarianism is its easy disregard of considerations that we take to be normal: loyalty to family and friends, *sympathy* with the needs of others and a particular regard for what is *just*. This is no doubt what made **D. D. Raphael** say that 'the personal character of human life has a central importance for morality which is neglected by utilitarianism'.

In this connection, it is something of a travesty of serious morality to select absurd situations to prove the 'correctness' of utilitarianism. These usually involve dilemmas about 'saving your mother or a drowning scientist', or 'whether a group of sadists are entitled to torture an innocent victim', or 'whether in a fire you should save the Mona Lisa or your cat'. Such situations bear little relation to real-life crises, and only serve to put utilitarianism in a bad light.

True utilitarianism was recognised by **Mill** as something that was better achieved by less direct, more 'traditionally moral' means. For him, the principle of utility was best served by developing the 'higher qualities' that produce the *noble character*. Mill was speaking of qualities such as cultural refinement, friendship, honesty, benevolence, loyalty, integrity and so on. It is in these qualities that true utilitarian benefits lie, immediately to the enrichment of the individual, and ultimately of society. This is why Mill argued for the development of those cultural pleasures that are found in art, music, literature and indeed education. Mill assumed, as **Plato** did, that the forming of an elite *cultural* class would also mean the creation of an elite *moral* class to the benefit of all.

Defenders of utilitarianism often point to the prominent utilitarian strand in the teaching of the Bible, particularly in the teaching of Jesus. The heart of Jesus' teaching was love of God, expressed through love of *neighbour*. On a number of occasions he made it clear that this overrode allegiance to man-made law. But it is only rarely, if at all, that allegiance to divine law would conflict with love of neighbour.

It could be argued instead that laws such as the **Ten Commandments** are charters of human rights, designed to protect the interests and well-being of all of us, in all circumstances. This only shows that if the Bible is a charter of utilitarian benefits for others, it is so by a different route, and only by way of secondary effect. In the first place comes the primacy of God, on which everything else depends. Thus to invoke the Bible in support of utilitarianism is an oversimplification, but it also shows the extent to which the principle of utility can be served by other ethical perspectives.

Even Kant is sometimes invoked as a **crypto-utilitarian**. Kant indeed does seem to assess the morality of actions by asking 'What would happen if everyone did this?' This shows that Kant is not discounting the importance of maximising good consequences. But the difference is that he never sacrifices good *principles* for good consequences. In Kant's view, human welfare and happiness depend on allegiance to the moral law, *whatever* the short-term consequences. In other words, the moral law stands to reason *because* it brings good consequences, thus showing again that the pursuit of social utility is not exclusive to utilitarianism.

This seems to be recognised in the emergence of so-called **rule utilitarianism**. This version was developed initially from **Mill** on the grounds that certain **laws** are the best way to create the most happiness. Traditional **act utilitarianism** encouraged the performance of isolated acts, each one based on a calculation of likely consequences. However, it is important to remember that rule utilitarianism does not sacrifice the principle of utility. It merely sees law as its best servant.

This raises the question 'Why is law so important?' The suggestion that laws provide 'guidelines' that are helpful for simple people to follow is hardly a convincing justification. More significant is the question of what laws stand for. Traditional ethical laws have influenced morality not as 'guidelines', but as upholding *values* that are seen as being essential to human dignity and decency. If this is true, traditional ethical laws represent a profound wisdom about what the good life means. Therefore, the old Greek test has to be reckoned with. The good life is that which brings happiness because it leads to a sense of personal moral fulfilment. Its opposite brings unhappiness because it is guilt-creating, unsatisfying and ultimately unfulfilling.

It is this criticism of utilitarianism that has been highlighted by **Bernard Williams**, who has argued that the calculative nature of a system geared to utility is unlikely to bring moral fulfilment. This is because it is often likely to conflict with one's personal moral sense of what is right or wrong. He believes that the notion of sacrificing the individual for the so-called benefits of the majority can often lead to what is *morally repugnant* (going against our basic instincts). The traditional view of moral integrity as standing by one's instinctive moral sense makes it difficult to fit in with the calculating nature of the principle of utility. However, **Häyry** has tried to correct this by introducing the notion of 'immoral preferences'. But to introduce the distinction between **moral** and **immoral** preferences requires some reference point outside utilitarianism itself. This would suggest that the principle of utility cannot claim to be an independent basis for moral action.

Hare takes the opposite view, holding that to follow a personal moral sense, or conscience, amounts to 'instinctual' thinking, while a more detached and dispassionate view of a situation results in a more creditable 'critical' thinking. The latter is said to take the preferences of all involved into account. Why Hare elevates the calculating nature of utilitarian thinking to a superior position over instinctual thinking is difficult to see. A Kantian, religious or even Humean approach would put critical thinking firmly on the side of what our moral sensitivity tells us is right or wrong.

In conclusion, we have seen that **utility** is an important aspect of ethical acts. But we have also seen that other ethical systems, while incorporating the value of utility, refuse to make it a *guiding* principle on the grounds that intuitive principles of right and wrong take priority over the calculation of consequences. If consequences alone are elevated to the position of determining right and wrong, then what follows can result in the morally repugnant, or in what **Williams** called a violation of our personal integrity. A system that would encourage such a violation would seem to threaten the very basis of personal morality, and sometimes encourage what is morally questionable. This would suggest that utilitarianism on its own has significant shortcomings as an ethical system.

Related questions:

1 Assess the view that utilitarianism is an unsuitable system for making decisions in personal morality.

2 Evaluate the strengths and weaknesses of utilitarianism.

3 Refering to one religious tradition, discuss to what extent you find religious ethics consistent, or otherwise, with utilitarian ethics.

Situation Ethics

So-called '**situation ethics**' is based, at a superficial level, on the principle that situations alter cases. This seems quite reasonable. The principle is clearly acceptable within utilitarianism. It is also acceptable in the *practical* application of Kantianism, despite possible theoretical objections from Kant. It is also acceptable within religious and natural law ethics. God does not lay down the *unreasonable* application of laws that conflict with other laws in certain situations. Stealing food to help the starving, or killing in war or in self-defence, come to mind. Within the ordinary **justice** system, mitigating circumstances are always taken into consideration.

However, the system that we are going to look at is somewhat different. It's not so much that situations alter *cases* as situations alter *principles*. Or, put more accurately, traditional principles are made hostage to some *higher* principle called the primacy of love. Thus the exercise of love is said to override all established principles, such as the **sanctity of life**, the principle of innocence or, more widely, the principle of **justice**. Such principles, it seems, can be set aside depending on the *perceived* demands of the particular situation. Although the aims of situation ethics are theoretically good, since selfless **agape love** is its driving force, the theory has caused something of a furore in moral circles when its theoretical foundations are examined.

 How useful is Joseph Fletcher's situation ethics as a guide to human behaviour?

Situation ethics of the variety proposed by the American divine **Joseph Fletcher**, although a form of *religious* ethics, is generally regarded with suspicion by supporters of both deontological and traditional religious ethics. This is because of its basic presupposition that morality can be adjusted to meet the demands of particular situations. This in itself is not a new idea, and is not to be confused with the principle that circumstances can alter the morality of acts. For instance, while killing other human beings is wrong as a general principle, killing in war or in self-defence is not necessarily so. The justification here is that the killing is not the killing of the innocent, and is done primarily as a solution to a conflict situation in which the validity of a deontological principle is still recognised. In Fletcher's system, killing could be justified in *any* situation as long as it is perceived as the loving thing to do. Thus a **subjective** principle (what love requires) necessarily becomes equated with an **objective** reality, the greatest moral good.

There is something morally repugnant in the notion that you can decide to act as you see fit if you think the situation warrants it. At worst, this opens the door to allowing you to be a moral judge in your own case. In law, it is said that a person who conducts his or her own defence has a fool for a client! A woman in a prison camp can decide to get herself pregnant if by doing so will lead to reunion with her family. The line of reasoning here is that if more people benefit from an action being done, or not being done, than would otherwise be the case, then it follows that the act is justified. This is what Fletcher means by 'justice is love distributed'.

A serious problem lies in the assertion and claim that 'what love requires' should be that which benefits others. This makes situation ethics a covert form of utilitarianism (the parallels are numerous), and makes it run counter to the common-sense intuition, natural law principle and religious tradition that evil can never be justified in the pursuance of good. What if I decide that the loving thing to do is rob a bank, and even kill in the process, because of the benefits it might bring to my family, friends and associates? Because Fletcher's system has no way of *controlling* what love requires, it is open to this kind of abuse. The assumption that love has an inner cognitive 'sense of direction' is simply false. The obvious reply that the 'true' exercise of love will always avoid the morally absurd is simply to beg the question.

131

One of its greatest weaknesses, therefore, seems to be its readiness to abandon any form of moral principle 'if the situation requires.' It assumes that the **'divine command theory'** that lies at the heart of Christian ethics, and forms the background to Fletcher's system, can be put in opposition to the **'love of neighbour principle'**, on the grounds that 'love permits everything'. Therefore, Fletcher's declared aim to find a *middle* route between traditional **deontological** ethical rules on the one hand and a **nihilistic** ethics of *no rules* on the other is highly questionable.

Situation ethics takes love (**agape**) as the 'fixed law' element, and benefit of others as the objective guiding principle for how love is to be expressed. The more people to whom love is distributed (Fletcher's measuring stick for justice), the greater is the love. Indeed, this looks very like a prescriptive (directive) element in the system, that we *should* do that which will benefit the most people involved. For this reason, situation ethics is not as freewheeling and **subjective** as it might appear, thus exposing its utilitarian character.

To emphasise its *religious* character, Fletcher looks for support for his theory in the example of **Jesus**. He claims that Jesus disregarded rules in order to 'put people first'. Indeed, He appeared to do this on a few occasions, when He set aside certain 'rules' because they badly served the interests of people caught in some situations. However, the rules in question were to do with such things as Sabbath observance, and were more like religious conventions rather than moral laws. Jesus taught that where a Sabbath rule prevented giving help to someone, even an animal, in distress, common sense would say relieve the distress. At no time did Jesus set aside a significant **moral law**, such as those contained in the **Decalogue**, in order to help someone.

Rather, it was one of the presuppositions of Jesus' love of neighbour principle that such love is *dependent* on fidelity to God's law. Thus the 'greatest love' is an act of total **altruism**, laying down *one's own* life for others. In Fletcher's scheme, the greatest love could be laying down *someone else's* life, as in the example of the crying baby among the hiding fugitives. The appeal to Jesus therefore doesn't work, and the attempt to reconcile situation ethics with traditional Christian ethics fails at crucial points.

Fletcher's attempt to break away from rule-centred ethics brought early support from liberal thinkers such as **Bishop Robinson**, who hailed it as an ethic for 'man come of age'. By this, he meant that its reliance on personal judgement was more mature, and made it more appealing, than the more obedience-centred nature of traditional morality. Robinson later retracted his support when he saw that ignoring moral rules could lead to moral chaos. Besides, rules are not just guidelines to behaviour, but enshrine fundamental principles of *moral wisdom* that can only be ignored at the expense of doing *harm* to others.

In conclusion, Fletcher's situation ethics is seriously flawed because, in principle, it allows us to ignore the traditional rules of moral wisdom. Fletcher may have naively supposed that the world had enough love to guarantee a *moral* application of his ethical proposal. This supposition is sadly unjustified, taking into account both the fallen nature (natural egoism) of human beings, and the facts of experience. The only saving grace of a system that permits an individual to decide 'what love requires' is that some people will get it right. But in the absence of any cognitive guidelines to help people to know what love can and cannot permit, his theory can only be what many think it is, a recipe for moral confusion.

Related questions:

1 How justified is the claim that situation ethics is a recipe for moral chaos?

2 How far can situation ethics be considered an ethic 'for man come of age'?

3 Assess the strengths and weaknesses of situation ethics.

Natural Law Theory

Natural law is defined as the law of 'nature'. In the **physical** realm there is no problem about speaking of natural law. The aim of science is to discover and identify what the laws of nature are. But in the **moral** realm the situation is more complicated. Many see the idea of a moral law of nature as something of an invalid derivation from the physical laws of nature. For instance, in Catholic morality, the natural law governing sexuality follows from the physical realities of sexual reproduction. From the reality of the physical *functions* of the sexual organs, it is argued that the correct use of sex must allow for reproduction.

The natural law governing life and property follows from a common-sense understanding about the *purpose* and *aims* of living in the world. Human beings have a natural right to *life* to enable them to achieve their natural destiny, and a natural right to *property* to enable them to live with dignity and independence. While such an understanding of natural law is widely acceptable, many other of its presuppositions are open to question. Is there really a law of nature that is applicable at the moral level? Can the physical be a basis for the moral? The question 'Is there really a *moral* law based on nature?' sums up the challenge facing this theory.

Q | Assess the strengths and weakness of natural law as a guide to ethical decision-making.

Natural law theory derives from **Aristotle**, who taught that the good life was that which led to happiness and fulfilment. The latter comes from respecting the nature of things, and we can tell the nature of something by looking at its function, purpose, final cause or '***telos***'. In the case of human beings, we can tell from reason that our moral function is to live in harmony with ourselves and others. We do this by respecting the rights of others to those things that are also important to ourselves: life, property, sexuality, education, freedom and so on. So far, there is little to separate the idea of natural law from the sensible use of natural reason in moral matters.

Later, the question of mankind's ultimate happiness became a special focus of attention under the influence of religious faith. Ultimate happiness was not attainable in this life, so the good life was that which was directed to ultimate happiness in the hereafter. Nevertheless, the moral life that led to personal fulfilment here and now would at once guarantee our eternal fulfilment. This was the message of **St Paul** who, although writing from a faith perspective, insisted that ethical behaviour had a rational foundation. For St Paul, the good life was that which conformed to the will of God, but this could be known from common sense, because the law of God was, as St Paul said, 'written on the heart' and could be seen from 'the things God had made'. This meant that conscience ('the heart') provided a basic inner moral sense of right and wrong even for those ignorant of faith.

Building on St Paul's inner moral sense, and Aristotle's ideas about the purposes of nature, **St Thomas Aquinas** gave the natural law theory its classic formulation. Right and wrong were brought into sharper focus in the Bible, but it could be shown that they had a rational foundation based on human nature. Thus reason and revelation point in the same moral direction. We can see from reason that truth, justice and goodness are basic values, and that good should always be preferable to evil. Equally, respect for others, for human life, for the rights and property of others, for the right of everyone to live in a peaceful society, the right to marriage and a family – all are visible through the window of reason.

Aquinas distinguished between the primary and secondary laws of nature. How the latter can be derived from the former could be exemplified in the case of sex. If the natural function of sex is to lead to procreation, the moral use of sex must not interfere with this function. Since the use of contraceptives would be one way of doing this, their use would be **intrinsically** wrong. Critics of this application of natural law claim that it is too selective. After all, a sexual relationship has more than one function (love, pleasure and companionship), and the behaviour of persons cannot be decided by physical facts.

This suggests the relevance of the 'is–ought' objection initiated by **David Hume**, and later called the 'naturalistic fallacy' by **G. E. Moore**. This says that you cannot go from a fact to a value, from what is the case to what ought to be the case. Thus, to say that the purpose of nature is this or that (fact) cannot justify a moral conclusion (ought). However, this can be seen to be too fine a point. In our moral experience we find it normal to go from an 'is' to an 'ought'. In religious ethics, what is God's will ought to be obeyed. In **social ethics**, if something is unjust because it is discriminatory (say, racism) it ought to be outlawed and forbidden. In **personal ethics**, if something is against your basic principles, you ought not to do it.

At a more fundamental level, if the natural function of a person is to live a rational life, and to live in security with others, it would be wrong gratuitously to kill another person, or even oneself. Special situations such as self-defence and war would create exceptions arising from conflicts of interest, where more than one life is at stake. But in spite of this, certain principles such as respect for life would not lose their intrinsic validity.

An extra dimension to Aquinas' theory was his identification of natural law with divine law. What was right or wrong in regard to nature and its laws was also right or wrong in the eyes of God, the author of nature. Aquinas saw human destiny in terms of eternal happiness with God in the hereafter. But this is gained in the first instance through adherence to the law of nature, which forms a seamless robe with the divine law revealed in the Bible. For Aquinas, the Bible reveals two moral truths, our ultimate destiny as union with God in heaven, and the sort of behaviour that can enable us to achieve that destiny. The latter is codified in the Ten Commandments. But a basic knowledge of divine law can also be attained through reason. Hence divine law is the same as the law of reason, which follows from our nature.

The strength of Aquinas' scheme is its relative simplicity. Natural law ethics, if true, enable anyone in principle to see what is right and what is wrong. It claims to be able to base morality on objective criteria, which makes it open to inspection by all reasonable people. But the fact is that not all reasonable people agree with the reasoning behind the theory. The alleged weaknesses of natural law theory are threefold.

One is that it is aligned too closely to a religious metaphysic (view of reality). If mankind has no religious destiny, it could be argued that the idea of following a natural law ethic ultimately makes no sense. (Kant, of course, argued the other way around. The natural ethic facing us all shows that we have a religious destiny.)

Secondly, related to this is the disputed notion of happiness. From a secular viewpoint, happiness is only for the here and now. If natural law cannot guarantee present happiness, it cannot command support from those who think that ethics should lead to happiness. However, **Aristotle** had already suggested that the best road to happiness was following what moral reason dictated. Anyone who acts against reason (for Aquinas, nature) will not be happy. This was a point raised by **Joseph Butler**, whose criterion of good behaviour was the extent to which it led to happiness and fulfilment. The problem is, though, that not everybody agrees about what constitutes 'acting in accord with nature or reason', and not everyone agrees that happiness and fulfilment are found in this way. Many would argue that moral satisfaction comes from acting from personal conviction, not in conformity to some objective law.

Thirdly, the claim that there is some fixed law of nature, or indeed some fixed nature of things that can be rationally detected, is open to question in an age that accepts homosexuality, genetic engineering and the whole field of invasive medicine. Nature is seen today not as something fixed and monolithic, but as something flexible, that can be accommodated to the good of mankind. If this is so, then the notion of a 'natural law' is difficult to sustain.

Against this, it could be argued that there is significance in the fact that we do have some clear sense of how nature works, and are able to tell when it is defective or malfunctioning. This allows for medical intervention, not to interfere with nature, but to allow it to achieve its natural purpose. Where this line is crossed, and medicine is not seen as assisting nature (in cloning, for instance), or where our treatment of nature (the environment) is destructive, there is a recognised unease that we are 'playing God' (not recognising any law) or ignoring God (nature). From this, it could be argued that nature is not such a bad guide in moral matters.

On the other hand, it can be argued that what is called 'natural law' is really only an aspect of human reason. Yet, even if this is true it can still be argued that reason is dependent on some fundamental facts about the nature of ourselves and the world. After all, in **Kantian ethics** reasoning is used to identify fundamental aspects of our nature as persons, endowed with understanding and free will. From this, Kant drew conclusions about the universality of certain ethical principles, which are recognised today in terms of 'natural' human rights.

Aquinas, on his part, has been identified as the first Western philosopher to have forged the link between ethics and law, and between natural law, divine law and human law. His use of reason in the application of natural law principles is recognised as possibly the principal foundation on which international law rests. Notions such as 'human decency', 'human rights' or 'natural rights', 'human dignity', 'natural justice' and the importance of 'human standards' of right and wrong echo natural law principles.

The recognised purpose of law to uphold such standards, and to root out what degrades and dehumanises, to recognise what constitutes the corrupt, the base and the perverse, what amounts to fraud, exploitation and corruption (especially of the young, the vulnerable and the defenceless), and what was declared at Nuremberg to be 'crimes against humanity' – all these concepts can be said to owe much to natural law reasoning. But whether the idea of a 'natural law' can really provide a basis for ethical decision-making without the support of a religious metaphysic is not so easy to answer.

Related questions:

1 Evaluate the view that natural law ethics are an obstacle to medical progress.

2 To what extent is natural law theory dependent on a religious outlook?

3 Compare and contrast natural law and Kantian ethics.

Virtue Ethics

Virtue ethics is assumed to represent a different approach to ethical behaviour compared to established systems such as utilitarianism, natural law theory and Kantianism. The reality is that virtue ethics in many ways achieves the same results, and that other systems also make room for virtue. **John Stuart Mill** in particular saw the virtuous character as an important utilitarian resource benefiting the wider society. **William James** saw saintliness, an essentially virtue-centred character quality, as a great asset to others. The virtuous person is also likely to have all the qualities that **St Thomas Aquinas** or **Immanuel Kant** would have approved of.

What is especially different about virtue ethics is its *communal* character. Virtue is more a product of the group than of the individual alone. Those whose lives are oriented towards the great virtues – such as kindness, love of neighbour, respect for others and compassion for the less well-off – are likely to be products of some group training, or institution, where such virtues are valued and imitated. This could be a church, a school, an organisation or indeed a family. How far virtue ethics is dependent on a religious context for its inspiration is a separate but interesting question.

 How far is virtue ethics a satisfactory guide to moral behaviour?

'Virtue' comes from the Latin *virtus*, meaning strength, and is also related to the Greek word for 'excellence'. In traditional usage, 'virtue' came to stand for 'goodness', as when the Bible poetically describes the 'virtuous man' as being 'like a tree planted near running water whose leaves never fade'. **Aristotle** says that the well-being of mankind, which is happiness, is achieved by living virtuously. In saying this, Aristotle makes a direct link between happiness and goodness. In a similar way, **John Stuart Mill** argued for the utilitarian (happiness-creating) value of a good character, consisting of virtues such as benevolence, kindness, honesty and compassion. This was a way of saying that the virtuous life was one of the surest ways to create moral and social **utility**, a claim also made by **William James** in his approval of saintliness.

The focal point of the virtuous life is the development of a virtuous character orientated to goodness. Virtue ethics may therefore be distinguished from **deontological ethics**, where the stress is on rational sense of duty, and **utilitarian ethics**, where the stress is on bringing about happiness. At the same time it would be a mistake to overlook the place for the virtuous character that these systems allow for, and indeed help to create.

A virtuous person is one who has developed the different virtues or character qualities that people generally admire. For **Plato** there were four cardinal virtues, prudence, justice, fortitude and temperance. Although **Aristotle** preferred to see virtue as something involving the practice of moderation between extremes, the aim or '*telos*' of doing the good (virtue) was the making of a virtuous *person*. Aristotle distinguished between *moral* virtues such as courage and *intellectual* virtues such as knowledge. Christianity added to all these the three theological virtues – faith, hope and charity (**agape**) – to provide what it saw as the ideal framework within which all the virtues should be pursued.

G. E. M. Anscombe, stressing the importance of the moral character, distinguished between good actions and good persons. Good persons do good deeds, but good deeds do not necessarily make good persons. A similar idea is expressed by **Philippa Foot**, who held that a person's fundamental values or 'desires' were the practical root of good actions, thus stressing the way in which the *desire* for goodness comes before doing good deeds. This approach can be seen as much less rationalistic than that associated with the various ethical theories. Here, the character is trained to be good, and the rest follows. The great mystic **Meister Eckhart** made this point when he said 'if your being is just your works will be'. The virtuous character is generally driven by such things as personal integrity, a sense of justice, sensitivity to others and a desire to help the less well off.

The virtues, especially the cardinal virtues, are variously described as dispositions, inclinations or even instincts, which lead us to act rightly towards others and ourselves. **Prudence** is the virtue of being shrewd in matters of moral judgement. **Justice** is the virtue of being able to treat others fairly and with consideration. **Fortitude** is the virtue of having the courage, or strength, to keep doing what prudence demands. **Temperance** is the virtue of being able to do all things in moderation. It is fair to say that the different virtues overlap and interlink, and together lead to the development of the 'virtuous person'.

It was a basic assumption in medieval thought that acquisition of the virtues required a certain training (from which we get the term 'ascetic'). The idea of being trained in character formation has come to the fore in recent years in the wake of a perceived over-concern with the introspection and rationalising associated with the ethical theories. For **Immanuel Kant**, it was a matter of acting on the moral law. For **Jeremy Bentham** and **John Stuart Mill** it was a matter of making the world a better place. Forgotten in this maelstrom of theory was the practical task of how to make moral behaviour happen in real life. Perhaps **David Hume's** idea that morality was a matter of 'sympathy' with others and **G. E. Moore's** high estimate of friendship suggest the closest affinity to a virtue approach.

Today, there is new interest in the cultivation of good personal qualities such as sympathy with others, sincere friendship, honest dealing, respect for human dignity and so on. But the idea is not so new, considering the moral ideals of the New Testament, or Mill's admission that good moral character was the best way to achieve the utilitarian ideal of a better world for all.

In this way, moral education is brought about not by philosophical discussion and analysis, but through exposure to the inspiring qualities that we can see in others. This is seen as a 'narrative', or 'story', approach, typically found in religious traditions, but also found in all moral brotherhoods, whether in science, learning, art, sport or politics. The key to this ethical approach is to identify with the feelings and moral ideals of the group, something given little mention in other more theoretical approaches, and for which, apparently, there is a new need.

Alasdair McIntyre laments the way in which a moral vacuum has emerged on the heel of decades of moral theorising. Instead of moral virtues we have the 'practical' virtues, exemplified in the world of industry, finance and entertainment, all geared to the attainment of worldly prestige, success and pleasure. Overarching everything, in a world of superficiality and short-term aims, is the value of wealth, health, freedom, excitement and convenience – but not virtue in the old sense of character-building, based on respect for the moral ideals of equality and justice.

McIntyre sees the essence of virtue in doing things for their own sake rather than for ulterior gain, coupled with a concern for 'achievement' and 'excellence' as an end in itself. Stressing the importance of communal belonging and a regard for old traditions and the virtues that typified them, McIntyre believes that joining with others for common aims will combat the tendency for personal gain, and encourage those virtues that stress common ideals and values. This can be seen in the *esprit de corps* (group spirit) of army regiments, religious orders and mountaineering teams.

One problem, though, is how to distinguish between traditions, or groups, whose 'virtues' respect the rights and dignity of others, and those that trample on them (criminal fraternities, drug-pushing organisations or paedophile rings). Yet it could be argued that such groups simply pervert to their own ends a fraternal dynamism that should encourage what is noble, virtuous and good.

In this respect, virtue ethics is subject to moral judgement about what is noble and good. One form of protection that helps to ensure this comes from doing not what one personally thinks is right, but what the community to which one belongs believes is right. In the end, the real test is how far such a community is the object of admiration or contempt. Virtue ethics is therefore part of a *community* dynamic in which the example of the best is the model for all, as romantically portrayed in the chivalrous tradition of King Arthur's Camelot. All of the great moral communities are driven and inspired by some form of virtue ethics, where ideals and attitudes drawn from older traditions serve commonly acknowledged moral aims and values.

For this reason, virtue ethics finds a natural context in religious institutions, where morality is something linked to the imitation of those who have set an example in being virtuous people. The drawback of virtue ethics may be the moral difficulty of developing the habits of character that it represents, because of lack of the required communal structures. Its strength is in its value as a source of fulfilment for the individual and the group and – as both Mill and James noted – in the asset that the virtuous person is to society.

Related questions: _____

1 To what extent is virtue ethics consistent, or otherwise, with utilitarianism?

2 How convincing is the claim that virtue ethics is almost impossible for a single individual?

3 To what extent does virtue ethics overlap with other ethical theories?

8 Medical Ethics

In recent years, medical ethics has become one the most lively, if not contentious, areas of ethical debate. Many of the ethical concerns in modern medicine arise from the dramatic advances in medical science and technology. But scientific or medical advances are not necessarily moral advances. This has become apparent to many in relation to the new possibilities now offered in the treatment of infertility and the related area of embryology. The medical terminology to describe these issues has become familiar: embryo research, genetic engineering, gene therapy, cloning, pre-gender embryo diagnosis, *in vitro* fertilisation, surrogate motherhood and abortion.

At the heart of these issues is the question 'Can scientific medicine be allowed to go unchecked to investigate or create the possible?' To some extent, this question has already been answered at both the moral and legal levels. There is widespread agreement that these issues cannot be confined to, or settled by, what science can make possible. There is a universal sense that many practices give rise to *ethical* concerns that some things are simply not right. This in turn has led to a recognition that science needs to be restrained by means of *legislation* that will set down the scope and limits of what it is decent to do. In this respect, the law becomes a moral guide, or conscience, with the function of transcending cultural or credal differences to set down appropriate legal controls between what *can* be done and what *should* be done.

But despite the importance of controlling legislation in many areas of medicine, there is a sense that the law cannot settle all issues, and that there is still a gap between what is legal and what is moral. In matters of human life and death, there is the belief that what the law permits is not necessarily a guide to what is morally right and wrong. Many of the more serious concerns revolve around the area of embryology, which is now becoming one of the most controversial areas of medical ethics, especially since the advent of the possibilty of cloning.

Yet, despite their perceived inadequacies, legal guidelines have become accepted as the best that is possible in a pluralist society, in which limits to what is permissible are seen to be necessary to serve the common good. A sense that ethical questions are not just a matter for the individual conscience lies at the centre of public debate about many of the issues in medicine. The modern legislation that governs many areas of medical research and practice is designed to make sure that factors such as commercial interest, private gain, personal convenience or sometimes the 'interests of science' do not determine what is right or wrong.

Some principles are still regarded as crucial to what is 'decent', 'right', 'just' or 'in accordance with human dignity'. The expression 'playing God' suggests that humans must not act out of self-interest, but submit at least to the dominion of reason and justice in the way in which they act. At the same time, the law is not just a restraining force in regard to medical practice. It can also be seen as a liberalising force, making possible the just use of medical technology for the benefit of all.

In this process, deontological principles about respect for life combine and interact with utilitarian considerations about what can benefit the majority in the long run. Not surprisingly, Western legislators rarely ignore the accepted values of a society influenced by religious traditions. While religion is often seen as the enemy of progressive thinking, many theologians insist that what conforms to an overall respect for life as upheld by religion is central to pursuing utilitarian benefits to mankind, both now and in the future.

One of the concerns in medical science is the problem of 'interfering with nature'. This is an understandable concern in the light of the problems associated with BSE, genetically modified foods, global warming and environmental pollution. But interfering with nature is not necessarily going against nature. It may simply be *assisting* nature to achieve its ideal aim, namely to function to advantage. The latter has been the traditional task of scientific medicine. For this reason, many theologians have made the parallel distinction between playing God and responsibly assisting God. This distinction has grown out of the recognition that science and medicine have in their hands the power either to do harm or to do good. It is the aim of ethics, and in particular medical ethics, to ensure that the latter is done.

Abortion

Abortion is one of the more controversial issues in medical ethics. The practice can be carried out for serious or trivial reasons, and many see its morality as dependent on the seriousness of the reasons for its request. This was the moral assumption underlying the Abortion Act of 1967, which attempted to permit abortion for genuine reasons of health and welfare. One effect of the Act was to intensify debate about whether the law made abortion too easy or too difficult to obtain. Extreme liberals wanted 'abortion on demand', while at the other extreme abortion was condemned as an unqualified evil. The law tried to find a middle road, showing some respect for the sanctity of life on the one hand, and recognising the social need for safe and risk-free abortion on the other. The big question for many is whether the law is a sufficient guide to the moral complexities of an issue that touches on some of the essential values of humanity.

Assess the view that abortion is always wrong.

The view that abortion is always wrong is associated particularly with the **absolutist** position of the Catholic Church, which condemns abortion as intrinsically evil. This is based on the claim that it amounts to murder of the innocent (the word 'innocent' is from the Latin for 'harmless'). This position has been repeatedly stated by successive popes, and owes much to its respect for human life in all its stages, from beginning to end, not only for *moral* reasons based on natural law, but for *religious* reasons related especially to the Incarnation..

This rigorous position is based on the principle that one cannot deliberately kill a human being except in circumstances in which a human being loses his or her claim to innocence, such as in war, through crime or in self-defence. The common good in protecting innocent life was, ironically, the traditional reason for capital punishment. The right to protect one's own life against an unjust aggressor was the justification for killing in self-defence. The duty to defend one's country justified killing in war.

But in the case of abortion no such justification could be found, because the foetal life does not lose its innocence. Yet the Catholic Church's position has been challenged by some of its own theologians who argue that it is too sweeping. They question, for instance, whether the moral prohibition against abortion should be applied equally across all stages of foetal development, from the moment of fertilisation to the later stages of pregnancy. A key claim is that the **foetus** is a full human being with all the rights that follow. This 'high view' of the foetus is seen as the essential moral objection to both abortion and embryo research (the embryo becomes a foetus after eight weeks of pregnancy). But modern theologians are beginning to question the grounds for such a view. In the light of other factors, such as the health prospects of the embryo or foetus, or the medical welfare of the mother, there is a recognition that termination could theoretically be justified in such cases.

Since the seventeenth century, the Church has taught that a human being exists from the moment of conception. One problem with this position is that conception is not a single moment, but a process that involves several stages, some of which take place within the first 14 days. Within this period, a single identity is not yet established, and so the Human Fertilisation and Embryology Authority (the UK government watchdog) legally permits research on embryos up to the 14th day. This shows how modern medicine has influenced the law in recognising that time is a relevant factor in the debate about when a foetus has acquired the status of a human being.

The Catholic Church takes an 'essentialist' (that is, fixed) position, arguing that all the potency that later results in the unique identity of a human person is already present at the earliest moment of the process of fertilisation. Thus abortion is intrinsically wrong in all circumstances, even if the pregnancy has been caused by rape. Alternative views have favoured a more 'existentialist', or flexible, position. In this view, the foetus is seen to undergo a living process from a more primitive to a more developed stage of existence. Under the influence of **St Thomas Aquinas**, some have identified the moment of 'quickening' as a decisive point in foetal development. This occurs some 40 days after conception, and before this point the foetus is not yet thought to possess a human soul. This key moment is also significant for the formation of the brain, and the first appearance of the 'human icon', when the foetus begins to look like a human being. In the age of the electronic scan this may be a decisive moment, but many object that it ignores more fundamental aspects of the foetus' right to live.

143

Expanding on this issue, **Jurgen Moltmann** has distinguished between the 'vitality' and the 'humanity' of the foetus, while **Bernard Häring** uses the distinction between the 'biological' stage and the 'personal' stage of life. In each case there is a recognition that 'life' does not necessarily mean 'human life'. This became a relevant factor in the Warnock Report, which recognised that the early foetus was 'neither a person nor a thing', but for this reason that research was only permissible on embryos less than 14 days old. After this, the foetus was given a significant (but to many, insufficient) level of protection from the law.

Abortion would be illegal unless certain conditions were fulfilled relating to the welfare and future life prospects of the foetus, and the welfare of the mother or her family. From this, it is clear that the law takes a limited utilitarian position, looking at the welfare of all concerned as well as taking into account the dangers inherent in clandestine abortion outside the law. What is significant is an insistence that the foetus cannot be harmed except under certain conditions, a restriction that also owes something to the traditional deontological principle of respect for human life.

The answer to the question so far can be seen to hinge on the status of the foetus. Those who view the foetus as inviolable (untouchable) differ from those who see it as competing for its right to life against other considerations. So far, the emphasis has been on the objective issue of what sort of being the foetus is, and whether it can command an absolute right to life.

The most poignant dilemma possible, although rare, is where the mother's life is at risk. Cases are known where mothers have made the heroic sacrifice of their lives to save the foetus, but many today support the mother's right to protect her own life. This is usually reasoned by using a mixture of deonto-logical and utilitarian principles to claim that the mother's primary duty is to her own life. A possible case for saving the mother's life might be made through the **act of double effect** principle. This is a principle that allows an action to be done so long as any secondary (evil) effect of the action is not intended, and does not contribute to the achievement of its primary aim. The argument would go like this.

If the removal of the foetus is seen to risk its death (future technology might overcome this), this could be seen as an effect that was foreseen but not intended. The *aim* would be to save the mother's life, not to kill the foetus. This means that the death of the foetus would contribute nothing to saving the mother. Thus, if the survival of the mother is not dependent on the death of the foetus, the good effect would not be achieved at the *expense* of the evil effect. The mother could wish for the survival of the foetus despite the near certainty of its non-survival. In this narrow scenario, it would seem that the mother could be morally justified in saving her life, as long as she did not intend, or benefit from, the death of her foetus. (The author acknowledges that the act of double effect is not normally applied in this case but this argument seems compelling.)

144

In conclusion, abortion is an ethical issue that has attracted much moral and legal debate. The debate has largely centred on the question of how far the embryo–foetus can be accorded an absolute right to life. One view is that its right to life is non-negotiable, and that therefore abortion is intrinsically wrong. This view has been challenged on the grounds that some discrimination is needed with regard to what stage of development has been reached by the foetus. In the earlier stages, it is argued, its moral status can be considered lower than at later stages. This view has the support of some eminent moralists, but is not meant to suggest that abortion is ever other than a regrettable last resort. The extent to which abortion can be chosen as a solution to birth control, or to serve personal convenience, remains especially controversial.

Related questions:

1 'Every pregnant woman has an absolute right to choose to have an abortion'. Discuss.

2 The use of the categorical imperative makes no room for compassionate treatment of women who want abortions. Discuss.

3 Assess the application of either a consequentialist or a deontological approach to the issue of abortion.

Euthanasia

The term 'eu-thanasia' is derived from the Greek, and means 'good-death'. In ethical debate it refers to the intervention of a third party, usually a doctor, directly and deliberately to bring about the death of a patient at the patient's request. This practice is to be strictly distinguished from any other form of intervention where the death of the patient may be desired, but is not intended to be the direct result of a medical action. Thus the administration of pain-killing drugs that may possibly shorten the life of the patient should not be called euthanasia, or even indirect euthanasia. It should also be distinguished from the situation in which a patient requests the ending of treatment. In this case the decision is to let 'nature take its course', so that the patient is 'allowed to die' naturally. In this essay, therefore, the word 'euthanasia' will stand for the deliberate killing of a patient at his or her request, and nothing else. In the light of this definition, it is possible to consider euthanasia as 'assisted suicide'.

Assess the arguments for and against euthanasia.

As the law stands, euthanasia is forbidden in many countries, including the UK. Fears about the impossibility of preventing abuses under a legalised system have made legislators wary of making it approved under law. A patient's wishes may be anticipated, fabricated or misunderstood by third parties. Besides, there is reluctance in many countries, especially those influenced by the Christian tradition, to legalise a practice that has been frowned on in the past, and which is seen to conflict with the traditionally held view of the sanctity of human life.

Despite this, there is increasing pressure today to have euthanasia legalised. The legalisation of euthanasia has been the persistent aim of the Voluntary Euthanasia Society, founded in 1936. At the time of writing, euthanasia has just been legalised under Dutch law, but indications are that no such legislation is being planned in the UK.

Opponents of euthanasia hold that it can never be right, because it is the direct taking of human life. From a secular (non-religious) viewpoint, euthanasia is neither right or wrong in principle, but even from a utilitarian perspective it is not clear whether making it legal would be good or bad for society. Under Kantian ethics, it would be a direct attack on the integrity of an innocent person, whether that person requested it or not. **Immanuel Kant** has argued against any form of suicide on the grounds that it involves the misdirection of the will.

Kant's reasoning is that the will can only correctly be used to perform one's duty. This means that the idea of having a duty to kill myself would be self-contradictory since I would be killing my capacity for moral action. In other words, the will should always be directed away from the self. Kant saw it as being analogous to a 'sentry leaving his post'. However, it is questionable whether euthanasia could never be seen as a duty, or that it could never be reconciled with a good will. A person could conceivably see it as a duty to end his or her life, say, out of love for others, or to save the distress of friends, and to see it as an act of good will to do so. However, this is not to be confused with what Jesus meant by 'giving up one's life for one's friends'. Jesus was talking about risking one's life, not deliberately causing one's death.

Under **natural law** theory, euthanasia is considered wrong because it is the direct taking of an innocent life. Our function is to live and use our lives as a once-given gift, to be preserved to the end. To wilfully shorten that life is to go against the basic instinct of self-preservation. A counter-argument, however, could be that human reason sees nothing abhorrent in a person wanting to end a life that is seen as intolerable. Here, the **sanctity of life** principle gives way to the **quality of life** principle, on the grounds that a life that is no longer tolerable has lost any meaningful sanctity. Besides, it can be argued, the sanctity of life principle is normally about respecting the life of *another*, and is not meant to exclude a person who wants to hasten the end of his or her own life for personal reasons, whose outcome is inevitable anyway.

Under some forms of Christian ethics, euthanasia has been seen as intrinsically evil on the grounds – based on revelation – that we are not the owners of our lives. Our lives are given on trust by God, and we are under an obligation to

God to live our lives morally to the end. In Catholic theology, natural law reasoning has been used to argue that euthanasia is wrong because it implies a rejection of the gift of life and, by extension, an offence against the divine Creator of life. Repeated condemnations of euthanasia – from the Council of Arles in AD 314 to the recent Vatican Declaration on Euthanasia in 1980 – have underlined the special dignity of the human person 'made in God's image'. The dignity of the human person is also a consequence of the immortality of the soul, in the light of which any temporal action of doubtful morality must be viewed *sub specie aeternitatis* (in the perspective of eternity).

Some liberal Christian moralists, such as **Anthony Dyson**, question whether euthanasia would necessarily undermine the sanctity of life. He argues that, all things being equal, one should respect such principles, but that conditions of extreme suffering can significantly alter their meaning. A life that is inevitably ending, and with its joy and meaning for an individual lost, could arguably have lost its dignity, and hence its moral sanctity.

Besides, if the sanctity or dignity of human life is dependent on the immortality of the soul created by God, it cannot then be dependent on the continuation of bodily life. The compassion shown by Jesus in trying to alleviate suffering can give a big impetus to this view. Jesus made it clear enough that suffering is something that one is entitled to avoid if possible, even though those are indeed 'blessed' whose suffering is unavoidable. **Karl Barth's** argument that the value of human life to its natural end must be maintained because its value is 'God's secret' is laudable, but cannot be an argument for the continuation of human suffering.

Ironically, the immortality of the soul offers the possibility of putting euthanasia into a different perspective. The words of Jesus – 'Fear not him who kills the body but him who kills the soul' – suggest that the sanctity of life relates more to the spiritual dimension of life than to its physical reality. From this perspective, it seems that euthanasia would not necessarily be incompatible with a genuine religious sense of the value of one's life before God. This religious sense implies the love of God, and is often revealed in the desire to 'be with God', a desire frequently expressed by religious people. This is a legitimate desire, and one that is not necessarily inconsistent with wanting euthanasia. Such liberal thinking need not imply that euthanasia should in any way be the norm or that it should be encouraged, but – seen in the wider perspective of faith – the wished-for death of the body can be given a certain Christian legitimacy.

From the perspective of secular humanism, there are no restraints on the wish to have euthanasia if the circumstances demand it. Many feel that there are strong utilitarian reasons to justify it. One is the right to have personal relief from the pain of a long drawn-out death. A second reason takes into account the suffering of relatives, and the possible benefits to them of a patient's early death. A third reason counts the costs to society of keeping alive a 'useless' citizen, while more 'deserving' cases lose out on medical resources. A fourth reason is that euthanasia is the mark of a 'civilised' and 'liberal' democracy, in which individuals are allowed to have their choices respected, happiness is promoted and pain is eliminated. However, these reasons are not as compelling as they might appear. Utilitarian counter-arguments can be made against euthanasia, such as the view that the practice would only encourage a 'culture of death' and the devaluation of life.

Rule utilitarians tend to be influenced by traditional attitudes, in which a premium is put on the preservation of life. They would only reluctantly be converted to the 'happiness now' cult, because it might be seen as leading to the undervaluing of human life in the long run. Those who would make life easily disposable now might be on the receiving end later. This might put a different complexion on how a 'civilised' society might be judged in the future. Once the principle is granted that human life is disposable, it is argued, this might be the 'thin end of the wedge', the creation of a **slippery slope**' or a 'domino effect', where eventually only the 'survival of the fittest' is accepted.

From a religious perspective, any form of 'playing God' by taking life away is bound to raise fears and anxieties. This can explain why religious people are in principle reluctant to consider euthanasia, and partly why the **hospice movement**, devoted to the cheerful care of the terminally ill, has been seen as a compassionate alternative to euthanasia.

One aspect that cannot be left out of the euthanasia debate is the practical question of its execution. The question about whether *doctors* can appropriately be involved arises from whether euthanasia is a medical or anti-medical issue. In this respect, euthanasia is different from solitary suicide. Medicine has traditionally been concerned with the saving of life, a greater priority even than the alleviation of pain. Many doctors see their possible involvement in euthanasia as repugnant and distasteful, the opposite of what the medical profession stands for. Yet there is increasing pressure on doctors to accept that euthanasia is a 'medical' procedure, however oxymoronic. This involves the difficulty of squaring two principles contained in the **Hippocratic Oath**, the principle 'not to do harm' and the principle to 'help' the patient. If the patient's idea of help is to be given euthanasia, the doctor faces a dilemma, for whatever he does he can be accused of 'breaking' the Oath.

In conclusion, there are those who see euthanasia as a right that people should have in circumstances in which terminal illness causes extreme unhappiness, leaving the sufferer with no real quality of life. They argue that everyone should be given the right to end such a life, a right that is self-evident since our lives belong to us. Others oppose this, and argue from rational principles that euthanasia is a form of suicide that makes it incompatible with the proper use of free will. Others see euthanasia as a violation of the sanctity of life and a denial of the divine command not to kill.

Yet we have seen that a liberal religious view is possible that attempts to reconcile euthanasia with a genuine religious desire to 'be with God'. This is seen by some as providing the basis for a positive view of euthanasia that takes religious principles into account. On the other hand, the overwhelming weight of religious

148

opinion is opposed to euthanasia. The general consensus is that euthanasia is wrong because it is interfering with the God-given gift of human life. Finally, the idea of someone having to carry out the 'death sentence' on a fellow human being is somehow distasteful. The idea that doctors may be in the front line of its administration is a disturbing aspect of a subject that many see as the antithesis of medical care, which is about healing, not taking away, human life.

Related questions:

1 To what extent is utilitarianism a useful guide for making decisions about euthanasia?

2 'Everyone has a natural right to have euthanasia.' Discuss.

3 How far should medical staff who care for the terminally ill allow their own views to influence their involvement?

Embryology

The origins of fertility treatment go back to the so-called 'test-tube babies', when it became possible to bring about the fertilisation of an embryo *in vitro* (in glass). The aim was then for the embryo to be implanted into a woman's womb to develop into a child. The practice became more complicated with the creation of 'spare embryos', which gave rise to the problem of whose embryos they were, whether they were of any significance and what should be done with them. This led to the idea of deliberately creating embryos, not for implantation but for research, which in turn led to the idea that embryos could be manipulated and used to provide cells and tissue for the treatment of different ailments.

This proved to be a short step from the possibility of creating embryos to order to produce 'designer babies'. It is also a possible short step to the advent of **cloning**, producing a genetic copy of an existing or dead person. In view of the fact that the human embryo represents the 'genesis' or beginning of human life, a creation that echoes the past of every human being and contains the origins of every human being's future life history, it is not surprising that this area of **bioethics** should attract such attention, or cause such concern.

 What ethical principles should govern bioethical issues such as *in vitro* fertilisation, embryo research, embryo selection, stem-cell research, cloning and surrogacy?

Technical advances in modern medicine have made possible the creation of human **embryos** by the artificial method known as *in vitro* (glass) **fertilisation,**

a procedure that takes place in a test tube or Petri dish. The method makes it possible to remove the process of fertilisation from its natural setting in a personal sexual relationship. By contrast, the human embryo is created by a technically impersonal method in which the contributors of the sperm and ovum are not necessarily related in any way. Thus the sperm and ovum may not be related biologically to, say, a couple in an established relationship of any kind, and the resulting embryo may not even be destined for birth. It may instead be destined for use as an object of research, or be scanned for suitability as part of a search for a more desirable embryo. A further twist is added if it is decided to use the embryo for implantation and birth. The receiving womb may not be that of someone biologically related to it, but may belong to strangers who will function as **surrogate** parents to a child of unknown background. Hence the question of 'embryo creation' and the medical use of 'spare' embryos have become major ethical issues. The debate concerns the immediate fate of embryos created in this way, and the fate of those who will later be born by such artificial methods.

The Catholic Church believes that the sanctity of life demands that an embryo should only be produced by the biological parents, within a married relationship. This only allows the creation of embryos by married parents, and forbids the creation of embryos with a view to their procreational use within other possible relationships. Here, the Catholic Church appeals to the supposed natural law principle that children should be a natural product of a loving relationship. It also appeals to the biblical view that the normal method of procreation is through a sexual relationship in marriage. The command 'thou shalt not commit adultery' was seen as the mainstay of family solidarity, and of a stable society.

However, critics point to the suffering caused by infertility, and also to the way in which the Bible did not condemn Abraham for his adultery in order to have a child. Today, they insist that there is technology to overcome infertility and improve the genetic gene pool, and that it should be used. They would not accept that embryos should be restricted to those who are married, and that a number of permutations are legitimate for the production of children, whether surrogate motherhood or donor sperm banks made available to all for the creation of embryos – for research, procreation or cloning.

The counter-argument to this completely liberal view appeals to the nature and status of the human embryo itself. The extreme conservative view held by the Catholic Church is that the embryo is a human person from the 'first moment of conception'. This gives it an entitlement to full human rights, and to be treated in accordance with the principle of the sanctity of life. In this view, an embryo can never be treated as a means to an end, and interference with it must only be for the good of the embryo itself. But there are many critics of this position, who see it as unwarranted by genetic findings.

The Catholic theologian **Bernard Häring**, backed up by non-Catholic theologians such as **John Habgood**, has argued that the status of the embryo is not so clear-cut, so that strict rules about its treatment are difficult to formulate. Häring believes that the embryo has an ambiguous status, and can hardly be regarded as a person at least until the stage of individuation, known as the 'primitive streak', has been reached. This is the point before which the embryo can still split into twins or more. A similar view was held by **St Thomas Aquinas**, who adopted **Aristotle's** distinction between vegetable, animal and human stages of life. The 'human' stage was not considered to be reached until a development called 'ensoulment', 'forming', 'animation' or 'quickening' took place, something that usually did not happen before the 40th day after conception. Habgood sees confirmation of this in the traditional attitude to **miscarriage**, which is accepted as a natural event, and is not marked by a funeral, burial or mourning. By contrast, these ceremonies and rituals normally follow the death of a child.

John Habgood concedes that there may be good utilitarian reasons for doing such research for the benefits of future generations provided certain guidelines are respected. One such guideline is not to deliberately create an embryo specifically for the purposes of research. This would devalue the embryo to the status of an object. For this reason he counsels the need for utilitarian considerations to be combined on the one hand with **Christian** principles which uphold the sanctity of life, and, on the other, with **Kantian** principles that forbid the reduction of the human to a mere *commodity*, treating it as a means rather than an end. This danger is perceived to exist with the growing practice of *pre-implantation genetic diagnosis* (PGD). This is a practice integral to the search for a certain type of ('designer') embryo, one genetically endowed with, say, the 'right' gender, eye-colour, height, and so on.

Another procedure causing ethical concern is so-called **stem-cell** research and development. Stem cells have the ability to divide for indefinite periods in culture and to give rise to specialised cells. Hence new cells can be grown from stem cells to replace damaged ones and bring medical relief. They may be taken from an adult, but with some difficulty. Alternatively, they may be grown in an embryo, then extracted, or 'harvested', for medical purposes. Ethical concerns have been heightened by the growing practice of creating embryos specifically for the purpose of providing stem cells to be harvested. Once again, the ethical issue is whether a human embryo can be 'used' in this way or, as many see it, deliberately created to provide 'spare parts' for the use of others, thus degrading it by treating it as a means to an end.

The agreed legal view, arrived at by the Human Fertilisation and Embryology Authority in 1990, is that embryos are not considered to be fully human. This would permit respectful research for the purposes of, say, gene therapy for the sake of the common good. In 1994, the Warnock Committee accepted embryo research in principle, but limited such research to the first 14 days of the embryo's life. However, recognising that the human embryo is 'neither a person nor a thing' – thus deserving some measure of moral respect – this does not permit the deliberate creation of embryos for the purposes of research. At the time of writing, however, HFEA has come under strong criticism for permitting the **screening** of embryos in the hope of finding one genetically compatible with a living sibling. This has caused a storm of protest because it sanctions the destruction of embryos, and for seemingly opening the gates to the quest for so-called 'designer babies'. The ethical seriousness of the practice is reflected in a statement by the eminent geneticist **Professor Robert Winston**, who has condemned the practice, saying that it 'produces a frisson that we are on the road to a very dark journey'.

Another possible development that is beginning to cause concern is that of human **cloning**. A form of cloning already takes place at a natural level, with the natural division of the ovum into twins or more. Artificial cloning is the attempt to create genetic copies of other human beings by interfering with the egg's nucleus. Although spiritual qualities, such as an individual's personality, character, soul or will, cannot be copied, many find the idea of a physical copy of another person repugnant. Legislators already distinguish between *therapeutic* and *reproductive* cloning. In the former, an embryo is cloned with the desired genes implanted in its nucleus. The aim is to use those genes as compatible tissue for the treatment of other recipients. In the latter, the nucleus is cloned with the intention of implanting the cloned embryo in the desired womb. While reproductive cloning is still illegal in most countries, and is likely to remain so, there is serious concern about the possible wastage of embryos that attempted cloning would involve. Even animal cloning is highly hit and miss, with the odds normally stacked against success.

Subjecting the embryo to a form of **gene therapy** is less controversial than cloning. In its most respectable form, this means the attempted identification and removal of genes that lie at the root of many conditions, such as spina bifida, Down's syndrome or Alzheimer's disease. There is widespread approval of this technique, on the grounds that it offers the possibility of removing the causes of later disability and suffering and, significantly, because it is done for the benefit of the embryo itself.

A major moral consideration that arises from new biotechnology is concern about the children who are produced by these methods. Once procreation is removed from the traditional setting of a married or loving relationship, many argue that such concerns are not misplaced. If there is no longer any need for 'natural parents', and traditionally valued elements such as love, commitment, natural bonding and blood relationship are no longer important, what guarantees are left to ensure the healthy and safe upbringing of the children who are being born by artificial means?

If embryos can so easily be created by scientific methods, especially in pursuit of the 'right to have a child', it is natural that there should be concern that the interests of the resulting children will be left out of account. Where a natural background is being replaced by an artificial one, and where technology has taken over from natural procreation, there is a sense that a moral vacuum will result in which the notion of a child's right not to be born into any sort of background or relationship is disregarded.

For this reason, many argue that the traditional principle that a child has a right to be born into a loving relationship with its natural parents acquires a special force. With regard to cloning, the danger of a child being born who will understandably resent the reasons behind his or her coming to be can only be seen as very real. Again, while the religious principle that each individual is a separate creation with its own unique dignity is not absolutely denied by cloning, it is at least in danger of being undermined. However, the main arguments against cloning do not depend on religious principles as such. They are universal arguments that reflect a common agreement that issues of natural justice are involved. Who really wants to be a copy of somebody else? The fact that children have no say in the matter makes the question yet more rhetorical.

A particular cause of concern is bound to be the prospects for the child's nurture and fosterage. If a child is to be born with the assistance of science, surely it has a right that everything possible is done to protect its interests. The alternative is to allow the production of new life to be at the whim of those already alive. The argument here is that natural justice should ensure that each child is born into circumstances that provide the best opportunity for its future welfare and development.

A disturbing aspect of the new biotechnology is its essential blindness to all ethical concerns about the human welfare of its end 'product', the resulting child. It need take no account of future parent–guardian suitability, no account of the problems of genetic anonymity (the child not knowing the identity of its genetic, or surrogate, father or mother), and of course no account of the possibility of legal disputes about the future custody, if not 'ownership', of the child. Does it belong to the surrogate mother, or the natural mother – and who really is the natural mother? In the case of clones, there is no mother at all since only a single gene is involved.

These concerns are heightened by what is known about the conditions required for healthy human development. It is common knowledge that a child has well-established emotional and psychological needs that are crucial to its healthy development. These needs are closely related to the unique sensitivity that marks out the human being from other animals. It seems a matter of justice, therefore, that a child that is being produced by scientific means should have as little as possible about which to be sensitive. Here are some examples.

How would the child feel if a surrogacy contract involved a tug-of-war between two 'mothers' or, worse, if the biological mother were to abandon the child to an unwilling surrogate mother? What if a child born under a prior legal agreement were later to discover that a row about its 'ownership' had made the global news headlines? How would a child feel on being told that its biological father will never be known, or that its genetic, or surrogate, mother will never be known? We are now a long way from moral issues about the status of the embryo or the foetus. Now we are looking at the issue of the welfare of a human being left to the mercy of others. It is not enough to say 'there but for the grace of God go I', because here everything is determined by the deliberate intentions and wishes of existing human beings.

In conclusion, we have seen that embryo creation and embryo research are ethical issues boil down to the question about the status of the embryo itself. How far can it be considered human? Those who may be called 'pro life' see the embryo as deserving of the highest respect due to a human being. From a religious angle it can be seen as an issue of the sanctity of life. Others see the embryo as occupying a no man's land between vegetable, animal and human. Those who may be called 'pro choice' see no restrictions on treating it as a means to an end. Those who hold a moderate position see the embryo as deserving of respect, but allow for limited interference with it for the benefit of others, provided that the embryo is not deliberately created for this purpose.

Those who favour the creation of embryos for research purposes, or for stem-cell harvesting, or as part of a search for one of the 'right' kind stand accused of embryo exploitation. 'If the embryo is merely a commodity, or a commercial commodity to be itemised and used for the benefit of others, then it stands degraded to the level of the sub-human. Those who reject this view may appeal to Kantian or Christian principles which forbid the reduction of what is human to the level of an object or a means to an end. They would argue that there can be no more ultimate end than what is human, and what is human can never be a means. To ignore this principle, they would say, is simply to endorse the oppression of the weak by the strong, a practice widely recognised as contrary to natural justice.

The division between 'pro life' and 'pro choice' raises the issue of whether utilitarian principles on their own can be decisive in settling these issues. The answer may be yes, but it depends on what is meant by utilitarianism. If a short-term view is taken, it would seem that embryos can be used and disposed of at will. If a longer-term view is taken, it is possible that 'playing God' now may have consequences of a detrimental kind in the future. In the end, utilitarian principles may have to take more account of mankind's spiritual dimensions than was previously realised, if harm is not to be done.

Related questions: _____

1 To what extent is utilitarianism a valid method of making decisions about fertility treatment?

2 To what extent are ethical concerns about scientific advances in fertility treatment justified?

3 Assess the arguments for and against embryo research and gene therapy.

Bibliography

Reference Works

Clarke, P. J. (2001) *Questions about God*, 2nd edn. Cheltenham: Nelson Thornes.
Copleston, F. C. (1946–75) *A History of Philosophy*, 9 vols. London.
Craig, E. (ed.) (1998) *The Routledge Encyclopedia of Philosophy*, 10 vols. London: Routledge.
Flew, A. and MacIntyre, A. (eds) (1955) *Essays in Philosophical Theology*. London: S.C.M. Press.
Gilbey, T. (ed.) (1951) *Aquinas, Philosophical Texts*. London: Oxford University Press.
Gilbey, T. (ed.) (1955) *Aquinas, Theological Texts*. London.
Helm, P. (ed.) (1999) *Faith and Reason*. Oxford: Oxford University Press.
Hick, J. (ed.) (1964) *The Existence of God (Philosophical Texts)*. New York: Macmillan.
Lacey, A. R. (ed.) (1986) *A Dictionary of Philosophy*, 2nd edn. London: Routledge & Kegan Paul.
Macquarrie, J. (1966) *Principles of Christian Theology*. London: S.C.M. Press.
Macquarrie, J. and Childress, J. (eds.) (1990) *A New Dictionary of Christian Ethics*. London: SCM.
McGrath, A. E. (ed.) (1993) *The Blackwell Encyclopedia of Modern Christian Thought*. Oxford: Blackwell.
Richardson, J. (ed.) (1969) *A Dictionary of Christian Theology*. London: S.C.M. Press.
Russell, B. (1984) *A History of Western Philosophy*. London: Unwin Paperbacks (first published 1946).
Wakefield, G. S. (ed.) (1983) *A Dictionary of Christian Spirituality*. London: SCM.

The Existence and Nature of God

Craig, W. L. (2001) *The Cosmological Argument from Plato to Leibniz*. London: Macmillan.
Descartes, R. [1647] *Philosophical Writings*. London.
Evans, C. S. (1998) *Faith beyond Reason*. Edinburgh: Edinburgh University Press.
Flew, A. (1966) *God and Philosophy*. London: Hutchinson.
Hick, J. (1963) *Philosophy of Religion*. Englewood Cliffs, NJ: Prentice-Hall.
Hume, D. [1746] Dialogues concerning natural religion. In *Hume Selections*. New York (1955 edition).
Kant, I. [1781] *The Critique of Pure Reason*. London (1961 edition).
Kenny, A. (1983) *Faith and Reason*. New York: Columbia University Press.
Kierkegaard, S. [1846] *Philosophical Fragments*. Princeton, NJ: Princeton University Press (1962 edition).
Mackie, J. L. (1982) *The Miracle of Theism: Arguments For and Against the Existence of God*. Oxford: Clarendon Press.
Owen, H. P. (1965) *The Moral Argument for Christian Theism*. London: George Allen & Unwin.

Pannenberg, W. [1960] *What is Man?* Philadelphia: Fortress Press (1970 edition).

Pannenberg, W. [1961] *Revelation as History*. London: Sheed and Ward (1969 edition).

Pannenberg, W. [1964] *Jesus: God and Man*. Philadelphia: Westminster Press (1977 edition).

Pascal, B. [1670] *Pensees*. Harmondsworth: Penguin (1966 edition).

Rahner, K. (1978) *Foundations of Christian Faith: an Introduction to the Idea of Christianity*. New York: Crossroad.

Swinburne, R. (1979) *The Existence of God*. Oxford: Clarendon Press.

Tennant, F. R. (1968) *Philosophical Theology*. Cambridge: Cambridge University Press.

Religion and Experience

Buber, M. [1923] *I and Thou*. Edinburgh: T. Clark (1960 edition).

Freud, S. [1927] *The Future of an Illusion*. London: Hogarth (1962 edition).

Hick, J. (1968) *Evil and the God of Love*. London: Macmillan.

James, W. [1902] *The Varieties of Religious Experience*. London: Longman (1945 edition).

Jung, C. G. [1935] *Psychology and Religion; West and East*. London: Routledge & Kegan Paul (1955 edition).

Marx, K. and Engels, F. [1849] *On Religion*. New York: Shocken Books (1964 edition).

McGinn, B. (1992) *The Foundations of Mysticism*. London: SCM.

Moltmann, J. (1974) *The Crucified God*. London: S.C.M. Press.

Otto, R. [1917] *The Idea of the Holy*. Harmondsworth: Penguin (1959 edition).

Plantinga, A. (1975) *God, Freedom and Evil*. London: George Allen & Unwin.

Schleiermacher, F. [1799] *On Religion: Speeches to its Cultured Despisers*. New York: Harper & Row (1958 edition).

Religion and Science

Brooke, J. H. (1991) *Science and Religion: Some Historical Perspectives*. Cambridge: Cambridge University Press.

Craig, W. L. and Smith, Q. (1995) *Theism, Atheism and Big Bang Cosmology*. Oxford: Clarendon Press.

Cupitt, D. (1976) *The Worlds of Science and Religion*. London: Sheldon Press.

Ford, A. (1986) *Universe: God, Man and Science*. London: Hodder and Stoughton.

Hooykaas, R. (1973) *Religion and the Rise of Modern Science*. Edinburgh: Scottish Academic Press.

Peacock, A. R. (1979) *Creation and the World of Science*. London.

Polkinghorne, J. C. (1991) *Reason and Reality*. London: SPCK.

Wilkes, K. (1969) *The Rise of Modern Science*. Oxford.

Religion and Language

Ayer, A. J. (1936) *Language, Truth and Logic*. London.

Clack, B. R. (1999) *An Introduction to Wittgenstein's Philosophy of Religion*. Edinburgh.

Kerr, F. (1986) *Theology after Wittgenstein*. Oxford: Blackwell.

Maquarrie, J. (1967) *God-Talk: an Examination of the Language and Logic of Theology*. London: S.C.M. Press.

Martin, J. (1966) *The New Dialogue between Philosophy and Theology*. London: Black.

Phillips, D. Z. (1976) *Religion without Explanation*. Oxford: Blackwell.

Ramsey, I. (1965) *Religious Language*. London: S.C.M. Press.

Soskice, J. M. (1985) *Metaphor and Religious Language*. Oxford: Clarendon Press.

Religion and Ethics

Dyson, A. and Harris, R. (eds) (1990) *Experiments on Embryos*. London: Routledge.

Häring, B. (1954–63) *The Law of Christ*. Cork: Mercier Press.

Häyry, M. (1994) *Liberal Utilitarianism and Applied Ethics*. London: Routledge.

Hooker, B. (2001) *Morality, Rules and Consequences*. Edinburgh: Edinburgh University Press.

MacIntyre, A. (1981) *After Virtue: a Study in Moral Theory*. London: Duckworth.

Nussbaum, J. and Sunstein, B. (eds) (1998) *Clones and Clones: Facts and Fantasies about Human Cloning*. New York: W. W. Norton.

Raphael, D. D. (1981) *Utilitarianism*. Oxford.

Singer, P. (1986) *Applied Ethics*. Oxford: Oxford University Press.

Profiles of Key Names

Anselm, St (1033–1109)   Born in Aosta in Italy, Anselm later studied in France. He became Archbishop of Canterbury in 1093. A man of great intellect, he wrote on many subjects, such as truth, logic and other philosophical problems. He is best remembered, however, for his ontological argument of God's existence.

Aquinas, St Thomas (1224–1274)   Italian by birth, he studied at the Universities of Cologne and Paris. He later returned to Paris as a teacher. His life's mission to defend the Christian faith is recorded for posterity in his massive *Summa Theologica* and *Summa Contra Gentiles*, both written between 1259 and 1273. He used the philosophy of Aristotle to show that religious faith is consistent with the insights of reason. He is probably best remembered by students for his Five Ways for proving the existence of God and for his theory of natural law.

Aristotle (382–322 BC)   A pupil of Plato, Aristotle went on to make his own name in the history of philosophy. In 335 BC he founded the Lyceum in Athens, an academy of learning. He contributed not only to philosophical thinking but also to natural science and the study of logic. He is contrasted with Plato by stressing empirical forms of knowledge, unlike his teacher who saw the *ideal* world as the most real.

Augustine, St (AD 354–430)   Born in North Africa into a pagan background (although his mother became a Christian), he was initially interested in philosophy. After taking up teaching posts in Italian universities, notably Milan, Augustine converted to Christianity. In AD 359 he became Bishop of Hippo, from where he established himself as one of the outstanding leaders of the early Church. An intellectual giant, he made a major contribution to showing how Christianity brings about inner change in the believer. Under the influence of Plato, he stressed the spiritual nature of all human beings, and his ideas had a significant influence on Luther and the Reformers. His writing output was vast, but he is often most associated with the theodicy that bears his name.

Ayer, A. J. (1910–1980)   Sometimes called the apostle of logical positivism, Ayer is generally regarded as the person who popularised linguistic philosophy in Britain. He was strongly influenced by empiricism, and was one of the first to formulate the **verification principle**. He was dismissive of metaphysics and religion, both of which he considered meaningless. He believed that ethical statements were equally *non-cognitive*, but could be explained merely as expressions of feeling. He is therefore generally credited with the metaethical theory of **emotivism**.

Barth, Karl (1886–1978)   Born in Basle, Switzerland, Barth spent most of his academic life in German universities. He considered the horrors of the First World War as evidence of the poverty of so-called **liberal theology** that had shifted the centre of gravity from God to mankind. Barth reacted strongly by insisting that God must come first, and human beings must humbly submit themselves to His Word, first in the Bible. His *Church Dogmatics* (1932–1968) was a thorough presentation of his Word of God theology. Many considered his position to be too dogmatic and

158

uncompromising, and therefore unsuitable for the secular age in which he lived. Yet he was highly regarded and greatly influential. A man of outstanding generosity, he believed that theology was a sublime discipline and would say to his students 'freely you have received, freely give'.

Bentham, Jeremy (1748–1832)   Born in London where he mainly worked, Bentham was a moral, political and legal philosopher. His **utilitarianism** was mainly applied to social reform, although he believed that the principle of utility should underlie all moral decisions. His views on happiness, however, left him at odds with religious ethics, which saw happiness in less empirical terms, and with Kant, who stressed moral principles.

Bonhoeffer, Dietrich (1906–1945)   One of the most endearing theologians of the twentieth century because his life was cut short, Bonhoeffer was born in Germany and decided to return there in its darkest days, although he could have stayed in Britain or America. A Lutheran pastor, he believed that faith must be costly, and should involve a moral struggle without the help of what he called 'cheap grace'. Life must be lived in a secular age as Jesus did, without official structures such as the Church. After joining in a plot to assassinate Hitler, he was executed by hanging, but his voice is still heard in his writings.

Buber, Martin (1868–1965)   Born in Austria, Buber established himself as a Jewish theologian and philosopher. He was forced by the Nazis to leave his teaching post in Frankfurt and he settled in the Hebrew University in Jerusalem. He is famous for his book *I and Thou*, in which he stated his basic view that God cannot be reduced to an object. On the contrary, God is a *subject* who can only be addressed in a personal relationship. His ideas influenced Karl Barth and other theologians of his time.

Butler, Joseph (1692–1752)   Born in Wantage in England, Butler became bishop of Bristol and then Durham. His interest in moral psychology led him to notice the opposing strains of self-love on the one hand, and benevolence on the other, in moral decision-making. He saw conscience as having overriding authority, but he believed that reason can alert us to the dominance of self-love over benevolence. He also believed that nature provided an in-built guide to how we should act. To ignore it was to feel guilty, to follow it was to be happy.

Bultmann, Rudolf (1884–1976)   Born in Wiefelstede in Germany, Bultmann was one of the most outstanding New Testament scholars of his day. From this, developed his interest in the universal significance of Jesus Christ. In presenting this conviction he used current ideas popular in **existentialism**, especially in the writings of Martin Heidegger. This turned Bultmann into a theologian whose concern was to show how the Christian faith can throw light on the task of how to live a morally fulfilling life. This aspect of his thought has continuing relevance, but has been overtaken by developments that have overshadowed purely personal concerns about life. Such developments have been typified by movements such as **liberation theology**, which have stressed the need for more organised and communal concerns about social justice in a lop-sided world of rich and poor. Bultmann is also remembered for shifting attention away from *factual* concerns about the past, especially about Jesus, and for his call to *demythologise* the Bible. In this way, he hoped to side-step the factual challenges of science, and focus attention instead on what religion means for human life.

Comte, Auguste (1798–1857)   Born in Montpellier in France, Comte lived mainly in Paris, where a statue of him stands opposite the Sorbonne. He is generally regarded as the father of **positivism**, the view that empirical science is the only true path to truth about the world. He was dismissive of religion as belonging to a primitive stage of human development. His linguistic followers came to be called **logical positivists**.

Descartes, René (1596–1650)   Descartes was born at La Haye in France, but later moved to Holland. He is regarded as the founder of modern philosophy, having broken away from the influence of traditional truth-claims based on tradition. In their place, he erected a system of *rational* knowledge based on a sure foundation. He began as an extreme sceptic about the outside world and turned to the thinking mind as the source of sure knowledge. His famous first conviction was that he existed, for only an existing thing could think (*cogito ergo sum*). He believed that the existence of God was an innate idea, something of which he could not be more certain. His sure and certain idea of God became the basis of his assurance that all rational knowledge was reliable.

Feuerbach, Ludwig (1804–1872)   Born in Germany, Feuerbach began as a student of theology at Heidelberg, but later went to Berlin, where he attended the lectures of Hegel. He was struck by Hegel's attempt to locate God in human consciousness, and got the idea that God may just be an idea in the mind. His famous theory that God is *man writ large*, and is really only a projection of our own powers on to an imaginary transcendent being, became a key influence in the thought of later writers such as Marx and Freud.

Freud, Sigmund (1856–1939)   Freud was brought up in a poor Jewish family in Vienna. After deciding to follow a medical career, he became interested in the problems of the mind. He developed the method of **psychoanalysis**, by which the unconscious is explored through dreams and conscious association techniques. His theory of religion attracted considerable interest because it claimed to show that faith was the result of repressed childhood frustrations around what he called the **Oedipus Complex**. Freud became famous for his uncovering the role of the unconscious, but his dismissal of religion as an *illusion*, based on childhood wishes for a protective father, no longer commands the attention that it once did.

Hegel, Georg W. F. (1770–1831)   Hegel was born in Stuttgart, and went on to become one of the most outstanding philosophers of all time. He became professor at the University of Heidelberg, and later in Berlin. Influenced by the critical idealism (the importance of the mind in understanding reality) of Kant, he developed the idea that all reality is mind-conditioned. History, in particular, is dominated by mind, or Spirit, which follows a process of thesis, antithesis and synthesis. In other words, events follow a scheme characterised by a state of affairs, followed by a reaction, followed by a resolution. The Absolute Spirit is God, who is the driving force of history through the agency of human consciousness. Hegel's **idealism** was highly influential among other thinkers, but his ideas were used by some – and famously by Marx and Feuerbach – to argue that the human spirit is all that there is, thus eliminating God from the picture completely.

Heidegger, Martin (1889–1976)   Born in Baden, Heidegger lived and taught in Germany, especially in Freiburg. As an **existentialist** he studied the meaning of being human. He believed that human beings were characterised by three things, a condition of *fallenness*, a state of finding themselves in situations not of their making (*facticity*) and a *potentiality* to overcome all negative forces to live an *authentic* existence. He became renowned for the complexity of his writings, but his ideas were used by Bultmann and Tillich to show how Christ could help transform the human spirit, and later by other thinkers such as Sartre, who extended his ideas on taking personal responsibility for our existence.

Hume, David (1711–1776)   Born in Edinburgh in Scotland, Hume is generally regarded as the greatest of all empiricist philosophers. He was also an historian, statesman, economist and army officer. Always seeming to take a tongue-in-cheek position, he exposed the futility of being over-confident about applying reason or observation to prove religious truths. He had much in common with Kant, who credited him with 'waking me from my dogmatic slumbers'. Both became towering figures in the so-called **Enlightenment critique** of religion, showing that arguments about things outside of human experience were doomed to failure. Hume was also influential in the field of ethics, where he applied a thoroughgoing empiricism to show that ethical statements had no objective validity.

James, William (1842–1910)   Born in New York, James spent most of his life travelling or working at Harvard, where he became professor of psychology, and later, philosophy. He made a significant contribution to the understanding of religious experience, refusing to question its objective validity, preferring instead to recognise its significance for moral and spiritual growth. He defended the importance of risk in matters of faith, whether religious or otherwise, recognising that some things could never be conclusively proved, but also questioning the propriety of looking for proof at all in many matters. He was strongly opposed to any attempt to apply a scientific method to understanding human experience.

Kant, Immanuel (1724–1804)   Regarded as the greatest philosopher since Plato and Aristotle, Kant spent most of his life as a professor of logic in Konigsberg in Prussia. A major figure of the Enlightenment, he combined the **empiricism** of Hume with a **rationalism** focused on how the mind works in decoding experience. His so-called **critical idealism** resulted in his rejection of all claims to know what lies outside experience. He thus rejected all attempts to prove the existence of God by reason. But he held that God could be known by *faith*. This is a kind of trust that our sense of moral duty is not futile. From this emerged his moral argument for God's existence.

Kierkegaard, Søren (1813–1855)   Born in Copenhagen in Denmark, Kierkegaard spent some time as a pastor in the city. His writings established him as a profound thinker about religion and its significance for human life. This made him the first great **existentialist**, but unlike other existentialists he worked out the meaning of life within the framework of his Christian faith. Following Augustine and Luther, he saw faith as a matter of personal choice that involved a profound inner change. He was violently opposed to the 'membership' type of Christianity, which he accused the Danish Church of promoting (to his cost). Faith was a blind leap, or risk, that had to be taken before its significance could become apparent. To some, this made him a **fideist**, but his understanding of the *existential* value of faith suggests that he was not, because its truth was open to experience. He is remembered for rejecting the system-building of Hegel, who saw God's revelation as a logical development within history. For Kierkegaard, Christianity was not the outcome of any system, but an unexpected bolt from the blue, a *paradox*, or near contradiction, supremely exemplified in the idea of God becoming man. For this reason, he rejected **natural theology** as a futile and insulting attempt to know the mystery of God.

Locke, John (1673–1704)   Born in Somerset in England, Locke worked mostly in Oxford and London. He was influenced by Descartes to the extent that he believed that all knowledge should be well-founded, but he had his own ideas about rational knowledge. He believed that the latter came from *experience* rather than from pure thought, a view that put him firmly within the empiricist tradition. His later attempted apology for the Christian faith, by appealing to prophecy and miracle, became one of the main targets of Hume's attack on miracles, and on other uses of reason and experience to support religious belief.

Luther, Martin (1483–1546)   Born in Germany, Luther is remembered for his powerful attack on the Roman Church, which led to the Reformation. Luther opposed the pretentions, as he saw them, of people setting themselves up as spokespersons for God. He saw human nature as too corrupt for such a task, and set up the Bible as the sole rule of faith. Following St Augustine, he saw faith as prior to all human knowledge, a view that led him to oppose the use of reason in matters of faith. His ideas had profound influence among later thinkers, such as Kierkegaard and Barth.

Marx, Karl (1818–1883)   Born in Trier in Germany, Marx worked in various cities in Europe, and eventually in London. Strongly influenced by Hegel's philosophy of history, he believed that economic conditions were the explanatory factor behind beliefs such as religion. This motivated him to outline a plan for social and political change that would bring about justice for the exploited masses, and remove their dependence on the wishful promises of religious faith. Under the influence of Feuerbach, he saw religion as an alienating force that slowed down social change. His ideas were ruthlessly applied by Lenin and his followers in the suppression of religion throughout Russia.

Mill, John Stuart (1806–1873)   Born in London, Mill became a noted **empiricist**, and follower of Bentham's utilitarianism. His own version of utilitarianism introduced a distinction between 'higher' and 'lower' pleasures, which gave rise to the philosophical problem of how to justify the distinction. This meant that Mill saw utility in more complex terms than Bentham. In particular, he highlighted the indirect utility potential of other approaches, such as the well-developed character. This brought him close to a form of virtue ethics. He also believed in the utilitarian benefits of *rules*, which led to rule utilitarianism.

Moore, George E. (1873–1958)   Born in London, Moore spent most of his life in Cambridge, where he became prominent in analytical circles. His contribution to ethics was his attack on the **naturalistic fallacy**, the view that goodness could be defined in terms of something else. Peace might be good, but goodness is not peace – in the same way that lemons are yellow, but yellow is not a lemon. This was also an application of the 'is–ought' debate started by Hume, in which a fact cannot be the basis of a value. These seem to be technical points that add little to ethical debate. More interesting than Moore's **non-naturalism** was his theory of **intuition**, the view that goodness can never be reasoned, but only known by intuition. Although he never defined intuition, others might have seen his views as confirming what was otherwise called **reason**, or **natural law**.

Nietzsche, Friedrich (1844–1900)   Born in Germany, Nietzsche was a brilliant student who went on to teach classics at Basle in Switzerland. He retired due to ill-health in 1879, and died after 11 years of insanity. His ideas have had a significant influence on politics, literature and religion. He was strongly anti-religious on the grounds that religion encouraged a 'slave' morality. The true 'will to live' required a break with the restraints of religion, and its replacement with an autonomous 'master' morality based on instinctive values created by each individual. His ideas provoked strong reactions from theologians such as Tillich, who set out to rebut his atheism by showing that religion was the true source of moral potential, both for the individual and the human race.

Otto, Rudolf (1869–1937)   Born in Germany, Otto became a Lutheran theologian, and held posts in various German universities. His ideas reflect the influence of Kant and Schleiermacher. His contribution to religion lay in his notion of the *numinous*. This was an inner sense of the *holy* that lay at the root of all of the great religions. The experience of the holy was an experience of *mystery*, which gave rise to a sense of both fear and fascination, at once attracting and repelling. Otto helped to restore a certain objectivity to religion and religious experience, thus countering the claim that religion was either an historical, psychological or sociological phenomenon. His ideas were influential in the psychological understanding of religion of Carl Gustav Jung.

Pannenberg, Wolfhart (b.1928)   Born in German-occupied Poland, Pannenberg began his theological studies in Berlin and later taught at several leading German universities. His outstanding contribution to philosophy and theology has been his carefully worked out view that the Resurrection of Jesus was an *historical* event, open to historical investigation. This set him apart from more fashionable views held by Bultmann and others, who refused to grant that the Resurrection was properly historical. From this, Pannenberg argued that the Resurrection was of universal significance, and that it held the key to the meaning of history and human destiny.

Pascal, Blaise (1623–1662)   Pascal was a French mathematician, philosopher and religious writer. He was a realist who had no time for Cartesian certainties. He rejected natural theology and the idea that God's existence could be proved by reason, believing in any case that in real life people are more concerned with hunting, fishing and gambling. This gave him the idea that, if nothing else, people could be shown what the stakes were. The result was his famous **wager**, in which he argued that the prize was eternal, but the stakes were only temporal. The idea, however, that this was an unworthy approach to gaining eternity is to overlook the deeper implications of his proposal.

Plato (428–348 BC)   Plato was a pupil of Socrates and later founded the Academy, a centre of learning in Athens, in 385 BC. He is famous for his theory of **forms**, in which he distinguished between the real world of ideal types and the illusory world of the senses. His *allegory of the cave* is meant to illustrate the difference between the two worlds, although it is also used to distinguish between the enlightened few and the unenlightened mass that characterise human society. Plato's ideas have also contributed to arguments for God's existence, such as his view that the ultimate origin of everything must be self-moving, and therefore a living *soul*.

Rahner, Karl (1904–1984)   Born in Freiburg in Germany, Rahner became a distinguished philosopher and theologian of the Catholic Church, but whose fame extended across denominational boundaries. His outstanding contribution to religious philosophy has been his theory of **transcendence**. This is the view that all human beings have an unconscious awareness of striving beyond all existing situations towards a mysterious horizon that is never reached. This striving is an implicit search for ultimate fulfilment, which is called God. This enabled Rahner to credit with implicit religious faith those who lived lives of honesty and integrity, although outwardly they might call themselves atheists or agnostics. This he called *anonymous Christianity*.

Russell, Bertrand   (1872–1970)   Russell spent most of his academic life in Cambridge, where he became a distinguished professor of philosophy. Among his pupils was Wittgenstein, who was influenced by his views on language and metaphysics. A well-known atheist, he is remembered for debating on religious matters with Copleston on the radio. When he refused to discuss the possibility of an ultimate origin of the universe, replying that 'it was a brute fact', Copleston retorted by saying 'if you refuse to play chess you can never be checkmated'!

Schleiermacher, Friedrich (1768–1834)   Often called the 'father of modern theology', Schleiermacher was responsible for changing theology from concern with the outside world to concern with inner *experience*. Where reason formerly ruled, it was now the emotions and inner intuition. He believed that religion was the outcome of an inner sense of *absolute dependence* that it was possible to obtain through reflection. He disagreed with Kant's idea that religion appeared from the sense of moral awareness, preferring to see it as a special area of awareness on its own. His ideas encouraged the search for God in terms of what was human, thus laying himself open to Feuerbach's conclusion that religion was merely a human projection to an imaginary God.

Teilhard de Chardin, Pierre (1881–1955)   Geologist, palaeontologist, priest, theologian and visionary, Teilhard was born in south-west France, but became a world figure due to his efforts to reconcile evolution with religious faith. His ideas were not well received by his religious superiors, who accused him of embracing scientific views too uncritically. He believed that all matter was sacred, and was destined to develop into conscious life. The evolutionary process would not be complete until an end (omega) point was reached, which was exemplified in the spiritual and moral development achieved by Jesus Christ. Perhaps it was his tendency to see the divine in an overly humanistic way that led to a ban on his writings, but his lasting legacy was his attempt to show that evolution was compatible with religious faith.

Tillich, Paul (1883–1965)   One of the most outstanding philosopher–theologians of the twentieth century, Tillich was born in Starzeddel, Germany. He served as a military chaplain in the First World War, but fled from the Nazis to spend his life in America, where he had a distinguished career. His great mission was to show the credibility of faith in the face of an atheistic culture. He reacted to the criticisms of Nietzsche by insisting that true moral courage was made possible by faith, not prevented by it. He is remembered for phrases such as 'ultimate concern' and 'Being Itself' to describe the nature of God.

Wittgenstein, Ludwig (1889–1951)   Born in Vienna, Wittgenstein came to Cambridge to study engineering, and met Russell. His subsequent interest in the philosophy of language owed much to this meeting. Regarded as one of the greatest intellects of his time, his ideas on language created wide interest, and led to the formation of the **Vienna Circle** and logical positivism. Initially, he saw language as being only valid for empirical uses, but later granted that language could have validity to the user when expressing experiences that belonged to various *forms of life*. This view, called **language games**, was taken up by many theologians to argue that religious language had its own validity for its users. His ideas about the *mystical* also provided a basis for the language of religion, as when he said 'It is not *how* the world is that is mystical, but *that* it is ('Nicht *wie* die Welt ist, ist das Mystische, sondern *dass* sie ist').

a posteriori	An argument based on, or *after*, **experience**; for example, the **teleological** argument.
a priori	An argument based on ideas prior to, or *before*, **experience**; for example, the **ontological** argument.
Abortion	The direct removal of a **foetus** from the womb, with the intention of ending its life.
Absolute	Unconditioned, free from limitations, not **contingent**. The term was applied by Hegel to refer to the highest reality, which he identified with spirit.
Absolutism	The view that some principles are **absolute**. A feature of **deontological ethics**, such as Kantianism and **Christian ethics**. Since most principles allow for exceptions, absolutism is regarded as too idealistic. Defenders would insist that treating others as '**ends**' and not as '**means**' only (Kant), and that innocent human life should never be deliberately taken, are absolute principles. In **medical ethics**, the dispute as to whether a life is fully 'human', especially at the **embryo** stage, is regarded as impossible to decide absolutely.
Act of double effect	A moral act done for a good **motive**, but which may involve an undesirable side-effect. A classic example may be the removal of the cancerous womb of a pregnant woman, or a so-called ectopic pregnancy. Appeal to this principle allows the removal of the womb or the fallopian tube, as long as the loss of the **foetus** although foreseen is not intended.
Act utilitarianism	The view that the **principle of utility** should govern all single actions. The opposite of **rule utilitarianism**.
Acts and omissions	A distinction in **ethics**. Acts are positive interventions say, in deciding to abort, or commit euthanasia. Omissions are decisions not to intervene, say, to allow a patient to die naturally by withdrawing treatment.
Agape	A term that belongs to **Christian ethics**. It is derived from St Paul and is based on the Greek word for 'selfless love', as distinct from other terms such as 'eros' (sexual love), or 'philia' (friendship). Marriage is said to involve all three, but agape love is used as a defining idea in **situation ethics**.

Agnosticism	Literally from the Greek *a*, 'against', and *gnosis*, 'knowledge'; an agnostic holds that some things, such as God's existence, cannot be fully known.
Altruism	From the Latin *alter*, 'the other', meaning 'other-regarding'. The practice of **agape** love is always altruistic.
Amoral	This term, rarely used in **ethics**, strictly means non-moral – being outside the sphere of morality. We use terms such as 'good' and 'bad' in an amoral way when we apply them to describe, say, a pen, car, footballer and so on.
Analogy	A method used in religious language of applying to God qualities based on those valued within human **experience**; for example, **goodness**, love, wisdom, care, **justice**, and so on.
Analytical statement	Used in association with linguistic analysis. Analysis' means 'pulling apart'. Statements of mathematics and explanations of words are analytical. An analytical statement is said to be significant but trivial, because it says nothing new.
Angst	An **existential** term that denotes a fundamental malaise or anxiety about existence in the light of man's awareness of his potentialities in the face of **finitude** and death.
Anthropology	From the Greek *anthropos*, 'man'; the study of human behaviour and human nature.
Anthropomorphism	From the Greek, meaning 'in human form'; in theology it means the tendency to speak of God in human terms – for example, when we call God *father*, or when we say God is *angry*.
Anthropic principle	A principle associated with the fact that the universe couldn't be understood without man being here to observe it. That the universe seems 'made for man' is seen by many as theologically significant.
Aristotelianism	A system of thinking about reality derived from Aristotle (384–322 BC), which gives priority to sense **experience** as the basis of all knowledge. It was highly influential in the thought of St Thomas Aquinas (see **Thomism**), and can be contrasted with **Platonism**.
Asceticism	From the Greek *ascesis*, 'training'; the practice of fasting and self-denial, which has been a common feature of Christianity

since the time of Jesus. It is closely linked to **mysticism** through the 'mystic way', and is generally regarded by most writers as a condition of progress in the spiritual life.

Aseity   From the Latin *a*, 'by', and *se*, 'itself'; God's capacity to exist necessarily, or by Himself.

Atheism   From the Greek *a*, 'against', and *theos*, 'God'; the view that there is no God.

Atonement   Literally 'at-one-ment'; the **doctrine** that Christ by His death reconciled, or made one, man and God.

Autonomy   From the Greek *auto*, 'self', and *nomos*, 'law'; the idea of being able to determine for oneself one's **beliefs** and values. It is associated with **liberalism** and revisionism.

Being   A concept used by some existentialist thinkers, such as Heidegger, to mean that which lies behind every particular being, and in which all beings participate. It may be compared with the way in which light may be distinguished from particular lights. Tillich defined God as 'Being Itself'.

Belief   A state of mind in which confidence, trust or **faith** is placed in a person, idea or thing.

Bioethics   The area of **ethics** concerning questions of human life (*bios*), especially genetics and procreation. Sometimes called biomedical ethics.

Blik   A word used by R. M. Hare to denote a **belief** that cannot be shaken.

Cardinal virtues   The term goes back to Plato and Aristotle, who recognised **prudence**, **justice**, **fortitude** and **temperance** as the hinge (cardinal) on which human life should turn.

Categorical imperative   A famous term used by Kant to mean an unconditional (categorical) requirement (imperative) to do one's duty. It should be distinguished from a hypothetical imperative, which is conditional on wanting to achieve an objective ('If you don't do crime, you won't do time'). Only a categorical imperative belongs to the **moral** life (duty for duty's sake).

Character   The **moral** qualities that define what a person is like. Expressions such as 'character building', 'character qualities' or 'character faults' give an indication of what is meant. In **virtue ethics**, the aim is to create a virtuous character.

Child The legal term to denote someone who is already born. A child is a subject of full human rights, unlike the unborn **foetus**, which has a lower legal status.

Christian ethics The **ethics** derived from the New Testament, but also associated with ecclesiastical (**church**) teachings.

Church The Christian organisation that sees itself as responsible for the message and the theology surrounding Jesus Christ, and as guardian of the Bible. Historically, it has clarified **beliefs** about Christ in Creeds and Councils.

Classical theism A term identified with the philosophical analysis of God from medieval times. It defines God as real, timeless, eternal, infinite, omnipotent, omniscient and perfectly **good**. It has been challenged by **process theology** and non-realist forms of theism.

Cognitive statement From the Latin, meaning 'knowledgeable'; statements restricted by logical positivists to what can be empirically verified. Religious statements are alleged to be 'non-cognitive' because there is said to be no **empirical** test for their truth or falsity.

Conscience An inner sense of **moral** awareness given moral, theological and psychological explanations. Aquinas called it 'the mind of man making moral judgements'. Newman saw it as the 'voice of God', but Freud saw it as a product of early human conditioning with no metaphysical significance.

Consequentialism The view that morality should be judged by results or consequences. This is usually associated with utilitarianism, and contrasted with **deontological ethics** where principles are put first, allegedly at the expense of consequences.

Contingent From the Latin, meaning 'to happen'; used to suggest something happening fortuitously or by circumstances. Events or beings in the world are said to be contingent, since they might not have happened. God is said to be a non-contingent, or necessary, Being.

Conversion An **experience** of the supernatural that results in a change of life towards the service of God.

Cosmological From the Greek *cosmos*, 'world' or 'universe'. The cosmological argument is based on facts about the world. Cosmology refers to the study of the universe.

Creationism The view that reality is ultimately explicable only in terms of a divine Creator. In modern usage, it denotes the view that Genesis should be taken literally as a description of how the world was created by God. In its more **liberal** sense, it is consistent with scientific views of the world.

Crime A legal term to mean an offence against the law.

Decalogue Another name for the Ten Commandments.

Deduction A method of reasoning in which general *a priori* principles are applied to individual situations; for example, because everything has a cause, this event must have a cause. Deductive reasoning is a well-known feature of the traditional arguments for God's existence.

Deism From the Latin *deus*, 'God'; the view that God created the world but left it to run according to its own laws. In deism, God does not interfere in the world.

Deontological ethics From *deon*, meaning 'duty', this refers to an ethical system that stresses duty and fixed laws. It is classically represented by **Kantian ethics**, and by certain features of traditional **Christian ethics**.

Descriptive ethics The view that **ethics** can only describe behaviour or, as held by some, that ethical truth describes certain (true, factual) aspects of reality. In the former, ethics is about what people believe to be right or wrong. In the latter, ethics is about doing what is objectively right or wrong. For instance, in Christian ethics right and wrong have a metaphysical significance since they depend on doing, or not doing, the will of God.

Determinism The view that all ethical behaviour is merely the outcome of pre-existing forces. It is incompatible with the view that ethical behaviour is freely chosen.

Divine command theory The view that right and wrong are determined by the will of God.

Doctrine From the Latin, meaning 'to teach'; the official teachings of the first Councils of the **Church**. For Catholics, it refers to all official teachings of the Church to the present day.

Dualism From the Latin *duo*, 'two'; a system involving two principles or forces. One system of dualism divides reality into **good** and evil. Descartes divided reality into mind and matter (Cartesian dualism).

170

Egoism   The view that ethical behaviour either is (descriptively), or should be (normatively), determined by selfish interests.

Embryo   A creature of the human species up to the first eight weeks of pregnancy, or before implantation takes place.

Emotivism   A theory of **metaethics** that right and wrong are only matters of the emotions, and are merely expressions or approval or disapproval ('hurrah–boo'), and only reveal one's **personal** attitude.

Empirical   From the Greek, meaning 'to try' or 'trial'; refers to **experience** as opposed to reason. Empirical evidence is the evidence of experience obtained through experiment and observation, and is identified with the methods of **science**.

Empiricism   A philosophical view that only things belonging to the ordinary world of sense have true reality. Its typical exponent is David Hume. The theory underlies the ethical theory of **emotivism**, since only 'expression' can be verified.

Enlightenment, the   A period from roughly 1650 to 1780, characterised by the rejection of authority in favour of reason. Often used as a simple term for the challenge to **religion** typified by Hume and Kant.

Epistemic   From the Greek *episteme*, 'knowledge'; a so-called epistemic distance separates man and God.

Epistemology   Theories of knowledge such as **idealism** and **empiricism**.

Eschatological perspective   The view that reality extends beyond the world of space and time to include the after-life. It is relevant to an understanding of ethical behaviour as subject to the judgement of God.

Eschatological verification   From the Greek *eschaton*, 'the end time' or 'the after-life'; associated with the theory of John Hick that religious **beliefs** will be verified in the next life.

Essence   From the Latin *esse*, 'to be'; that which makes something what it is. God's existence is said to be identical with his essence, or His essence is to exist. Existentialist thinkers have argued that man's essence is not fixed, but must be created or shaped by the manner of his existence.

Ethics   A Greek word for human behaviour corresponding to the Latin word *mores*, meaning 'morals'.

ex nihilo   From the Latin, meaning 'from nothing'; used in connection with the **belief** that the world was created from nothing by God.

Existential ethics   The understanding of the ethical life in terms of how one decides for oneself how life is to be lived.

Existentialism   A continental movement in **philosophy** that analyses the meaning of human existence. It claims that the individual must create his or her own form of existence, and take responsibility for his or her lifestyle and **beliefs**. It is traceable to Kierkegaard, who stressed **personal** subjectivity as the key to human existence. It exerts a strong influence in philosophy and theology.

Experience   From the Latin *ex per iri*, 'from going through'; that which is perceived through the senses rather than deduced from reason. It is associated with the approach to **religion** established first by Kant, and later by Schleiermacher and Otto. It is non-controversial when concerned with what is **empirical** and verifiable, but controversial when interpreted in terms of aesthetics, morality and religion.

Exploitation   A term of ethical judgement that means taking unjust advantage of others.

Expressivism   The view that religious **beliefs** are merely expressions of an individual's convictions, and do not necessarily relate to reality.

Extrinsically good/evil   A judgement that something is good or bad because of factors that lie incidental to (extrinsic to) the action being considered. Something not intrinsically evil (not evil in itself) may be extrinsically evil because of its effects. For instance, war may be seen as extrinsically evil because it causes destruction and death.

Faith   A conviction not necessarily based on **empirical** evidence, but considered not contrary to such evidence, and usually associated with religious **beliefs**. It is widely claimed to provide access to important truths about reality, and is often contrasted with proven certainty. It forms part of an important debate about its relation to reason.

Fall, the   The theological theory about the events surrounding Adam and Eve in Genesis 2–3. It refers to man's 'Fall' from grace following Adam's disobedience, and is key to Paul's explanation of the Redemption by Christ in Romans 5.

Falsification	Associated with the claim that religious **beliefs** cannot be proved wrong by **empirical** evidence. The reverse of **verification**.
Fideism	The position that **faith** is immune to **rational** investigation, and can be internally justified; associated with Luther and Kierkegaard.
Fiducia	From the Latin, meaning 'trust'; highlighted by Luther as the **essence** of **faith** being trust in God as opposed to assent to religious truths.
Finite	From the Latin, meaning 'end'; the nature of the world and of man. It is contrasted with the nature of God as infinite.
Finitude	A term used by **existential** writers to denote the human awareness of death. It is seen as a disturbing aspect of human life that contributes to *Angst* or anxiety. It has been used by Tillich and others to raise the question of God's existence.
Foetus	A human creature after eight weeks of pregnancy.
Fortitude	The second of the **cardinal virtues**, this is the virtue that makes possible the doing of **good** (it could be called the engine of ethical behaviour).
Fundamentalism	A term derived from a movement in America based on certain fundamentals about the Bible, such as the literal truth of the creation story of Genesis. It is identified with the view that the Bible should be interpreted literally, regardless of the findings of **science**. It regards the theory of evolution and other related scientific discoveries as reductionist in nature, and as a threat to the status of man as the child of God. It is totally committed to preserving the **spiritual values** of the Bible.
Genetic fallacy	The mistaken belief that because the origin of something can be explained, its full reality is also explained. An example would be the view that **conscience** is illusory because it begins from childhood fears.
Golden Rule	'Do unto others as you would have them do unto you.'
Good/Goodness	Normally, that which is approved as praiseworthy, right, just or in accordance with God's will. It is said by G. E. Moore to be a 'non-natural quality' in a thing, and impossible to define in terms of something else, but it can be recognised

173

intuitively, in the form of friendship, honesty, courage, kindness and so on.

Hedonism The view that pleasure is the highest **good**.

Hippocratic Oath An oath traced to Hippocrates (460–377 BC), to be taken by doctors as the standard of good medical practice in relation to the treatment of patients. It forbids anything that is inconsistent with the curing of illness and disease, and it forbids doing injury. The Oath became controversial with the dawn of **abortion** and euthanasia, because it enjoined both the duty 'not to harm' and to work for the 'benefit' of the patient, thus setting a dilemma for doctors. Today, it is largely abandoned in its original form.

Idealism So-called 'critical idealism' refers to Kant's distinction between what we are given in **experience** and the part played by the mind in making experience possible. In this view, not only is the mind a major element in how we come to know things, but we can only know what is first in experience. Thus **metaphysics**, and any attempt to know what lies outside experience (such as God), becomes impossible.

Illusion A **belief** that is seen as a source of comfort, which may be true or false. It should be distinguished from 'delusion', which is contrary to reality. Freud called **religion** an illusion, but believed it to be false.

Immanent From the Latin, meaning 'to dwell in'; the **belief** that God is not separate from the world, but is somehow in the world.

Induction A method of reasoning in which general laws are derived from individual instances. Thus, if one sample of water boils at a certain temperature, all samples will be assumed to boil at that temperature. Inductive reasoning is typical of the scientific method of experimentation, which leads to general conclusions. Whether the first cause argument of Aquinas is inductive or deductive reasoning is not so clear if the claim 'every event must have a cause' is not distinguished from the **empirical** observation that 'every event has a cause'.

Immoral This means doing something against **moral** principles, but it is often interpreted as sexual misbehaviour. The term is not quite the same as unethical, which has a wider meaning.

Ineffable From the Latin *effabilis*, 'speakable'; that which cannot be described in words. It is associated with claims of mystics,

and people who claim that religious experiences defy verbal expression.

Intrinsically good/evil This refers to actions that are right or wrong in themselves, regardless of other considerations. **Abortion** and euthanasia are sometimes claimed to be intrinsically wrong. Kant held actions against the **moral law** to be intrinsically wrong.

Intuitionism A theory of **metaethics** associated with G. E. Moore. He held that ethical judgements could only be intuited, as opposed to the view that they could be reasoned by reference to other things, such as the will of God.

Justice The second of the **cardinal virtues**, this is the ability to give others their proper due. In ordinary usage it means the fair and proper treatment of others. It is linked to human rights.

Kantian ethics The deontological ethical system associated with Immanuel Kant.

Language game A term used by Wittgenstein to show that language functions differently in different contexts; for example, physics, poetry, **ethics** and **religion**.

Legalism A pejorative term suggesting excessive attachment to rules and regulations at the expense of the interests of others. Jesus appeared to be a critic of legalism, but did not underplay the importance of law, a point overlooked by **situation ethics**, which claims to be a corrective to legalism.

Liberal/Liberalism From the Latin, meaning 'free'; it refers to viewpoints that differ from traditional or conservative teachings, and is the opposite of **fundamentalism**. Liberal interpretations of Scripture take into account the latest findings of scholars. So-called 'liberal theology' in nineteenth-century Germany followed Schleiermacher in basing religious knowledge on human **experience**, but was strongly rejected by Barth as being too humanistic.

Logical positivism A movement in **philosophy** based on positivist principles, that the only reality is the **empirical**, and therefore the only reality that can be spoken about.

Material values This refers to worldly things such as money, fame or power. It can be contrasted with **spiritual values**, which are those related to the human spirit, such as **justice**, **goodness**, education, morality and so on.

Materialism	The philosophical view that reality does not go beyond the material world, and that all living organisms, including human beings, are ultimately material substances.
Means and ends	In ethical debate, these terms refer to the way in which values are pursued. Kant held that human beings should always be treated as ends, and never as means only. 'The end cannot justify the means' is a principle held in certain ethical theories. In utilitarianism and **situation ethics**, it appears that the end *can* justify the means.
Medical ethics	The principles that should govern procedures in medical **science**, especially in regard to practices such as fertility treatment, **embryo** research, **abortion** and euthanasia.
Metaethics	The area of ethical debate that looks at the language of **ethics**, and analyses the meaning of ethical claims. Includes **intuitionism, emotivism**, the nature and extent of free will, and the extent to which ethical behaviour is governed by principles that are relative or **absolute**.
Metaphysics	The study of basic issues that go beyond scientific questions about things in the world. Religious claims are seen as part of metaphysics. Many see the need for a necessary being, or first cause, (God) to explain existing things, and to answer Leibniz's question 'Why is there something, and not just nothing?' Hume said that metaphysical questions yielded no fruit and that books on the subject should be 'consigned to the flames', but not everyone agrees. Theories about realities beyond the physical world were discredited by Kant as impossible, since we can supposedly only know about appearances. Others see metaphysical questions as evidence of the mind's relentless search for truth.
Miracle	From the Latin, meaning 'to wonder'; it traditionally meant an event caused by God which was contrary to the laws of nature, but it now has a wider meaning to include ordinary events seen as (indirect) evidence of divine intervention.
Miscarriage	The unavoidable loss of an **embryo** or **foetus** by natural occurrence.
Moral	A term that corresponds to 'ethical', but with certain differences. A person may be described as moral (**good**) but not ethical.

Moral argument	An argument based on the reality of ethical or **moral** awareness. It was used famously by Immanuel Kant to argue for God's existence, and by later thinkers such as J. H. Newman, who appealed to the **personal** nature of **conscience**.
Moral law	A term used by Kant to indicate the existence of a law that was self-evident to reason and ethical perception. The test of its rationality was if its denial would create **moral** chaos in society.
Moral sense	The claim that the rightness or wrongness of an action can be detected (intuited). Hume held that this amounted to our being able to feel agreeable or disagreeable 'sentiments' from the actions of others, but rejected the claim that morality had any religious or metaphysical foundation.
Motive	The reason why an action is performed. In **Kantian ethics**, motive determines the **ultimate** morality of an action, for without a good motive there can be no good will, an idea central to the **categorical imperative**.
Mystery	From the Greek, meaning 'secret'; associated with the sense of the divine or holy spoken of by religious thinkers.
Mysticism	An alleged **experience** of oneness with God, as claimed by mystics.
Myth	An event that need not be understood to have happened as described, but which contains a deeper truth. The term is associated with Rudolf Bultmann, who saw a myth as any biblical event in which God is described in anthropomorphic (human) terms. To 'demythologise' is to extract the hidden (**existential** and religious) truth from the myth.
Natural law ethics	The ethical system associated with Aristotle, Aquinas and Butler. It is based on the claim that nature is a guide to right and wrong by taking the natural functions of things into account.
Natural theology	Attempting to know about God by reason alone. The term is associated with **proofs** for God's existence.
Naturalism	(1) The view that **ethical values** can be derived from natural facts (as in natural law). It was rejected by Hume and Moore, who called this the '**naturalistic fallacy**'. (2) A philosophical view that reality does not go beyond the things and events of the natural world. It logically implies **atheism**.

Naturalistic fallacy	The alleged mistake of claiming that what is **good** or evil is dependent on things in the natural world. An example would be to say that whatever brings happiness, peace or brotherhood is good. Moore's test was the 'open question argument'. It may be good to have peace, but it remains an open question whether the reverse, 'peace is good', is true.
Nihilism	An ethical pseudo-theory that nothing (*nihil*) has permanence, value or validity. It is associated with Nietzsche, who forecast but also advocated the overthrow of all traditional systems of ethics, especially those with a religious connection, to be replaced by a free-for-all struggle for human dominance. Oscar Wilde expressed the paradoxical nature of nihilism when he described the nihilist as 'that strange martyr who has no faith, who goes to the stake without enthusiasm, and dies for what he does not believe in'.
Noetic	From the Greek, meaning 'mind' or 'intellect'; used in connection with **mysticism**, in the claim that the mystical **experience** is a source of knowledge.
Numinous	A term used to denote that which is beyond the **empirical**, but can still be an object of **experience**. It is sometimes used to describe that which is perceived to be mysterious, and is associated with the thought of Rudolf Otto.
Objectivism	A term meaning that **ethical values** have objective validity, corresponding to the claim that truth has a similar validity. In **Kantian ethics** the **moral law** has objective validity, and in religious ethics it has cosmic significance in relation to the will of God. The notion is rejected by those who claim that ethical values are at most subjective, confined to the mind of the speaker, or mere social conventions dependent on temporal agreement.
Ontological	From the Greek *onta*, 'being'; having to do with being and reality. The ontological argument is an attempt to establish that God's being involves His existence.
Pantheism	From the Greek *pan*, 'all', and *theos*, 'God'; the view that the world and God are identical – that God is all, or everything. It is associated with Spinoza.
Panentheism	This differs from **pantheism** by seeing God in everything (from the Greek prefix *en*, meaning 'in'), suggested perhaps by the way in which salt is in seawater. It is typical of the view, held by process theologians, that God is in the world.

Parable   A story that illustrates a truth or a point.

Paradox   An apparent contradiction. The term is associated with Kierkegaard, who used it to denote something almost impossible to understand, such as the idea of God becoming man.

Personal   Having the characteristics of a person. It can be contrasted with an objective thing. In Buber's thought, the personal 'You' is contrasted with the impersonal 'It'. In Christian theology, God is seen as personal. The alternative to a personal cause of the world, it is argued, must be that of chance.

Personal ethics   This refers to the **ethics** or morality of personal living. It can be contrasted with **social ethics** (ethics governing the way in which society is ruled), or **medical ethics** (ethics governing medical practices).

Personalism   The view that **ethics** should be directed to the **good** of persons, or that ethics is about respecting not so much rules, but the will of a **personal** God.

Phenomenology   Rooted in the Greek *phainomenon*, 'to appear'; a philosophical system associated with Edmund Husserl, which attempts to describe human experiences as they appear to consciousness. It represents a reaction to the impersonal nature of **science**, which seeks to establish objective facts at the expense of how things appear to people in ordinary life as imbued with meaning. While science might describe a house, phenomenology would describe a home.

Philosophy   From the Greek, meaning 'love of wisdom'; the search for truth in all its forms by using reason alone. What the subject matter of philosophy should be is itself a philosophical question.

Philosophical theology   The study of the meaning and coherence of theological **beliefs** from a **rational** point of view.

Philosophy of religion   The critical study of the foundations of religious **beliefs** from a philosophical point of view. It is associated with study and criticism of the arguments for God's existence.

Physicalism   From the Greek *physis*, 'nature'; similar to **materialism** and **naturalism**, the view that the only reality is that which is physical.

179

Platonism A system of thinking about reality, derived from Plato (417–347 BC), in which the world of sense **experience** is considered inferior to the world of Ideal Forms on which it is based. It has been influential in Christian thought since Augustine, and it has led to a disparagement of the material in favour of the spiritual.

Positivism A philosophical movement that rejects **metaphysics** and **religion**, claiming that the only true knowledge is that obtained by observation and **experience**.

Predicate In ordinary usage, that which is said about something – for example, An elephant is an animal'. It was disputed by Kant in his criticism of Anselm that 'existence' was a predicate, since a concept does not require that it actually exists – for example, elephants may be extinct. It has been counter-argued that existence is a necessary and defining predicate in the unique case of God.

Prescriptivism An addition to **emotivism** made by R. M. Hare, who pointed out that ethical expressions laid down prescriptions for behaviour that were meant to be universalised.

***Prima facie* duties** A term used by W. D. Ross to indicate basic duties that are obvious (*prima facie*) to everyone, such as honesty, **justice** and respect for life.

Principles, ethical This refers to general laws that are widely recognised as self-evident, such as **justice**, equality and respect for persons. In utilitarianism, happiness is a key ethical principle; in **Kantian ethics**, the **moral law** is the source of key ethical principles; and in religious ethics, the Ten Commandments are a statement of primary ethical principles.

Process theology A theological system based on the idea that reality is in process rather than being already fixed, and that God is acting within the process. It stresses God's immanence rather than His **transcendence**.

Proof **Empirical** evidence that something is true or false.

Proportionalism A modern suggestion in ethical decision-making where an attempt is made to find a proportion between the good and bad effects of an action. It is not widely accepted, and should be distinguished from the **act of double effect**.

Prudence The first of the **cardinal virtues**, it originally meant the ability to know right from wrong. For Aquinas, it meant the ability to know how to order the **moral** life in accordance

with natural law, and with God's will. The idea of acting with prudence – that is, in one's own best interests – still echoes its original meaning.

Psychology A system of thought based on a study of the working of the human psyche, particularly the unconscious. It is associated with Sigmund Freud, who pioneered the method of psychoanalysis, and has become linked with theories about the nature of **religion**.

Quality of life An idea that has arisen particularly in relation to both **abortion** and euthanasia, and is used in contrast to the more traditional concept of **sanctity of life**. It is meant to suggest that a life that has no prospect of having an alleged minimum of happiness or well-being is not worthwhile. It is used to argue for the abortion of the severely handicapped, and for the use of euthanasia for those who are undergoing severe suffering.

Rational In accordance with reason. **Rationalism** is associated with thinkers such as Descartes, who held that certain ideas were innate (in-built) and did not depend on **experience** for their truth to be understood; for example, the truths of mathematics.

Rationalism The philosophical approach that gives priority to reason as the primary source of truth; in contrast to **experience**, which is seen as a less reliable source.

Realism/ Non-realism A modern term in theology related to the idea that God can be understood in either an objective (realist) or subjective (non-realist) way. Traditional theism saw God in a realist way, meaning that God was a Being with objective reality. Non-realism locates God in the subjective consciousness and appears to deny His objective reality.

Reductionism The practice of explaining events exclusively in terms of the natural or social sciences. A religious explanation is incompatible with an explanation that 'reduces' an event to a natural phenomenon, or a subjective **experience**. Explaining events in terms of natural phenomena – for example, in terms of psychological needs – does not necessarily involve reductionism.

Relativism The view that **moral** claims about right and wrong are always relative to particular times, persons or circumstances. It is opposed to the view that some moral claims are **absolute**, admitting of no exceptions through appeal to what is

relative. Both concepts call for qualification, but some systems of **ethics** tend towards one or the other.

Religion A word that is almost impossible to define; generally, a system of **belief** about the supernatural. Monotheistic religion such as Christianity focuses on belief in a supernatural Being called God.

Revealed theology The study of **beliefs** based on God's **revelation** of Himself in the Bible. It includes use of philosophical ideas to explain the significance of such beliefs and their coherence.

Revelation A technical theological term meaning the disclosure by God of certain truths about His nature and will that are not accessible to reason. The precise nature of revelation is a matter of dispute.

Revisionist A modern term used to denote controversial ideas that revise, or break away from, traditional ones. An example is the modern idea that God can be understood in a non-realist way.

Righteousness As applied to God, this means that He is always in the right. It is supposedly challenged by the existence of evil and suffering, and answered by **theodicy**.

Rule utilitarianism A variation in the approach to the **principle of utility** in which respect for certain rules of living are seen as the best way to achieve that principle.

Sanctity of life The principle that human life has an entitlement to respect because it is sacred or holy (an object of sanctity). The principle underlies **Kantian ethics** on the grounds of **rational** self-evidence, and religious ethics on the grounds that human life is sacred in the eyes of God. The principle is also reflected in laws governing human rights and **medical ethics**.

Science From the Latin *scientia*, 'knowledge'; it has come to be identified with **empirical** knowledge. The so-called 'scientific method' refers to the obtaining of knowledge about the world through experimentation and **experience**. It is often contrasted with **religion** and **metaphysics**.

Secular ethics The name given to any ethical system that makes no reference to **religion**.

Secularisation	From the Latin *saeculum*, 'an earthly time'. A modern *de facto* trend characterised by a non-religious view of the world. The supposedly modern 'secular age' is contrasted with the 'age of faith'.
Secularism	An ideology that opposes religious influences, and attempts to replace **religion** with 'secular' or worldly ideas.
Sexual ethics	The area that deals with ethical questions about practices such as homosexuality, sex outside marriage, birth control and so on.
Sin	A religious term that denotes an action contrary to the will of God.
Situation ethics	An ethical system that claims that ethical behaviour should be altered in accordance with particular circumstances or situations. One form controversially advocates **agape** love as the controlling factor in all situations, and considers actions that are motivated by agape love to be intrinsically justified.
Slippery slope argument	The argument that once an exception is made to a **moral law**, a tendency follows to make further exceptions, thus setting up a 'slippery slope'. The term is used in **medical ethics**, and echoes Kant's refusal to make any exceptions to the moral law.
Social ethics	The area of **ethics** relating to the just governing of people's interests in society.
Spiritual values	Those values which are not related to material benefits, such as love for others, a sense of **justice**, or respect for the will of God. Both the **cardinal** and **theological virtues** exemplify spiritual values.
Stoicism	A Greek religious ethical system popularised by Cicero, and based on the concept that everything is willed by God. The ethical task for human beings is to conform to what God wills by acting with reason rather than emotion. This explains the popular idea of Stoicism as encouraging the acceptance of pain without complaint, because it is the will of God.
Subjectivism	The view that ethical awareness is only in the mind, and has no objective reality.
Summum bonum	A term associated with Kant, meaning the 'highest **good**', by which he meant the state of affairs in which **virtue** would be

rewarded with happiness. Although a **rational** concept, its realisation is beyond the bounds of earthly possibility, and so it suggests the existence of God to make it possible.

Supernaturalism　From the Latin *super*, 'over' or 'above'; the **belief** in a **transcendent** God who exists above and beyond the material or physical world.

Symbol　Something from the **empirical** world used as a key to refer to the supernatural world of religious **faith**. The Cross is the outstanding Christian symbol. Other realities such as light have been used as symbols to express truths about God.

Synthetic statement　From the Greek, meaning 'bringing together'. Such statements bring together subject and **predicate** in such a way that they can be verified or falsified. Religious statements are alleged not to be properly synthetic.

Teleological　From the Greek *telos*, an 'end' or 'goal'. The term has become identified with the notion of design or purpose. The teleological argument is based on the contention that the world exhibits evidence of design or purpose, and so points to God.

Teleological ethics　The view that **ethics** should have a '*telos*', or aim. It is associated with utilitarianism, but Kantian and religious ethics also have a **teleological** aspect. In religious ethics the aim is twofold – to show love for others and to serve God.

Temperance　The fourth **cardinal virtue**, this means being temperate, or showing moderation in all things. For Aristotle, it was the **essence** of **virtue**, which consisted of moderation between extremes.

Theodicy　From the Greek *theos*, 'God', and *dike*, 'justice'; the attempt to vindicate the **goodness** and **justice** of God in ordaining or allowing **moral** and natural evil and the human suffering that they cause.

Theological virtues　**Faith**, hope and charity (**agape**).

Thomism　The system of thought derived from St Thomas Aquinas. Under the influence of Aristotle, Aquinas attempted to throw light on the world of sense **experience**. This led to his conviction that the material world needs an explanation from beyond itself. The result was his Five Ways for proving God's existence.

Transcendence (1) A term used in **ethics** to indicate the reality that ethical awareness does not belong to the material world, but is a function of the human spirit. It was used by Kant to argue that the human will reaches beyond (transcends) the natural world in response to the **moral law**. (2) A quality belonging to human beings by which they are capable of going beyond their limitations, unlike the lower animals. It has been used by some thinkers to claim that only God can fulfil man's restless transcendence.

Transcendent From the Latin, meaning 'to go beyond'; associated with the claim that God is completely beyond the world and is totally different from man.

Trinity The Christian **belief** that God is three persons in one nature, Father, Son and Holy Spirit.

Ultimate From the Latin, meaning 'last'; used in the context 'ultimate cause' or 'ultimate explanation'. From a theological point of view, God is the ultimate cause of the world. Non-believers deny the need for such a cause or explanation.

Universalisability A term that is prominent in **Kantian ethics**, to indicate that **moral** rules are applied universally. If a rule cannot be universalised it is flawed, and it must be restated. The telling of lies cannot be universalised without causing moral chaos. R. M. Hare saw this as the defining characteristic of *moral* prescriptions.

Utilitarian ethics An ethical system based on the principle that happiness must be the aim of ethical behaviour.

Utility, principle of The principle that ethical behaviour must be useful to others, not a slavish attachment to rules and regulations.

Values, ethical Values that are considered to be important from an ethical point of view. In **Kantian ethics**, such values follow from the **moral law**.

Verification From the Latin *veritas*, 'truth'; associated with **empiricism**, to mean the process by which something can be shown to be true or false. According to logical positivists, religious statements are incapable of **empirical** verification and are therefore meaningless.

via negativa An aspect of the *via positiva*, it means qualifying all positive statements about God on the understanding that God is a

185

mystery whose being cannot adequately be expressed in human language. In a sense, both ways go together.

via positiva The method of speaking about God that goes back to Pseudo-Dionysius. Typically, it is based on the highest human qualities, which are then applied to God in a pre-eminent way (hence the *via eminentiae*) – for example, God is perfectly wise, just, and so on.

Virtue A term that derives from the Latin *virtus*, meaning 'strength', and originally referred to strength of **character**. The corresponding Greek word meant a form of excellence. In **ethics**, it refers to what is **good**. A virtuous person is one who shows the **virtues**, or character qualities, that are esteemed by others.

Virtues This term refers to the character qualities that are summed up in the **cardinal virtues**. Aquinas added the virtues of **faith**, hope and charity, and considered Jesus as the embodiment of all the human virtues.

Index

Page numbers in italics indicate illustrations